Class, Crisis and the State

Class, Crisis and the State

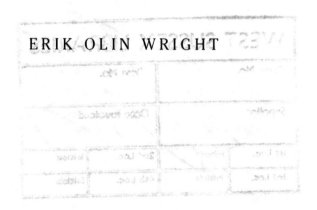

ERIK OLIN WRIGHT

VERSO

London · New York

To my parents

First published by New Left Books 1978
Paperback edition published by Verso 1979
Third impression 1993
© Erik Olin Wright 1978
All rights reserved

Verso
UK: 6 Meard Street, London W1V 3HR
USA: 29 West 35th Street, New York, NY 10001–2291

Verso is the imprint of New Left Books

ISBN 0–86091–719–3 (pbk)

British Library Cataloguing in Publication Data
A catalogue record for this book is available from the British Library

Library of Congress Cataloging-in-Publication Data
A catalogue record for this book is available from the Library of Congress

Printed in Great Britain by Biddles Ltd

Contents

Chapter 3

Historical Transformations of Capitalist Crisis Tendencies

Chapter 4

Bureaucracy and the State

Chapter 5

Conclusion: Socialist Strategies and the State in Advanced Capitalist Societies

Acknowledgements

All intellectual production is ultimately a social process, but I feel that this book has been especially shaped by the collective exchanges I have had over the past five years. Each of the chapters in this book went through many versions before completion, and each version benefited tremendously from the critical comments I received from many people. I am especially indebted to the San Francisco Bay Area *Kapitalistate* Collective, which has unquestionably been the richest forum for the development of many of the ideas in this book. I would also like to express my special gratitude to Michael Burawoy, Manuel Castells, Roger Friedland, David Gold, Andy Levine and Luca Perrone for the intensive debates we have had on all aspects of this work. In addition, the following people have read various pieces of the book and given me comments and suggestions which in one way or another are embodied in the final product: Daniel Bertaux, Kathy Blee, Sam Bowles, Amy Bridges, Winnie Breines, Jens Christiansen, Al Gedicks, Barbara Heyns, Alex Hicks, Rebecca Kharkov, Robert L. Kahn, Ira Katznelson, Margaret Levi, Clarence Lo, John Mollenkopf, Jim O'Connor, Claus Offe, Nicos Poulantzas, Adam Przeworski, Michael Reich, Jesse Schwartz, Michael Soref, Arthur Stinchcombe, Al Szymanski, Göran Therborn, Kay Trimberger, Alan Wolfe, Marcia Kahn Wright, Glen Yago, and Maurice Zeitlin. Finally, I would like to thank the editors of *New Left Review*, especially Perry Anderson, for their extremely conscientious and insightful comments on the original manuscript of this book. Most of the theoretical developments in the text over the past year were directly provoked by their criticisms.

1

Methodological Introduction

The essays in this book have been heavily shaped by the academic context in which they were written. As a graduate student in sociology I constantly confronted the hegemony of an empiricist, positivist epistemology in the social sciences. In virtually every debate over Marxist ideas, at some point I would be asked, "prove it!" To the extent that Marxist categories could be crystallized into "testable hypotheses", non-Marxists were willing (sometimes) to take those ideas seriously; to the extent that debate raged simply at the level of theory, non-Marxists found it relatively easy to dismiss our challenges.

Marxists in the social sciences reacted to these pressures in several distinct ways. Perhaps the dominant response was to dismiss the attacks of non-Marxist social scientists as reflecting bourgeois ideology and/or a positivist methodology. It was common in Marxist student circles to argue that the very enterprise of formulating "testable hypotheses" was inimical to a Marxist methodology. Historical and dialectical explanation was counterposed to predictive, linear explanations. Particular hostility was reserved for the battery of quantitative techniques used in American sociology: even to use regression equations in a research project was to abandon the essence of Marxism. The demand that we prove theoretical claims through empirically testable propositions, therefore, was treated as purely ideological. To accept the demand would be to give up the battle by accepting the methodological principles of positivist social science.

A second response was to try to generate empirical studies which would prove our arguments to even the most stubborn opponent. Of particular importance in this vein was the large number of "power structure" studies produced in the 1960s and early 1970s criticizing pluralist interest-group theory. Such studies contributed greatly to legitimating the use of certain Marxist categories in social research and to demonstrating the ideological character of much pluralist theory. But as many Marxist critics of such research have stressed, much of the dialectical character of Marxist theory was lost in the process. In a sense, a large part of such Marxist empirical work can be seen as using Marxist categories without using Marxist theory.

Naturally, there is a third alternative: the attempt to develop empirical research agendas firmly rooted within not only the categories, but the logic, of Marxist theory. Such an approach would reject the positivist premise that theory construction is simply a process of empirical generalization of law-like regularities, but would also insist that Marxist theory should generate propositions about the real world which can be empirically studied.

This third strategy is only beginning in the United States. In effect it is an attempt simultaneously to engage in debate with mainstream social theory and to develop a style of empirical research which advances Marxist theory. Potentially, the research generated by this orientation may become an important contribution by North American Marxists to Marxist social science.[1]

1. A few examples of empirical studies in this third mode include: Michael Reich, *Racial Discrimination and the White Income Distribution*, Ph.D. Dissertation, Department of Economics, Harvard University, 1973; Roger Friedland, "Class Power and Social Control: the War on Poverty", *Politics and Society*, Vol. 6, No. 4, 1976, and *Class Power and the Central City: The Contradictions of Urban Growth*, Ph.D. Dissertation, Department of Sociology, University of Wisconsin, 1977; Michael Burawoy, *The Organization of Consent: Changing Patterns of Conflict on the Shop Floor, 1945-1975*, Ph.D. Dissertation, Department of Sociology, University of Chicago, 1976; Erik Olin Wright and Luca Perrone, "Classi Sociale, Scuola, Occupazione e Reddito in U.S.A.", *Quaderni di Sociologia*, Vol. XXIV, No. 1-2, 1975, and "Marxist Class Categories and Income Inequality", *American Sociological Review*, Vol. 42, No. 1, 1977; Sam Bowles and Herb Gintis, *Schooling in Capitalist America*, New York 1976; and Alfredo Del Rio, *Class Struggle and Electoral Politics in Chile, 1958-1973*, Ph.D. Dissertation, Department of Sociology, University of Wisconsin, (forthcoming).

The essays in this book should be seen, in part, as contributing to the formation of this third response to positivist social science. While none of the essays constitutes an empirical investigation of a specific historical or structural problem, they are all intended to help establish the theoretical preconditions for such investigations.

The development of a stronger tradition of theoretically-structured empirical investigation within Marxism has three important preconditions: first, it is necessary that Marxists develop a broad range of research competences so that they can in fact conduct empirical investigations in a sophisticated and sensitive way. Second, it is essential to have a deep grasp of Marxist theory, so that the propositions developed do not merely tap the surface level of Marxist categories but are in fact systematically linked to the inner logic of the theory itself. Finally, it is important to know how to link that theory to concrete research agendas. The essays in this book are primarily relevant to the second and third of these issues. In order to understand how they attempt to accomplish this, it will be helpful to examine briefly the methodology of theory-construction which underlies them.

Linking Theory to Data in Social Research

One of the central epistemological premises of Marxist theory is the distinction between the "level of appearances" and the underlying social reality which produces those appearances.[2] This is not to say that "appearances" are purely ephemeral, inconsequential mystifications. On the contrary, the immediately encountered social experience of everyday life is extremely important. People starve "at the level of appearances", even if that starvation is produced through a social dynamic which is not immediately observable. The point of the distinction between appearances and underlying reality is not

2. In making the distinction between "appearances" and an underlying structural reality, I am not intending to argue for a Hegelian image of appearances as the outward expression of essences. The point of the distinction is to emphasize that there are structural mechanisms which generate immediately encountered reality, and that a Marxist social theory should be grounded in a revelation of the dynamics of those structures, not simply in a generalization about the appearances themselves.

to dismiss appearances, but rather to provide a basis for their explanation. The central claim is that the vast array of empirical phenomena immediately observable in social life can only be explained if we analyse the social reality hidden behind those appearances. If we remain entirely at the level of appearances we might be able to describe social phenomena, and even predict those phenomena, but we cannot explain them.[3]

Marxists, then, have generally stressed the importance of elaborating a theory of the underlying structures of social relations, of the contradictions embedded in those structures, of the ways in which those underlying structures generate the appearances which people encounter in everyday life. The classic example of such an analysis is, of course, Marx's discussion of surplus value in *Capital*: the equality of exchange relations (commodity relations) in the capitalist market hides the real relations of exploitation within production. One can very easily *predict* exchange relations by simply investigating characteristics operating at the level of the market (indeed, this is one of the essential projects of neoclassical economics) but in order to *explain* them it is necessary to explore the dynamics embedded in production relations themselves.

It is one thing to make the epistemological claim that explanation requires the decoding of hidden contradictions; it is another to develop a strategy for studying the social world which allows one to link systematically such underlying structural processes to empirically observable phenomena. General maxims about moving from the concrete to the abstract and back to the concrete are not very helpful. The problem is *how* to move from the concrete to the abstract, and how to move back.

In the absence of a coherent strategy for linking systematically the abstractions of Marxist theory to concrete research, two problems are likely to arise. On the one hand, Marxist theory often tends to become very ideological and immutable to transformation from empirical study. The fre-

3. There is a vast literature in the philosophy of sciences which deals with these questions of the relationship between explanation, prediction and description. One of the hallmarks of positivist social science, in these terms, is the collapsing of the distinction between explanation and prediction. Marxism, on the other hand, insists on the radical distinction between the two. For a useful discussion of these issues see Russel Keat and John Urry, *Social Theory as Science*, London 1976, especially part I.

quent impression in Marxist research that all of the answers are pre-given, are "known" prior to the investigation, is at least partially the result of the methodological distance between the general theory and the "facts" of history. On the other hand, Marxist research often becomes purely descriptive, contributing only marginally to the development of Marxist theory. Historical movements are richly described using Marxist categories, but those descriptions are difficult to translate into transformations of theory. While one should not exaggerate these two tendencies, nevertheless the advancement of Marxist theory is at least in part retarded by the lack of clear strategies for linking theory and research.[4]

In order to facilitate the development of such strategies within Marxism, two general tasks are important. First, it is essential that Marxist theory be formulated in a comprehensible way. This may seem trivial, but the opacity of much Marxist theoretical work is a tremendous obstacle to using such work as a basis for systematic empirical investigation. In particular, it is critical to distinguish within Marxism between assumptions or premises which are not subject to transformation by historical investigation, and propositions which are;[5] and it is important to distinguish between definitions of concepts and propositions about those concepts. To be sure, theoretical debates over the definitions of concepts and theoretical debates about the actual dynamics of the social world are related. Definitions should not be arbitrary, and a theory of social structures influences the very definitions of those structures. Nevertheless, the two types of theoretical discussion should not be confused, at least if the goal is to develop a

4. In many ways this issue is similar to the problem of linking theory and practice. It is easy enough to say that theories are tested in practice, that theory comes from practice, that theory is a form of practice, etc. It is much more difficult to specify rigorously the ways in which theory and practice are in fact dialectically related, the ways in which they shape either, interpenetrate, and so on.

5. Throughout this discussion the expression "historical investigation" will refer to investigations of the dynamics of social change, not simply investigations of the past. To analyse a problem historically is to study contradictions and change, not simply to uncover "origins". While it is true that an historical investigation will typically involve gathering data from the past, the critical issue is not the temporality of the data but the way in which they are analysed. It is entirely possible to conduct ahistorical investigations of the past and historical investigations of the present.

conceptual apparatus that can be used in empirical research.

Clarity, however, is not enough. It is also important to develop a more systematic way of understanding the causal relations between the structural categories of Marxist theory and the level of appearances tapped in empirical investigation.[6] That is, historical investigation gathers data at the level of appearances (by definition): events, personal ties, manifest economic variables, institutional arrangements, demographic distributions, and so on. In some sense these phenomena constitute "effects" of structural relations. The problem is to define more systematically what "effects" means. If empirical investigation is to be directly linked to the logic of the theory itself, then much greater rigour in understanding the logic of causality implicit in the theory is necessary.

Some steps in this direction have been made by Louis Althusser and other so-called structuralist Marxists. The concepts of over-determination and, more broadly, structural causality, have provided at least a preliminary formulation of the relationship between structures and their manifest effects.[7] This concept of causality, however, has been very difficult to use explicitly in empirical studies. While this may be due partially to the high level of abstraction at which Althusser and others have discussed these concepts, it is also due to certain problems in the conceptualization of structural causality itself. In particular, the global notion of structural causality contains within itself several distinct forms of causality. In order to make the concept of structural causality accessible for empirical research, therefore, it needs to be broken down into this plurality of types of causation.

---

6. The idea of trying to formulate a systematic language for capturing the causal imagery of Marxist theory was initially stimulated by the work of Arthur Stinchcombe, especially in his book *Constructing Social Theories*, New York 1968. In particular, his discussion of the logic of functional causation and historicist causation was important in suggesting the utility of distinguishing between types of causal relations. The specific typology of determination presented here has been most influenced by the work of Poulantzas and other "structuralist" Marxists and the work of Claus Offe. For an earlier attempt at symbolically representing the causal logic of Marxist theory, see Luca Perrone and Erik Olin Wright, "Lo Stato nella Teoria Funzionalista e Marxista-Strutturalista", *Studi di Sociologia*, Vol. XI, 1973.

7. See especially Louis Althusser and Etienne Balibar, *Reading Capital*, London 1970, pp. 186, 188.

Modes of Determination and Models of Determination

What follows is a provisional attempt at elaborating a more differentiated schema of structural causality compatible with Marxist theory. The discussion will revolve around what I shall label "modes of determination", that is, a series of distinct relationships of determination among the structural categories of Marxist theory and between those categories and the appearances of empirical investigation. These diverse modes of determination will then be organized into what can be called "models of determination", that is, schematic representations of the complex interconnections of the various modes of determination involved in a given structural process. Such models of determination can be considered symbolic maps of what Althusserians have generally referred to as "structured totalities".

Before discussing these diverse modes of determination, it must be emphasized that the schematic diagrams representing the models of determination are largely heuristic devices. They are designed to make explicit those linkages among categories which are either vague or implicit in theoretical statements. The diagrams themselves may appear to be highly mechanistic and rigid, not allowing for the dynamic movements which lie at the heart of a dialectical view of history. The intention, however, is to develop a way of representing the structural constraints and contradictions present in a given society which make that dynamic movement a non-random process.

At least six basic modes of determination can be distinguished within the global concept of structural causality: structural limitation, selection, reproduction/nonreproduction, limits of functional compatibility, transformation and mediation. While these modes of determination are highly interdependent, and thus a full understanding of any one of them presupposes an understanding of all, nevertheless it will be helpful to define each of them.

1. Structural Limitation: This constitutes a pattern of determination in which some social structure establishes limits within which some other structure or process can vary, and establishes probabilities for the specific structures or processes that are possible within those limits. That is, structural limitation implies that certain forms of the determined structure have been excluded entirely and some possible forms are more likely than others. This pattern of determination is especially important for understanding the sense in which economic structures "ultimately" determine political and ideological structures: economic structures set limits on the possible forms of political and ideological structures, and make some of those possible forms more likely than others, but they do not rigidly determine in a mechanistic manner any given form of political and ideological relations.

A good example of such structural limitation determination is the relationship between the economic structure and the forms of the state in feudal society. Given the nature of economic relations in classical feudalism—the control of the immediate means of production by the peasantry, the appropriation of the surplus product through coercion, the limited amount of surplus available, etc.—a representative democracy with universal suffrage was structurally impossible as a form of the state, i.e. it fell outside the structural limits established by economic structures. Within those limits, however, a fairly wide variety of state forms could occur, ranging from highly decentralized manorial systems of political rule, to relatively centralized Absolutist states. While the given structure of feudal economic relations may have shaped the likelihood of different specific forms of the feudal state, it did not determine uniquely which form occurred.

Structural limitation does not imply that every structurally *possible* form of the state (or other structure determined by a relation of structural limitation) is necessarily *functional* for the reproduction of the determining structure. We shall deal with this question in some detail below in the discussion of "limits of functional compatibility" as a mode of determination. For the moment it is simply important to note that the range of structurally limited possibilities and the range of functional possibilities do not necessarily coincide. In fact, part of our understanding of the concept of "contradiction" will hinge on the various ways in which a non-correspondence between structural and functional limitation is generated. More on this later.

2. *Selection*: Selection constitutes those social mechanisms that concretely determine ranges of outcomes, or in the extreme case specific outcomes, within a structurally limited range of possibilities. In a sense, selection can be seen as a form of second-order limitation: the setting of limits within limits. Much of the analysis of specific historical conjunctures can be thought of as investigations of the concrete patterns of selection that occur within broadly defined structural limits.

There are two complementary forms of "selection", which can be termed "positive" and "negative" selections.[8] Negative selection involves those mechanisms which *exclude* certain possibilities. Positive selection, on the other hand, involves mechanisms which determine specific outcomes among those that are possible. What is typically referred to as "decision-making processes" revolve around processes of positive selection. Taken together, positive and negative selection determine the concrete structural outcomes within limits determined by structural limitation.

A good illustration of selection can be seen in the inter-relationship between the economic structure (forces and relations of production), the state structure and class struggle: the economic structure establishes limits of variation on both class struggle and the structure of the state: the state in turn acts as a selection mechanism on forms of class struggle, shaping those struggles within limits established by the underlying economic structure. These patterns of determination are illustrated in the simple model of determination in Figure 1.1

8. This distinction between positive and negative selection derives largely from the work of Claus Offe. See his "Structural Problems of the Capitalist State" in Von Beyme (ed.), *German Political Studies*, Vol. I, Los Angeles 1974, and "The Theory of the Capitalist State and the Problem of Policy Formation" in Leon Lindberg *et al* (eds), *Stress and Contradiction in Modern Capitalism*, Lexington, 1972. Offe has used the term with particular effectiveness in his analysis of the internal structures of the state apparatus and how they select specific forms of state activity, but the concept can be generalized to cover all processes of selection with respect to structural limitation. Göran Therborn's discussion of "input" and "transformation" mechanisms in the state apparatus is also closely related to this discussion of selection determination, in *What does the Ruling Class do when it Rules?* London 1978.

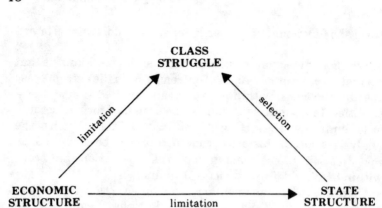

Figure 1.1   Illustration of Selection and Structural Limitation

In the case of feudal economic structures, this model of determination would read as follows: Given the basic structure of feudal economic relations, only certain forms of class struggle are possible, and different specific forms have greater probability than others. For example, the possibility of revolutionary socialist struggles organized through political parties is beyond the limits of variation imposed by feudal economic relations. Within the broad range of possible class struggles that could occur, the structure of the state was an important selection mechanism which determined whether struggles would take the form of land invasions, grain riots, millenarian movements, peasant flight from landlords, etc.

3. *Reproduction/non-reproduction*:   Reproduction/non-reproduction is a more complex mode of determination than structural limitation and selection. To say that one structure functions to reproduce another implies that the reproducing structure *prevents* the reproduced structure from changing in certain fundamental ways. To say that the capitalist state, for example, reproduces capitalist economic relations means that it prevents those economic relations from changing into non-capitalist economic relations, and furthermore, that in the absence of such a reproduction process the economic structure potentially (but not inevitably) would change in such ways. Reproduction thus is also a kind of limiting process: it main-

tains the reproduced structure within certain limits of variation. The essential difference from structural limitation is that in the latter case there is no presumption that the determined structure would necessarily change in the absence of the specific structural limitation process, whereas in the case of reproduction such changes would normally occur. Reproduction/non-reproduction is symbolized in Figure 1.2.

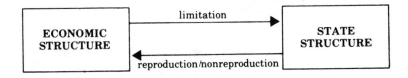

Figure 1.2 Illustration of Reproduction/non-reproduction and Limitation as Modes of Determination

To say that the capitalist state is necessary for the reproduction of capitalist economic relations is not to say that the capitalist state always functions in a perfectly optimal way for the reproduction of those economic relations. It is quite possible for the effects of the state to be far less than optimal, and even under certain circumstances, for it to become non-reproductive. Reproduction/non-reproduction must therefore be understood as a variable relation of determination, not an absolute one.

4. *Limits of functional compatibility*: If the state is not always optimally functional for the reproduction of economic relations—indeed, if it is possible for the state to become non-reproductive—then we need some way of expressing the processes which determine which forms of the state will be functional and in what ways. This is what is meant by "limits of functional compatibility": the mode of determination which determines which forms of the state will be reproductive and which non-reproductive. Stated in somewhat different terms, limits of functional compatibility determine what the effects of a given structure of the state will be on economic structures. This relation is illustrated in Figure 1.3 over the page.

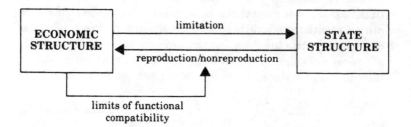

Figure 1.3   Illustration of Limits of Functional Compatibility

As expressed in this model of determination, the economic structure both sets limits of variation on the structure of the state, and determines the extent to which it will itself be reproduced by the actual structure of the state which emerges. The crucial issue is that these two modes of determination do not necessarily coincide. The limits of functional compatibility are not intrinsically coordinated with the limits of structural variation. This is precisely what makes it possible for a form of the state to emerge which is non-reproductive of economic structures, and thus for a structural contradiction to exist between economic and political structures. When such a situation arises, either there will occur a fairly rapid transformation of the economic structures or the structures of the state will be altered in ways which make it once more reproductive. To a large extent, class struggle determines which of these outcomes will in fact occur.

A good example of limits of functional compatibility as a mode of determination is the relationship of the state to economic structures in the transition from feudalism to capitalism: In the early periods of the Absolutist state in Western Europe, these state structures could be considered reproductive of a limited development of the capitalist mode of production within a still largely feudal social structure. Perry Anderson describes this relation as follows: "The apparent paradox of Absolutism in Western Europe was that it fundamentally represented an apparatus for the protection of aristocratic property and privileges, yet at the same time the means whereby this protection was promoted could *simultaneously* ensure the basic interests of the nascent mercantile and manufacturing classes. . . . There was always a potential field of *compatibility* at this stage between the nature and programme of the Absolutist State and the operations of mercantile and manufacturing capital."[9] As capitalism expanded, however, the Absolutist state increasingly became an obstacle to capital accumulation. "Its feudal character constantly ended by frustrating and falsifying its promises for capital". In our terms, this structure of the state gradually became non-reproductive of the emerging economic relations even though it still fell within the structural limits of variation. The eventual result was the bourgeois revolutions: the resolution of the functional incompatibility of the Absolutist state through its violent transformation.

5. *Transformation*: Transformation refers to a mode of determination by which class struggle (practices) directly affect the processes of structural limitation, selection and reproduction/non-reproduction. Transformation is thus fundamental to the dialectical character of patterns of determination as understood in Marxist theory: class struggle, which is itself structurally limited and selected by various social structures, simultaneously reshapes those structures. The word "simultaneously" is important in this formulation: social structures do not first structurally limit and select class struggle, after which class struggle transforms those structures. Class struggle is intrinsically a process of transformation of structures, and thus the very process which sets limits on class struggle is at the same time transformed by the struggles so limited. This dialectical relationship between transformation and limitation is represented in Figure 1.4.

It is especially important to understand the relationship between the concept of "contradiction" and the notion of transformation. In our discussion of limits of functional compatibility, I argued that the potential non-correspondence between structural limitation and limits of functional compatibility as modes of determination made *possible* the contradictions between structures. For that possibility to become actualized,

9. *Lineages of the Absolutist State*, London 1974, pp. 40–41.

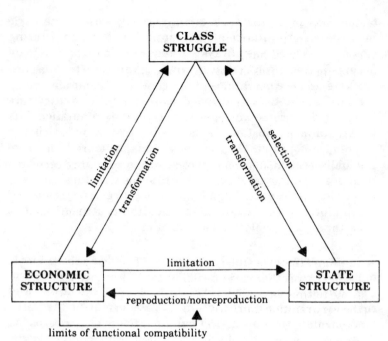

Figure 1.4   Illustration of Transformation as a Mode of Determination

however, class struggle must affect social structures through relations of transformation. Class struggles are, above all, struggles over social structures. This means that even if at a given point in time the structure of the state falls within the limits of functional compatibility determined by economic structures, there is no reason for that compatibility to be automatically reproduced over time. Class struggles transform economic relations, thus changing the reproduction requirements themselves; and class struggle transforms the state, thus making it potentially less reproductive over time. There is thus a systematic tendency for the contradictions between *classes* (class struggle) to generate contradictions between social structures (non-reproductive relations of determination).

To describe a mode of determination as transformation does not imply that a particular structure will in fact necessarily be transformed. In the case illustrated in Figure 1.4, the transformation of state structures is a consequence of class *struggle*, and it may well happen that the forces for the maintenance of existing structures of the state may be stronger than the forces for transformation. Defining a mode of determination as a relationship of transformation means that what is at issue is the transformation of structures, not that such transformation always takes place.

6. *Mediation*: Mediation is in some ways the most complex mode of determination. It defines a mode of determination in which a given social process shapes the consequences of other social processes. A mediating process must be distinguished from what is commonly called an "intervening" process or variable in sociology. This distinction is illustrated in Figure 1.5. An intervening variable is simply a variable which is causally situated between two other variables. X causes Y which in turn causes Z. A mediating variable, on the other hand, is one which shapes the very relationship between two other variables: Y causes the way in which X affects Z. In a sense a mediating process can be viewed as a "contextual variable": processes of mediation determine the terrain on which other modes of determination operate.

Mediation is especially important in analysing the relationship between class struggle and relations of structural limitation, selection and reproduction. For example, it is often

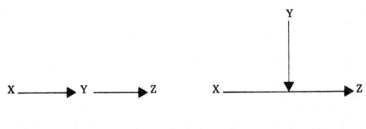

Y as an intervening variable   Y as a mediating variable

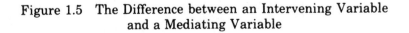

Figure 1.5   The Difference between an Intervening Variable and a Mediating Variable

argued that the bureaucratic structure of the capitalist state acts as an important selection mechanism in determining the actual activity of the state (policies, interventions, etc.). Class struggle decisively mediates this selection relation: the identical structures of the state will have very different consequences for state activity depending upon the relationship of class struggle to the state. When class struggles remain completely external to the institutions of the state, bureaucratic structures may effectively select state policies which optimally serve the interests of capital. When class struggles occur within the state apparatus itself—when civil service workers and teachers become unionized, state employees go on strike, welfare workers support their clients, etc.—the same formal state structure can select very different sorts of state interventions. This pattern is illustrated in Figure 1.6.

Class struggles similarly mediate reproduction determinations. The extent to which a given state structure is reproductive of economic relations may be conditioned by the kinds of class struggles in the society. Where class struggle is very intense and very politicized, bourgeois democratic structures may prove quite unreproductive; where class struggle is very

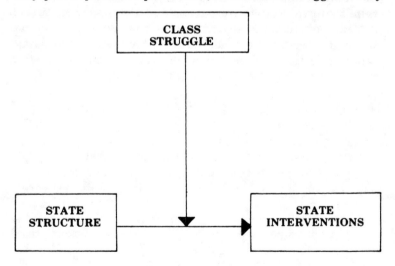

Figure 1.6 Illustration of Mediation as a Mode of Determination

economistic and apolitical, the identical structures may function very reproductively.

Finally, class struggle also mediates relations of structural limitation. Structural limitation does not simply define those forms of the determined structures which are impossible; it also determines the relative likelihood of various possible forms of that structure. Class struggle can mediate this relationship and alter the pattern of probabilities. This kind of mediation is particularly important in periods of revolutionary transformation of structures. For example, after a socialist revolution, a variety of new state forms are structurally possible. To the extent that the working class has a history of active participation in bourgeois democratic struggles, the likelihood that a genuinely democratic form of the socialist state will emerge is increased.

If we take all six of these modes of determination together, we can create a model of determination of the relationships among economic structures, state structures, state interventions and class struggle. This model is presented in Figure 1.7. This model could of course be made more complex. Other elements could be added, such as the role of ideology. Or, more complex interconnections among the elements could be posed. For example, it could be argued that the structures of the state themselves mediate the transformation relationship between class struggle and the state (i.e. the structures of the state shape the extent to which they can be transformed by class struggle).[10] In the present context, the issue is not so much the completeness of this specific model of determination, but the demonstration that this kind of model is a useful way of clarifying the relationships among elements in a theory.

Models of determination such as the one illustrated in Figure 1.7 should not be thought of as the end product of a serious historical investigation. Rather they are a prelude to such research. They are designed to lay out explicitly the logic of relations to be explored in a particular historical investigation. A model of determination charts the terrain of an investigation;

10. This kind of "auto-mediation" by state structures is analogous to the relationship between limits of functional compatibility and reproduction/non-reproduction; in both cases, the characteristics of a given structure determine the ways in which it is affected by another process or structure. This is very close

it does not provide the answers for that investigation. Concrete historical studies are essential to spell out how limitation and selection processes operate, how class struggle transforms and mediates those relations, how the transformation of social structures generates non-reproductive relations, and so on. The model helps to clarify the questions to be asked in research, and it may help to facilitate the theoretical integration of different research projects, but the actual historical research is still essential for any genuine understanding of historical development.

Themes of the Book

Even though I will use the modes of determination discussed above throughout this book, the essays should not be read exclusively as illustrations of a methodological strategy. The basic substantive concern of the analysis is to understand how the historically specific contradictions of advanced monopoly capitalism pose new possibilities and constraints for socialist movements. The three core essays in this book attempt to provide some of the critical ingredients for analysing this problem.

Chapter 2 explores the class structures of advanced capitalist societies. The pivotal issue in the chapter is how to analyse the

---

to Nicos Poulantzas's discussion of the relationship of class struggle to the state. He writes: "these state structures, as appear in the relation of the instances, carry inscribed within them a set of variations which in delimiting the class struggle achieve concrete reality according to the effects which this struggle has on the state within the limits thus set": *Political Power and Social Classes*, London 1973, p. 188. This extremely complex formulation might be stated symbolically in the following way:

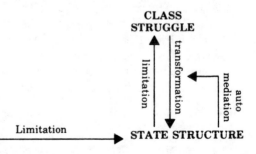

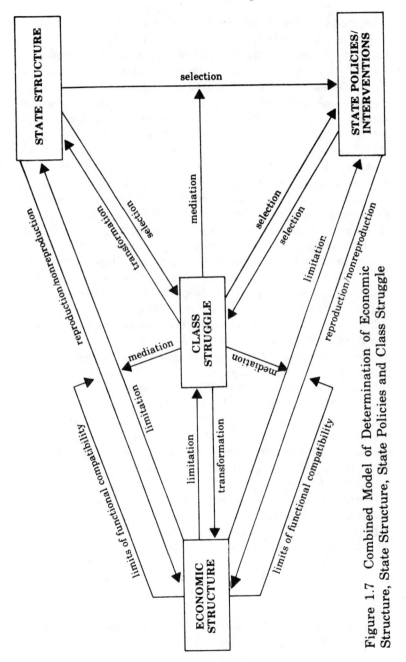

Figure 1.7 Combined Model of Determination of Economic Structure, State Structure, State Policies and Class Struggle

class location of those positions in the social structure which are often loosely labelled "middle class". The concept of "contradictory locations within class relations" is introduced as a way of understanding such positions. But classes are never simply "positions" in a social structure; classes are also social forces which transform social structures. To grasp these two aspects of class theoretically, the distinction between class interests and class capacities is developed towards the end of this chapter. This in turn provides us with the theoretical tools for tackling the fundamental question of the inter-relationship among class structure, class formation and class struggle.

Chapter 3 surveys a variety of Marxist theories of economic crisis and attempts to link them through an analysis of the historical transformations of the accumulation process. In different periods of capitalist development, the capital accumulation process faced qualitatively different impediments. In each period the structural solution to a given impediment became the basis for new contradictions and new impediments in subsequent periods. In these terms, advanced monopoly capitalism is characterized by impediments centred on the role of the state, the necessity for the capitalist state to move towards progressively more pervasive interventions in the accumulation process itself. This gradual politicization of the accumulation process has important implications for socialist movements in the advanced capitalist countries.

Chapter 4 centres on the problem of understanding the internal structures of the capitalist state, especially the bureaucratic character of those structures. The basic issue is to understand the ways in which those structures prevent the working class from using the capitalist state to realize its fundamental class interests. To analyse this problem, the theoretical statements of Lenin and Weber on the state are systematically compared.

Finally, Chapter 5 attempts to integrate the themes of the previous three chapters. Its essential question is: in what ways do the specific contradictions in accumulation in advanced monopoly capitalism affect the relationship between the state and the process of class formation? Is Lenin's basic assessment still correct—that the parliamentary-bureaucratic republic ultimately impedes the formation of the proletariat into a revolutionary class? Is it possible, given the new contradictions of advanced capitalism, for the left to use the capitalist state as part of a strategy for a socialist transition? What assumptions should be made about the nature of the advanced capitalist state in order for the political strategy of Eurocommunism to become a genuine strategy for socialism, and what conditions would have to be fulfilled for that strategy to succeed? I do not have adequate answers to these complex questions. But I hope that the analyses in these essays will help to give greater theoretical precision to the questions themselves and indicate what must be done to be able to answer them more fully.

2

The Class Structure of Advanced Capitalist Societies

All Marxists agree that manual workers directly engaged in the production of physical commodities for private capital fall into the working class. While there may be disagreement about the political and ideological significance of such workers in advanced capitalism, everyone acknowledges that they are in fact workers. There is no such agreement about any other category of wage-earners. Some Marxists have argued that only productive manual workers should be considered part of the proletariat.[1] Others have argued that the working class includes low-level, routinized white-collar employees as well.[2] Still others have argued that virtually all wage-labourers should be considered part of the working class.[3] If this disagreement were just a question of esoteric academic debates over how best to pigeon-hole different social positions, then it would matter little how these issues were eventually resolved. But classes are not merely analytical abstractions in Marxist theory; they are real social forces and they have real consequences. It matters a great deal for our understanding of class struggle and social change exactly how classes are conceptualized and which categories of social positions are placed in which classes. Above all, it matters for developing a viable

1. For example, Nicos Poulantzas in "On Social Classes", *New Left Review* 78, and in *Classes in Contemporary Capitalism*, NLB, London 1975.
2. For example, Al Szymanski, "Trends in the American Working Class", *Socialist Revolution* No. 10.
3. For example, Francesca Freedman, "The Internal Structure of the Proletariat," *Socialist Revolution* No. 26.

socialist politics how narrow or broad the working class is seen to be and how its relationship to other classes is understood.

This chapter will explore the problem of understanding class boundaries in advanced capitalist society. Rather than review the wide range of approaches Marxists have adopted in defining classes, I will focus primarily on the work of Nicos Poulantzas, in particular on his book *Classes in Contemporary Capitalism*.[3a] This work is, to my knowledge, the most systematic and thorough attempt to understand precisely the Marxist criteria for classes in capitalist society. While there are many points in Poulantzas's argument with which I disagree, his work has the considerable merit of sharply posing the problem of defining classes in advanced capitalism and of providing some stimulating solutions. A critical discussion of Poulantzas's work can, therefore, provide a very useful starting-point for the development of an explicit theory of classes in contemporary capitalism.

The first section below presents an outline exposition of Poulantzas's theory of the structural determination of class. Poulantzas's basic conclusion is that only manual, non-supervisory workers who produce surplus-value directly (productive labour) should be included in the proletariat. Other categories of wage-labourers (unproductive employees, mental labour, supervisory labour) must be placed in a separate class—either the "new" petty bourgeoisie, or in the case of managers, the bourgeoisie itself. This exposition of Poulantzas will be followed in the second section by a general assessment and critique of his argument. The third section presents the preliminary outlines of an alternative conceptualization of class boundaries, that hinges on the concept of *contradictory locations within class relations.* I will argue that not all positions in the social structure can be seen as firmly rooted in a single class; some positions occupy objectively contradictory locations between classes. The analytical task is to give such positions a precise theoretical meaning and to relate them systematically to questions of class struggle. The final section of the chapter links the concept of contradictory class locations to class struggle by developing a distinction between class interests and class capacities.

3a. For studies of classes not discussed here, see Bibliography, p. 255ff.

Poulantzas's Theory of the Structural Determination of Class

The following presentation of Poulantzas's ideas will necessarily be schematic and incomplete. I will discuss only the
essential elements of his views on class boundaries and not deal
with a variety of other important issues which he raises (such as
class fractions, the relationship of classes to state apparatuses,
etc.). While the exposition will lose many of the nuances of
Poulantzas's analysis, I hope that the basic contours of his
argument will stand out. Critical comments will be kept to a
minimum in this section.

General Framework

Poulantzas's analysis of social classes rests on three basic premises. 1. *Classes cannot be defined outside of class struggle*. This
is a fundamental point. Classes are not "things", nor are they
pigeon-holes in a static social structure. "Classes", Poulantzas
writes, "involve in one and the same process both class contradictions and class struggle; social classes do not firstly exist
as such and only then enter into class struggle. Social classes
coincide with class practices, i.e. the class struggle, and are only
defined in their mutual opposition."[4] Poulantzas does not mean
by this proposition that classes can only be understood in terms
of class *consciousness*. Class struggle, in Poulantzas's analysis,
does not refer to the conscious self-organization of a class as a
social force, but rather to the antagonistic, contradictory quality of the social relations which comprise the social division of
labour. Class struggle exists even when classes are disorganized. 2. *Classes designate objective positions in the social
division of labour*. These objective positions, Poulantzas
stresses, "are independent of the will of these agents".[5] It is
crucial not to confuse the analysis of the structure of these
objective class positions with the analysis of the individuals
(*agents* in Poulantzas's terminology) who occupy those positions. While both analyses are important, Poulantzas insists
that "the question of who occupies a given position, i.e. who is or
becomes a bourgeois, proletarian, petty bourgeois, poor peasant,

4. *Classes in Contemporary Capitalism*, p. 14.
5. Ibid.

etc., and how and when he does, *is subordinate to the first aspect*—the reproduction of the actual positions occupied by the social classes".[6] Poulantzas refers to the reproduction of these objective positions within the social division of labour as the "structural determination of class". These first two propositions taken together imply that in order to define classes it is necessary to unravel the objective positions within the antagonistic social relations comprising the social division of labour. 3. *Classes are structurally determined not only at the economic level, but at the political and ideological levels as well.* This is perhaps the most distinctive (and problematic) part of Poulantzas's analysis. While it is true that "the economic place of the social agents has a principal role in determining social classes",[7] their position in ideological and political relations of domination and subordination may be equally important: "It must be emphasized that ideological and political relations, i.e. the places of political and ideological domination and subordination, are themselves part of the structural determination of class: there is no question of the objective place being the result only of economic place within the relations of production, while political and ideological elements belong only to [class struggle]."[8] Political and ideological factors cannot be relegated to the transformation of a "class-in-itself" into a "class-for-itself", but lie at the heart of the very determination of class positions.[9] Given these premises, the basic theoretical strategy

6. "On Social Classes", pp. 49–50.
7. *Classes in Contemporary Capitalism*, p. 14.
8. Ibid., p. 16. In this particular passage, Poulantzas uses the expression "class position" rather than "class struggle" at the end. By class position in this context, Poulantzas refers to the concrete situation of a class in a specific historical conjuncture. Thus, for example, under certain historical circumstances, the labour aristocracy may assume the class position of the bourgeoisie, without actually changing its objective place in the class structure. This is a confusing use of the word "position" and Poulantzas himself is not always consistent in the way he uses it (note the quote under proposition 2 above). At any rate, throughout this discussion I will use the expression "class position" to refer to objective class location.
9. Poulantzas writes: "The analyses presented here have nothing in common with the Hegelian schema with its class-in-itself (economic class situation, uniquely objective determination of class by the process of production) and a class-for-itself (class endowed with its own 'class consciousness' and an autonomous political organization = class struggle), which in the Marxist tradition is associated with Lukács." (ibid.)

Poulantzas adopts for analysing class boundaries centres on elaborating the economic, political and ideological criteria which determine objective class positions within the social division of labour. We will first examine how Poulantzas does this for the working class and the new petty bourgeoisie, and then for the bourgeoisie.

Structural Determination of Working Class and New Petty Bourgeoisie

In the course of capitalist development the traditional petty bourgeoisie—independent artisans, small shopkeepers, etc.—has steadily dwindled. In its place there has arisen what Poulantzas calls the "new petty bourgeoisie", consisting of white-collar employees, technicians, supervisors, civil servants, etc. Under conditions of advanced capitalism, the crucial question for understanding the structural determination of the working class, Poulantzas argues, centres on analysing the boundary between the working class and this new segment of the petty bourgeoisie.

Poulantzas's argument proceeds in two steps. First, he discusses the economic, political and ideological criteria which separate the proletariat from the new petty bourgeoisie. The basic economic criterion he advances is the distinction between productive and unproductive labour. The basic political criterion is the distinction between non-supervisory and supervisory positions. The core ideological criterion is the division between mental and manual labour. Secondly, Poulantzas discusses why this "new" petty bourgeoisie belongs to the same class as the traditional petty bourgeoisie. He argues that, although they appear quite different at the economic level, both the old and new petty bourgeoisie bear the same ideological relationship to the class struggle between the proletariat and the bourgeoisie, and this common ideological relationship is sufficient to merge them into a single class. The first argument explains why certain categories of wage-labourers should be excluded from the working class; the second explains why they should be considered members of a common class, the petty bourgeoisie. We will examine the first of these arguments in some detail, the second more briefly.

Economic Criteria

Poulantzas argues that the distinction between productive and unproductive labour defines the boundary between the working class and the new petty bourgeoisie at the economic level. All workers are productive labourers and all unproductive labourers are new petty bourgeois (as we shall see, some productive labourers are also petty bourgeois). Poulantzas thus decisively rejects wage-labour *per se* as an appropriate criterion for the working class: "It is not wages that define the working class economically: wages are a form of distribution of the social product, corresponding to market relations and the forms of "contract" governing the purchase and sale of labour power. Although every worker is a wage-earner, every wage-earner is certainly not a worker, for not every wage-earner is engaged in productive labour."[10]

Poulantzas defines productive labour in a somewhat more restrictive way than most Marxist writers: "Productive labour, in the capitalist mode of production, is labour that produces surplus-value *while directly reproducing the material elements that serve as the substratum of the relation of exploitation: labour that is directly involved in material production by producing use-values that increase material wealth.*"[11] The conventional definition of productive labour by Marxists does not explicitly restrict it to labour directly implicated in material production. Poulantzas, however, argues that "labour producing surplus-value is broadly equivalent to the process of material production in its capitalist form of existence and reproduction".[12] He insists that this definition is consistent with Marx's usage of the concept of productive labour, since Marx always associated surplus-value creation with commodity production, and commodity production (according to Poulantzas) is always material production.

Given this definition of productive labour under capitalism, Poulantzas argues that unproductive wage-earners must be excluded from the ranks of the proletariat because they lie outside the basic capitalist relation of exploitation. In discussing commercial employees as an example of unproductive

10. Ibid., p. 20.
11. Ibid., p. 216. Italics in original.
12. Ibid., p. 221.

labour, Poulantzas writes: "Of course, these wage-earners are themselves exploited, and their wages correspond to the reproduction of their labour-power. 'The commercial worker . . . adds to the capitalist's income by helping him to reduce the cost of realizing surplus-value, inasmuch as he performs partly unpaid labour.' Surplus labour is thus extorted from wage-earners in commerce, but these are not directly exploited in the form of the dominant capitalist relation of exploitation, the creation of surplus-value."[13] The working class is defined by the fundamental class antagonism within capitalism between direct producers, who are separated from the means of production and produce the social surplus product in the form of surplus-value, and the bourgeoisie, which owns the means of production and appropriates surplus-value. Unproductive wage-earners, while clearly not members of the bourgeoisie, do not contribute to the production of the surplus product. Thus they are not directly exploited in the form of the dominant capitalist relation of exploitation and so, Poulantzas argues, cannot be included in the working class.

Political Criteria

As Poulantzas stresses time and time again, economic criteria alone are not sufficient to define the structural determination of class. In particular, political and/or ideological criteria exclude certain categories of productive wage-earners from the working class. The use of political criteria is especially important in Poulantzas's analysis of the class position of managerial and supervisory labour. Within the process of material production, supervisory labour is unquestionably productive because of its role in coordinating and integrating the production process. But within the *social* division of labour, supervisory activity represents the political domination of capital over the working class: "In a word, the despotism of the factory is precisely the form taken by the domination of the technical division of labour by the social, such as this exists under capitalism. The work of management and supervision, under capitalism, is the direct reproduction, within the process of production itself, of the poli-

13. Ibid., p. 212.

tical relations between the capitalist class and the working class."[14]

How then does Poulantzas reconcile these competing criteria? At the economic level, supervisory labour in commodity production is exploited in the same way that manual labour is exploited; but at the political level, supervisory labour participates in the domination of the working class. Poulantzas solves this problem by turning to the distinction between the *social division of labour* and the *technical division of labour*. While he never explicitly defines the differences between the two, the general sense is that the technical division of labour represents structural positions derived from the particular technologies used in production (or forces of production), whereas the social division of labour is derived from the social organization of production (or relations of production). Now, it is a basic proposition of Marxist theory that "in the actual organization of the labour process, the social division of labour, directly dependent upon the relations of production, dominates the technical division".[15] Poulantzas then argues that the position of supervisors as exploited productive labour reflects their role in the purely technical division of labour, whereas their position of political domination of the working class defines their role in the social division of labour. Given this assertion, he concludes that supervisors' "principal function is that of extracting surplus-value from the workers", and on this basis they must be excluded from the working class altogether.[16]

Supervisors, however, are also excluded from the bourgeoisie, for while they politically dominate the working class they are also politically dominated by capital itself. This specific position within political relations of domination and subordination—subordinated to capital while dominating the proletariat—defines the political criteria for the new petty bourgeoisie.

Ideological Criteria
The working class is not only exploited economically and dominated politically, it is also dominated ideologically. The central

14. Ibid., pp. 227–8.
15. Ibid., p. 225.
16. Ibid., p. 228.

axis of this ideological domination within the social division of labour is the division between *mental* and *manual* labour.[17] Poulantzas argues that the mental/manual division excludes the working class from the "secret knowledge" of the production process, and that this exclusion is necessary for the reproduction of capitalist social relations. "Experts" of various sorts at all stages of the production process help to legitimize the subordination of labour to capital, by making it appear natural that workers are incapable of organizing production themselves. The division between mental and manual labour thus represents the ideological prop for the exclusion of workers from the planning and direction of the production process.[18] Experts are the direct carriers of this ideological domination; thus, like supervisors, they are excluded from the working class.

This ideological criterion is especially important in determining the class position of certain categories of engineers and technicians. Engineers and technicians are generally productive wage-earners, and although many of them occupy positions within the supervisory structure (and thus are new petty bourgeois because of political criteria), there are subaltern technicians who do not directly supervise anyone. Nevertheless, Poulantzas argues, because of the primacy of the social division

17. In defining the mental/manual labour division, Poulantzas writes: "We could thus say that every form of work that takes the form of knowledge from which the direct producers are excluded, falls on the mental labour side of the capitalist production process, irrespective of its empirical/natural content; and that this is so whether the direct producers actually do know how to perform this work but do not do so (again not by chance), or whether they in fact do not know how to perform it (since they are systematically kept away from it) or whether again there is simply nothing that needs to be known." (Ibid., p. 238.) Poulantzas is thus very careful not to define mental labour as "brain work" and manual labour as "hand work". While there is a rough correspondence between these two distinctions, the mental/manual division must be considered an aspect of the social division of labour and not a technical fact of whether muscle or brain is primarily engaged in the labour process.

18. It is important to note that ideological domination, in Poulantzas's framework, has nothing to do with the consciousness of workers. Ideology is a material practice, not a belief system within the heads of workers. To say that the division of labour between mental and manual activities constitutes the ideological domination of the working class means that the material reality of this division excludes workers from the knowledge necessary for the direction of the production process. Of course, such an exclusion has consequences on consciousness—workers may come to believe that they are utterly incapable of gaining the necessary knowledge to organize production—but the ideological domination is real irrespective of the beliefs of workers.

of labour over the technical division, and because within the social division of labour even subaltern technicians (as mental labour) occupy a position of ideological domination over the working class, they must be excluded from the proletariat and considered part of the new petty bourgeoisie. The mental/manual division is central to the determination of the class position of all mental labourers, not just technicians, engineers and the like. White-collar workers in general participate, if only in residual ways, in the elevated status of mental labour, and thus participate in the ideological domination of the working class. Even low-level clerks and secretaries, Poulantzas insists, share in the ideological position of mental labour and thus belong to the new petty bourgeoisie rather than the proletariat.[19]

As in the case of political criteria, capital dominates the new petty bourgeoisie ideologically. The division between mental and manual labour simultaneously supports the ideological domination of manual labour by mental labour and the ideological subordination of mental labour to capital. Experts may participate in the "secret knowledge" of production, but that knowledge is always fragmented and dominated by the requirements of capitalist production and reproduction.

The Class Unity of the New and Traditional Petty Bourgeoisie
Poulantzas admits that it might seem strange to categorize the new and traditional petty bourgeoisie in a single class. He even agrees that the traditional petty bourgeoisie "does not belong to the capitalist mode of production, but to the simple commodity form which was historically the form of transition from the feudal to the capitalist mode".[20] How then can two groupings

19. This does not mean that Poulantzas regards the mental/manual division as operating uniformly on all categories of wage-labourers within the new petty bourgeoisie. He stresses that the mental/manual division is reproduced within the new petty bourgeoisie itself, and that many new petty bourgeois are themselves subordinated to mental labour within the category of mental labour: "The mental labour aspect does not affect the new petty bourgeoisie in an undifferentiated manner. Certain sections of it are affected directly. Others, subjected to the reproduction of the mental/manual division within mental labour itself, are only affected indirectly; and while these sections are still affected by the effects of the basic division, they also experience a hierarchy within mental labour itself." (Ibid., p. 256).

20. Ibid.. pp. 285–6.

which are rooted in such utterly different economic situations be amalgamated into a single class? Poulantzas argues that this class unity is a consequence of the relationship of both the traditional and the new bourgeoisie to the class struggle between the bourgeoisie and the proletariat: "If the traditional and the new petty bourgeoisie can be considered as belonging to the same class, this is because social classes are only determined in the class struggle, and because these groupings are precisely both polarized in relationship to the bourgeoisie and the proletariat."[21] This common polarization with respect to the bourgeoisie and the proletariat has the consequence of forging a rough ideological unity between the traditional and the new petty bourgeoisie. It is this ideological unity, Poulantzas maintains, which justifies placing both the traditional and the new petty bourgeoisie in the same class: "The structural determination of the new petty bourgeoisie in the social division of labour has certain effects on the ideology of its agents, which directly influences its class position . . . these ideological effects on the new petty bourgeoisie exhibit a remarkable affinity to those which the specific class determination of the traditional petty bourgeoisie has on the latter, thus justifying their attribution to one and the same class, the petty bourgeoisie."[22]

The core elements of this common petty-bourgeois ideology include reformism, individualism, and power fetishism. *Reformism*: Petty-bourgeois ideology tends to be anti-capitalist, but regards the problems of capitalism as solvable through institutional reform rather than revolutionary change. *Individualism*: "Afraid of proletarianization below, attracted towards the bourgeoisie above, the new petty bourgeoisie often aspires to promotion, a 'career', to 'upward mobility'."[23] The same individualism characterizes the traditional petty bourgeois, but takes the form of mobility through his becoming a

21. Ibid., p. 294.
22. Ibid., p. 287. Note that here Poulantzas is talking about the ideology *of* a class rather than the position of the class in the social division of labour at the ideological level. While it may be true that the traditional petty bourgeoisie occupies the place of mental labour in the mental/manual division (i.e. the old petty bourgeoisie is not separated from the "secret knowledge" of production even though many petty bourgeois artisans would be classified *technically* as manual labourers), Poulantzas is more concerned here with certain features of the ideology of agents within the petty bourgeoisie.
23. Ibid., p. 291.

successful small businessman. *Power Fetishism*: "As a result of the situation of the petty bourgeoisie as an intermediate class ... this class has a strong tendency to see the state as an inherently neutral force whose role is that of arbitrating between the various social classes."[24] While Poulantzas admits that in certain respects the ideologies of the two petty bourgeoisies are different, he insists that the unity is sufficiently strong as to warrant considering them a single class.

The Structural Determination of the Bourgeoisie

Whereas in his discussion of the boundary between the working class and the new petty bourgeoisie Poulantzas focuses on political and ideological criteria, in the discussion of the bourgeoisie he concentrates on the strictly economic level. His basic argument is that the bourgeoisie must be defined not in terms of formal legal categories of property ownership, but in terms of the substantive dimensions which characterize the social relations of production. Two such dimensions are particularly important. *Economic Ownership*: This refers to the "real economic control of the means of production, i.e. the power to assign the means of production to given uses and so to dispose of the products obtained".[25] Such economic ownership must not be confused with legal title to productive property: "This ownership is to be understood as real economic ownership, control of the means of production, to be distinguished from legal ownership, which is sanctioned by law and belongs to the superstructure. The law, of course, generally ratifies economic ownership, but it is possible for the forms of legal ownership not to coincide with real economic ownership."[26] *Possession*: This is defined as "the capacity to put the means of production into operation".[27] This refers to the actual control over the physical operation of production. In feudal society, the peasant generally retained possession of the means of production while the feudal ruling class maintained economic ownership; in capitalist society, on the other hand, the bourgeoisie has both economic ownership and

24. Ibid., p. 292.
25. Ibid., p. 18.
26. Ibid., p. 19.
27. Loc. cit.

possession of the means of production. The working class is separated from control not only over the product of labour, but over the very process of labour itself.

These two dimensions of social relations of production —economic ownership and possession—are particularly important in analysing the class position of managers.[28] Poulantzas argues that since these agents fulfil the *functions* of capital, they occupy the *place* of capital. Thus they belong to the bourgeoisie, regardless of any legal definitions of ownership: "It is the place of capital, defined as the articulation of relationships that bear certain powers, that determines the class memberships of the agents who fulfil these 'functions'. This refers us to two inter-connected aspects of the problem: (a) the powers involving either utilization of resources, allocation of the means of production to this or that use, or the direction of the labour process, are bound up with the relationships of economic ownership and possession, and these relationships define one particular place, the place of capital; (b) the directing agents who directly exercise these powers and who fulfil the 'functions of capital' occupy the place of capital and thus belong to the bourgeois class even if they do not hold formal legal ownership. *In all cases, therefore, the managers are an integral section of the bourgeois class.*"[29]

Poulantzas recognizes that the precise relationship between economic ownership and possession is not immutably fixed in capitalism. In particular, the process of centralization and concentration of capital characteristic of the development of monopoly capitalism generates a partial "dissociation" of economic ownership and possession. Especially in the developed monopoly corporation, where very heterogeneous production units are often united under a single economic ownership, managers of particular units will generally have possession of the means of production of that unit without directly having economic ownership.[30] Nevertheless, Poulantzas insists that the "dis-

28. When Poulantzas uses the term "managers", he is explicitly discussing those managerial personnel who directly participate in economic ownership and/or possession. When he discusses lower-level positions within the managerial hierarchy, he uses expression like "the work of management and supervision", or simply "supervisors".

29. Ibid., p. 180. Italics added.

30. Poulantzas provides an extremely interesting discussion of the trans-

sociations that we have analysed between the relationships of economic ownership and possession (i.e. the direction of the labour process) do not in any way mean that the latter, exercised by the managers, has become separated from the place of capital".[31] Capital remains a *unitary structural position* within class relations even if the *functions* of capital have become differentiated. It is this structural position which fundamentally determines the class location of managers as part of the bourgeoisie.

Poulantzas has very little to say about the specific ideological and political criteria defining the bourgeoisie, other than that they occupy the position of ideological and political domination in the social division of labour. The most important context in which Poulantzas explicitly treats such criteria is in the discussion of the heads of state apparatuses. Such positions belong in the bourgeoisie, Poulantzas argues, not because they directly occupy the place of capital at the economic level, but because "in a capitalist state, they manage the state functions in the service of capital".[32] The class position of such agents is thus not defined directly by their immediate social relations of production, but rather indirectly by the relationship of the state itself to the capitalist class.

Assessment and Critique of Poulantzas's Analysis

The following critique of Poulantzas's analysis will parallel the foregoing exposition.[33] First, the logic of his analysis of the

---

formations of the dissociation of economic ownership and possession in the course of the development of monopoly capitalism (ibid., pp. 116–130). He argues that during the initial stages of monopoly concentration, economic ownership became concentrated more rapidly than the labour process actually became centralized (i.e. under unified direction). The result was that during this initial phase of concentration, monopoly capital itself was characterized by economic ownership of the means of production with only partial powers of possession. It was not until what Poulantzas calls the restructuring period of monopoly capitalism that economic ownership and possession were fully reintegrated within monopoly capital itself.

31. Ibid., p. 181.

32. Ibid., p. 187.

33. This assessment of Poulantzas's analysis of classes will focus on the actual criteria he uses to understand classes in contemporary capitalism, rather than

boundary between the working class and the new petty bourgeoisie is examined. The discussion focuses on two criticisms: 1. that there is little basis for regarding the distinction between productive and unproductive labour as determining the boundary of the working class at the economic level; 2. that Poulantzas's use of political and ideological factors effectively undermines the primacy of economic relations in determining class position. Secondly, Poulantzas's claim that the traditional and new petty bourgeois are members of the same class is criticized on two grounds: 1. the ideological divisions between the two categories are at least as profound as the commonalities; 2. while ideological relations may play a part in the determination of class position, they cannot neutralize divergent class positions determined at the economic level. Finally, there is a brief examination of Poulantzas's treatment of the boundary of the bourgeoisie. The main criticism made here is that not all managers should be considered an integral part of the bourgeoisie, even if they participate in certain aspects of relations of possession.

The Boundary between Working Class and New Petty Bourgeoisie

It will be helpful in our discussion of Poulantzas's perspective to present schematically the criteria he uses in analysing the structural determination of classes. Table 2.1 presents the criteria by which he defines in the most general way the working class, the traditional and new petty bourgeoisie and the capitalist class. Table 2.2 examines in greater detail the various combinations of criteria which define different sub-categories within the new petty bourgeoisie. It is important not to interpret the categories in these typologies as constituting discrete, empirical "groups". This would certainly be a violation of

on the epistemological assumptions which underlie his analysis. I will thus not deal with the problem of his general concept of "class struggle" and his categorical rejection of "consciousness" as a useful category in a Marxist analysis. While it is important to deal with these issues (indeed, most reviews of Poulantzas's work are preoccupied with these questions rather than the substance of his argument), I feel that it is more useful at this point to engage Poulantzas's work at a lower level of abstraction.

Table 2.1 General Criteria for Class in Poulantzas's Analysis

	Economic criteria			Political criteria		Ideological criteria	
	Exploiter Appropriates Surplus-Value	Exploited* Surplus Labour Extorted	Exploited* Surplus-Value Extorted	Domination	Subordination	Domination	Subordination
Bourgeoisie	+	−	−	+	−	+	−
Proletariat	--	+	+	−	+	−	+
New petty bourgeoisie	−	+	− / +	+ / −	+	+ / −	+
Old petty bourgeoisie	−	−	−	−	+	+	+

+ criterion present   + / − criterion usually present, but sometimes absent
− criterion absent   − / + criterion usually absent, but sometimes present

*To say that 'surplus labour' is extorted from a wage-labourer, but not surplus-value, means that the worker performs unpaid labour for the capitalist, but does not produce actual commodities for exchange on the market. The worker is thus not formally productive, but nevertheless is exploited.

Table 2.2 Various Combinations of Criteria for the New Petty Bourgeoisie

	Economic criteria			Political criteria		Ideological criteria	
	Exploiter Appropriates Surplus-Value	Exploited Surplus Labour Extorted	Exploited Surplus-Value Extorted	Domination	Subordination	Domination	Subordination
Unproductive labour							
Supervisors in circulation and realization	−	+	−	+	+	+	+
Subaltern mental labour	−	+	−	−	+	+	+
*Unproductive manual labour**	−	+	−	−	+	−	+
Productive labour							
Supervisors in material production	−	+	+	+	+	+	+
Technicians and engineers in material production (who are not also supervisors)	−	+	+	−	+	+	+

*This category is not explicitly discussed by Poulantzas, but it is clearly a possibility (e.g. a janitor in a bank).

Poulantzas's view of social classes. The purpose of the typologies is to highlight the relationships among the various criteria, not to turn the analysis of classes and class struggle into a static exercise in categorization.

Let us now turn to the question of Poulantzas's use of the productive/unproductive labour distinction in his analysis of the boundary of the working class, and then to the logic of his use of political and ideological factors as criteria for class. Once these two tasks are completed, we will examine some statistical data on the size of the proletariat in the United States using Poulantzas's criteria.

Productive and Unproductive Labour

There are three basic difficulties in Poulantzas's discussion of productive and unproductive labour: 1. problems in his definition of productive labour; 2. the lack of correspondence between the productive/unproductive labour distinction and actual positions in the labour process; 3.—and most significantly—the lack of fundamentally different economic interests between productive and unproductive workers.[34]

Productive labour, to Poulantzas, is restricted to labour which both produces surplus-value and is directly involved in the process of material production. This definition rests on the claim that surplus-value is only generated in the production of physical commodities. This is an arbitrary assumption. If use-values take the form of services, and if those services are produced for the market, then there is no reason why surplus-value cannot be generated in non-material production as well as the production of physical commodities.[35]

The second difficulty with Poulantzas's use of productive/unproductive labour concerns the relationship of this distinction to positions in the social division of labour. If actual positions generally contain a mix of productive and unpro-

34. Many of the ideas for this section on productive and unproductive labour come directly from James O'Connor's very important essay "Productive and Unproductive Labor", in *Politics and Society*, Vol. 5, No. 2, and from numerous discussions within the San Francisco Bay Area *Kapitalistate* collective.

35. Marx's famous comparison of teaching factories and sausage factories makes this precise point: "The only worker who is productive is one who produces surplus-value for the capitalist, or in other words contributes towards the self-valorization of capital. If we may take an example from outside the sphere of material production, a schoolmaster is a productive worker when, in addition to

ductive activities, then the distinction between productive and unproductive labour becomes much less useful as a criterion for the class determination of those positions. A good example is grocery-store clerks. To the extent that clerks place commodities on shelves (and thus perform the last stage of the transportation of commodities), then they are productive; but to the extent that they operate cash registers, then they are unproductive. This dual quality of social positions as both productive and unproductive is not restricted to the circulation of commodities, but exists directly within the process of material production itself. Consider the case of the material production of the packaging for a commodity. Packaging serves two distinct functions. On the one hand, it is part of the use-value of a commodity. One can hardly drink milk without placing it in a transportable container. But packaging is also part of realization costs under capitalism, since much of the labour embodied in packaging goes into producing advertising. Such labour cannot be considered productive, because it does not produce any use-values (and thus cannot produce surplus-value). This is not a question of any historical normative judgement on the goodness of the labour. Labour which produces the most pointless luxuries can still be productive. But labour which merely serves to facilitate the realization of surplus-value is not, and at least part of the labour-time that is embodied in packaging falls into this category.[36]

---

belabouring the heads of his pupils, he works himself into the ground to enrich the owner of the school. That the latter has laid out his capital in a teaching factory, instead of a sausage factory, makes no difference to the relation." (*Capital*, Vol. I, Penguin/NLR, London 1976, p. 644). It would be hard to imagine a clearer statement that Marx did not restrict the concept of productive labour to labour directly involved in material production. It is surprising that Poulantzas never discusses this quotation, especially since he does cite Marx heavily to support his own use of the concept of productive labour.

36. Admittedly, such advertising-packaging labour is socially necessary labour time under capitalism and contributes to the costs of production of commodities. But this can be said about most realization labour, not just realization labour that becomes physically embodied in a material aspect of the commodity. Advertising labour should therefore be categorized as a *faux frais* of capitalist production, along with many other kinds of unproductive labour. For a fuller discussion of how to count unproductive labour in costs of production, see pp. 151–3 in chapter 3 below. For a discussion of advertising labour, see Baran and Sweezy's analysis of the interpenetration of sales and production in monopoly capitalism: *Monopoly Capital*, New York 1966, chapter 6.

While Poulantzas does admit that some labour has this dual productive/unproductive character, he sidesteps this problem in his analysis of classes by saying that labour is tendentially one or the other. In fact, a large proportion of labour in capitalist society has both productive and unproductive aspects, and there is no reason to assume that such mixed forms of labour are becoming less frequent. The productive/unproductive labour distinction should thus be thought of as reflecting two dimensions of labour activity rather than two types of labourers.

The most fundamental objection, however, to Poulantzas's use of the productive/unproductive distinction goes beyond questions of definition or the conceptual status of the distinction. For two positions within the social division of labour to be placed in different classes on the basis of economic criteria implies that they have fundamentally different class *interests* at the economic level.[37] Let us assume for the moment that the productive/unproductive labour distinction generally does correspond to different actual positions in the social division of labour. The key question then becomes whether this distinction represents a significant division of class interests. If we assume that the fundamental class interest of the proletariat is the destruction of capitalist relations of production and the construction of socialism, then the question becomes whether productive and unproductive workers have a different interest with respect to socialism. More precisely, do unproductive workers in general lack a class interest in socialism? One possible argument could be that many unproductive jobs would disappear in a socialist society and thus unproductive workers would be opposed to socialism. Aside from the problem that this argument confuses occupation with class, many jobs that are quite productive under capitalism would also disappear in a socialist society, while many unproductive jobs in capitalist society —doctors employed by the state for example—would not.

It could also be argued that since unproductive workers produce no surplus-value, they live off the surplus-value produced

37. The expression "fundamental" or "ultimate" class interests refers to interests involving the very structure of social relations; "immediate" class interests, on the other hand, refers to interests within a given structure of social relations. Expressed in slightly different terms, immediate class interests are interests defined within a mode of production, whereas ultimate class interests are interests defined between modes of production (see pp. 88–91 below).

by productive workers and thus indirectly participate in the exploitation of those workers. Taking the argument one step further, it is sometimes claimed that unproductive workers have a stake in increasing the social rate of exploitation, since this would make it easier for them to improve their own wages. This kind of argument is perhaps clearest in the case of state workers who are paid directly out of taxes. Since taxation comes at least partially out of surplus-value,[38] it appears that state workers live off the exploitation of productive labour. There is no question that there is some truth in this claim. Certainly in terms of immediate economic interests, state workers are often in conflict with private sector workers over questions of taxation. The bourgeois media have made much of this issue and have clearly used it as a divisive force in the labour movement. However, the question is not whether divisions of immediate interests exist between productive and unproductive workers, but whether such divisions generate different objective interests in socialism. Many divisions of immediate economic interest exist within the working class—between monopoly and competitive sector workers, between black and white workers, between workers in imperialist countries and workers in the third world, etc. But none of these divisions implies that the "privileged" group of workers has an interest in perpetuating the system of capitalist exploitation. None of these divisions changes the fundamental fact that all workers, by virtue of their position within the social relations of production, have a basic interest in socialism. I would argue that this is true for most unproductive workers as well.

Poulantzas agrees that, in general, both productive and unproductive workers are exploited; both have unpaid labour extorted from them. The only difference is that in the case of productive labour, unpaid labour time is appropriated as surplus-value; whereas in the case of unproductive labour, unpaid labour merely reduces the costs to the capitalist of appropriating part of the surplus-value produced elsewhere. In both cases, the capitalist will try to keep the wage bill as low as possible; in both cases, the capitalist will try to increase productivity by getting workers to work harder; in both cases, workers will be dispossessed of control over their labour process.

38. See pp. 154–5 in Chapter 3.

In both cases, socialism is a prerequisite for ending exploitation. It is hard to see where a fundamental divergence of economic interests emerges from the positions of unproductive and productive labour in capitalist relations of production. Certainly Poulantzas has not demonstrated that such a divergence exists. He has stated that the formal mechanisms of exploitation are different for the two types of workers; but he has not shown why this formal difference generates a difference in basic interests and thus can be considered a determinant of a class boundary.[39]

Another way of looking at this issue is from the point of view of capital. No one has ever suggested that the distinction between productive and unproductive capital represents a class boundary between the capitalist class and some other grouping. Typically, the productive/unproductive capital distinction is treated as one element defining a fractional boundary within the bourgeoisie (such as between banking and industrial capital). However, it could be argued, in much the same fashion as Poulantzas argues for the working class, that unproductive capital lies "outside the dominant capitalist relation of exploitation" and thus agents occupying the place of unproductive capital should not be considered members of the capitalist class. This argument, of course, would be absurd, because it is obvious that whatever short-run conflicts of interests there might be between productive and unproductive capital, their fundamental class interests are the same. The same can be said for the distinction between productive and unproductive labour.[40]

39. A concrete example may help to illustrate this argument. By every definition of unproductive labour, a janitor in a bank is unproductive. No surplus-value is produced in a bank and thus the labour of all bank employees is unproductive. A janitor in a factory, however, is productive, since cleaning up a work area is part of the socially necessary labour time in the actual production of commodities. Is it reasonable to say that these two janitors have a different class interest in socialism? Unless this is the case, it is arbitrary to place one janitor in the working class and the other in the new petty bourgeoisie. (See G. Carchedi, "On the Economic Identification of the New Middle Class", *Economy and Society*, Vol. IV (1975), No. 1, p. 19, for a similar critique of unproductive labour as a criterion for class.)

40. This critique of Poulantzas's use of the productive/unproductive labour distinction as a class criterion does not imply that the distinction has no relevance for Marxist theory in general. In particular, the distinction between productive and unproductive labour may play a central part in the analysis of the accumulation process and crisis tendencies in advanced capitalism. (See Chapter 3).

Political and Ideological Criteria

Poulantzas insists that while ideological and political criteria are important, economic criteria still play the principal role in determining classes.[41] If we look at Charts 1 and 2, this does not appear to be the case. As can be seen from the charts, the working class represents the polar opposite of the bourgeoisie: on every criterion they have opposite signs. *Any* deviation from the criteria which define the working class is enough to exclude an agent from the working class in Poulantzas's analysis. Thus, an agent who was like a worker on the economic and political criteria, but deviated on the ideological criteria, would on this basis alone be excluded from the proletariat (this is the case for subaltern technicians). In practice, therefore, the ideological and political criteria become co-equal with the economic criteria, since they can *always* pre-empt the structural determination of class at the economic level. (This is quite separate from the question of the correctness of the economic criteria themselves as discussed above.) It is difficult to see how, under these circumstances, this perspective maintains the primacy of economic relations in the definition of classes.

The treatment of ideological and political criteria as effectively coequal with economic criteria stems, at least in part, from Poulantzas's usage of the notion of the "technical" division of labour. Poulantzas very correctly stresses that the social division of labour has primacy over the technical division. But he incorrectly identifies the technical division of labour with economic criteria whenever he discusses the role of political and ideological factors. For example, in the discussion of technicians Poulantzas writes: "We have . . . seen the importance of the mental/manual labour division for the supervisory staff and for

41. In reading this critique of Poulantzas's use of political and ideological criteria in the definition of classes, it is important to remember the political and ideological context in which Poulantzas has developed his analysis. In a personal communication, Poulantzas writes: "I think that one of our most serious politico-theoretical adversaries is *economism*, which *always* pretends, as soon as we try (with all the theoretical difficulties we encounter here) to stress the importance of the politico-ideological, that we 'abandon the primacy of economics'." Poulantzas is absolutely correct in attacking economism and in attempting to integrate political and ideological considerations into the logic of a Marxist class analysis. The difficulty, as we shall see, is that he does not develop a clear criterion for the use of ideological and political criteria, and thus in practice they assume an almost equal footing with economic relations.

engineers and technicians. This played a decisive role in so far as, by way of the primacy of the social division of labour over the technical, it excluded these groupings from the working class despite the fact that they too perform 'capitalist productive labour'."[42] Poulantzas in effect equates the performance of productive labour with the technical division of labour. But if the "dominant capitalist relation of exploitation" constitutes the essential definition of productive labour, then it is unreasonable to treat productive labour as strictly a technical category. More generally, rather than viewing economic criteria as being rooted in the technical division of labour and political-ideological criteria in the social division, both should be considered dimensions of the social division of labour. If this is granted, then it is no longer at all obvious that ideological and political criteria should always pre-empt economic criteria in the structural determination of class. On the contrary: if economic criteria within the social division of labour are to be treated as the principal determinants of class, then they should generally pre-empt the ideological and political criteria.

Aside from undermining the economic basis of the theory of class, Poulantzas's use of political and ideological criteria has other difficulties. Especially in his discussion of political criteria, it is sometimes questionable whether these criteria are really "political" at all. The core political criterion Poulantzas emphasizes in his discussion of the new petty bourgeoisie is position within the supervisory hierarchy. Now, apart from the issue of supervision as technical coordination, there are two ways in which supervision can be conceptualized. Following Poulantzas, supervision can be conceived as the "direct reproduction, within the process of production itself, of the political relations between the capitalist class and the working class".[43] Alternatively, supervision can be seen as one aspect of the structural dissociation between economic ownership and possession at the economic level itself. That is, possession, as an aspect of the ownership of the means of production, involves (to use Poulantzas's own formulation) control over the labour process. In the development of monopoly capitalism, possession has become dissociated from economic ownership. But equally, pos-

42. *Classes in Contemporary Capitalism*, p. 251.
43. Ibid.. p. 228.

session has become internally differentiated, so that control over the entire labour process (top managers) has become separated from the immediate control of labour activity (supervision). Unless possession itself is to be considered an aspect of political relations, there is no reason to consider supervision a reflection of political relations within the social division of labour rather than a differentiated element of economic relations.[44]

In Poulantzas's use of ideological criteria, it is never clear exactly why the mental/manual division should be considered a determinant of an actual class boundary, rather than simply an internal division within the working class. It is also not clear why this particular ideological dimension was chosen over a variety of others as the essential axis of ideological domination/subordination within the social division of labour. For example, sexism, by identifying certain jobs as "women's work" and of inferior status to men's work, is also a dimension of ideological domination/subordination within the social division of labour. This puts men as a whole in a position of ideological domination, and yet this hardly makes a male worker not a worker. The same can be said of racism, nationalism and other ideologies of domination. All of these create important divisions within the proletariat; but, unless they correspond to different actual relations of production, they do not constitute criteria for class boundaries in their own right.

The Size of the Proletariat Using Poulantzas's Criteria

The upshot of Poulantzas's use of economic, political and ideological criteria is that the working class in the United States becomes a very small proportion of the total population. Of course, the validity of a conceptualization of class relations can hardly be judged by the number of people that fall into the working class. Nevertheless, since it is of considerable political importance how large or small the working class is seen to be, it

44. It is one thing to say that supervision has a political dimension and another to say that supervision is itself political relations within production. The former seems correct and is analogous to saying that possession and even economic ownership have political dimensions. The latter considerably expands the notion of the "political" and must, of necessity, make possession of the means of production itself part of the "reproduction of political relations within production".

is worth attempting to estimate the distribution of the population into classes using different criteria for class position.

While census data are of relatively little use in estimating the size of the working class, since they are not collected in terms of Marxist categories, there are other sources of data which are more useful. In particular, the University of Michigan Survey Research Center conducted a survey in 1969 on working conditions throughout the United States which included a number of questions which make it possible to reach a reasonably good estimate of the size of the working class using a variety of criteria. The survey contains data on: the respondent's occupation and the industry in which he/she works; whether or not the respondent has subordinates on the job whom he/she supervises; whether or not the respondent is self-employed, and if so, how many employees, if any, the respondent has.[45] On the basis of these questions, we can estimate the size of the working class according to Poulantzas's criteria if we make some rough assumptions about the relationship of occupational titles to the mental/manual labour division and the relationship of industrial categories to the productive/unproductive labour distinction.

For present purposes, we will use the following definitions: 1. *Mental Labour*: professionals, technicians, managers (by occupational title), clerks and salespeople. 2. *Manual Labour*: craftsmen, operatives, labourers, transportation and services (i.e. janitors, barbers, cooks, etc.). 3. *Unproductive sectors*: wholesale and retail trade, finance, insurance, real-estate, services and government. 4. *Productive sectors*: agriculture, fishing, mining, construction, manufacturing, transportation and communications.

This set of categories is not perfect, both because of limitations of the data and because the complex reality of class relations can only be approximated by statistical data. By Poulantzas's definition of mental labour, there are certainly some craftsmen who should be considered mental labourers (i.e. they are not separated from the "secret knowledge" of pro-

45. See my "Class Structure and Income Inequality", unpublished Ph.D. Dissertation, Department of Sociology, University of California, Berkeley (available from University Microfilms, Ann Arbor, Michigan), for a detailed discussion of the survey.

duction and use it in their labour process). There are also positions in trade and government which are clearly productive by any definition, and some positions in productive sector industries which are unproductive. Nevertheless, these categories can give us a pretty good idea of the size of the proletariat based on Poulantzas's analysis.

The results appear in Tables 2.3–2.5. Table 2.3 presents the proportion of the total economically active population (i.e. people working twenty hours a week or more) that fall into each combination of the criteria for class. (None of the results differs significantly if the analysis is restricted to full-time workers.) The working class—non-supervisory, manual wage-earners in the productive sector—constitutes less than 20 per cent of the American labour force. The new petty bourgeoisie, on the other hand, swells to a mammoth 70 per cent of the economically active population. Table 2.4 gives these same results for men and women separately. Less than 15 per cent of the economically active women in the American population are working-class according to Poulantzas's criteria, while among men the figure is still only 23 per cent.[46] Finally, Table 2.5 gives the proportion of the population which is working-class using a variety of different combinations of Poulantzas's criteria. If the productive/unproductive labour distinction is dropped, but the other criteria kept, the working class increases to over 30 per

46. A reasonable objection could be raised that the estimates according to Poulantzas's criteria are unrealistically low because I have used such a broad definition of supervision. Undoubtedly, some individuals say that they "supervise others on the job" when in fact they are simply the chief of a work team and have virtually no actual power within the labour process. As a result of the vagueness of the criterion for supervision, the estimates in Tables 1 and 2 indicate that well over a third of the labour force are supervisors. A second set of data enables us to adopt a more refined criterion for supervision. (However, the data set in question, the ISR Panel Study of Income Dynamics, is much less of a representative sample than the survey used in the above Tables, and thus is less adequate to gain a picture of the overall shape of the class structure.) In this second survey, individuals who said that they were supervisors were also asked if they had "any say in the pay and promotions of their subordinates". Approximately 65 per cent of all male blue-collar supervisors said that they did *not* have any say in pay and promotions (the data are not available for female supervisors). If we assume that all of these individuals should be classified as workers by Poulantzas's criteria, then the proportion of males in the working class increases from 23 per cent in Table 2 to about 33 per cent. Undoubtedly, the true proportion is somewhere in between these two estimates. In any event, even using this narrower definition of supervision, the working class remains a decided minority in Poulantzas's framework.

Table 2.3 Distribution of the Active Labour Force by Class Criteria (United States national random sample taken in 1969)

| | Self-Employed | | Wage-Earners | | |
	Em-ployers	Petty Bourgeoisie	Super-visors	Non-supervisors	TOTALS
Mental Labour					
Unproductive Sector	3·3%	1·9%	15·6%	16·5%	37·2%
Productive Sector	2·5%	0·4%	4·4%	4·5%	11·9%
Manual Labour					
Unproductive Sector	0·3%	0·3%	5·3%	11·2%	17·2%
Productive Sector	1·3%	1·8%	10·7%	19·7%	33·6%
TOTALS	7·5%	4·5%	36·1%	51·9%	100·0%
Number in Sample	110	65	526	758	1459

SOURCE: 1969 Survey of Working Conditions, Institute of Social Research, University of Michigan (for a detailed discussion of the sample, see my "Class Structure and Income Inequality", unpublished Ph.D Dissertation, Department of Sociology, University of California, Berkeley. Available from University Microfilms, Ann Arbor, Michigan).

DEFINITIONS:

Mental Labour: professionals, technicians, managers (by occupational title), clerks, sales
Manual Labour: craftsmen, operatives, labourers, transportation, services (i.e. janitors, etc.)
Unproductive Sectors: wholesale and retail trade, finance, insurance, real estate, services, government
Productive Sectors: agriculture, mining, fishing, construction, manufacturing, transportation, communications

Table 2.4 Distribution of Active Labour Force by Class Criteria for Men and for Women (1969)

| MEN | Self-Employed | | Wage-Earners | | |
	Em-ployers	Petty Bourgeoisie	Super-visors	Non-supervisors	TOTALS
Mental Labour					
Unproductive Sector	4·0%	1·7%	14·3%	9·0%	29·0%
Productive Sector	4·0%	0·6%	5·6%	3·0%	13·2%
Manual Labour					
Unproductive Sector	0·4%	0·2%	5·6%	8·7%	14·9%
Productive Sector	2·1%	2·7%	15·4%	22·7%	42·9%
TOTALS	10·5%	5·3%	40·8%	43·4%	100·0%
Number in Sample	98	49	380	404	931

(See Table 2.3 for definitions of the categories)

WOMEN	Self-Employed		Wage-Earners		
	Em-ployers	Petty Bourgeoisie	Super-visors	Non-supervisors	TOTALS
Mental Labour					
Unproductive Sector	2·2%	2·0%	18·1%	30·9%	53·1%
Productive Sector	0·0%	0·2%	2·4%	7·1%	9·6%
Manual Labour					
Unproductive Sector	0·2%	0·4%	5·1%	15·2%	20·9%
Productive Sector	0·0%	0·0%	1·8%	14·6%	16·3%
TOTALS	2·4%	2·6%	27·4%	67·7%	100·0%
Number in Sample	12	13	129	344	508

(See Table 2.3 for definitions of the categories)

Table 2.5 The Size of the American Working Class by Different Criteria, 1969

Criteria for the working class	Percentage of the economically active population which is working class by given criteria		
	TOTAL	MEN ONLY	WOMEN ONLY
All wage-earners	88·0%	83·6%	95·1%
All wage-earners who are not supervisors	51·9%	43·4%	67·7%
Blue-collar wage-earners (including blue-collar supervisors)	46·8%	52·4%	36·7%
Blue-collar, non-supervisory wage-earners	31·0%	31·4%	29·8%
Productive, non-supervisory manual labour (the working class in Poulantzas's analysis)	19·7%	22·7%	14·6%

SOURCE: Same as Table 2.3

cent of the population. If the manual/mental labour distinction is dropped, but the supervisory labour criterion kept, the proportion rises to over 50 per cent of the population (67 per cent for women). We will deal more thoroughly below with the question of alternative criteria for class. The important point in the present context is that it makes a tremendous difference which criteria are used to define the proletariat, and that using Poulantzas's criteria reduces the American working class to a small minority.

The Class Unity of the New and Traditional Petty Bourgeoisie

The relationship of economic to political and ideological criteria is even more important in Poulantzas's argument about the class unity of the old and new petty bourgeoisie than it is in his analysis of who should be excluded from the working class in the first place. At the economic level not only are the old and new petty bourgeoisie characterized by different economic situations, but those situations are in many ways fundamentally opposed to each other. In particular, the old petty bourgeoisie is constantly threatened by the growth of monopoly capitalism, while the new petty bourgeoisie is clearly dependent upon monopoly capital for its reproduction. At the political level their interests are also opposed: the new petty bourgeoisie in general has an interest in the expansion of the state; the old petty bourgeoisie is generally opposed to big government and large state budgets.

In order for these opposing interests of the old and new petty bourgeoisie at the economic and political levels to be neutralized by the ideological level, the ideological bonds between the old and new petty bourgeoisie would have to be very powerful indeed. In fact, Poulantzas provides a partial view of the ideologies of the old and new petty bourgeoisie, and it is equally plausible to characterize them as opposed at this level as well as at the economic and political levels. While it is true that individualism characterizes the ideology of both the new and old petty bourgeoisie, the individualism of the two categories is extremely different. The individualism of the old petty bourgeoisie stresses individual autonomy, be your own boss, control your own destiny, etc. The individualism of the new petty bourgeoisie, on the other hand, is a careerist individualism, an individualism geared towards organizational mobility. The archetypal new petty bourgeois is the "organization man" whose individualism is structured around the requirements of bureaucratic advancement; the archetypal traditional petty bourgeois is the "rugged individualist", who makes his/her own way outside of the internal demands of organizations. To call both of these "petty-bourgeois individualism" is to gloss over important distinctions.

The basic problem with Poulantzas's discussion of the old and new petty bourgeoisie, however, does not concern these ideological divisions between them. Even if the two categories could be said to have identical ideologies, it would still be very questionable on this basis to call them a single class. In what sense can the economic level be considered the "principal" determinant of class relations if two groups of agents with contradictory positions at the economic level—in fact, who exist in different modes of production at the economic level—can, on the basis of ideology alone, be grouped into a single class? In the end, the procedure Poulantzas adopts makes ideology itself the decisive criterion for class.

The Class Boundary of the Bourgeoisie

Table 2.6 presents the various combinations of criteria Poulantzas uses to define the bourgeoisie. The most valuable aspects of his discussion are the emphasis on the need to go below legal categories of ownership and the analysis of the historical transformations and dissociations of economic ownership and possession.

Poulantzas's discussion of the class position of managers, however, is inadequate. When a manager occupies a position in the relations of production that is characterized by *both* economic ownership and possession, it is certainly reasonable to categorize the manager as part of the bourgeoisie. The problem arises when a manager occupies a position characterized by possession but not economic ownership. Poulantzas's solution to this situation is to argue that, in spite of the structural differentiation of different functions of capital, the positions

Table 2.6 Detailed Criteria for the Bourgeoisie and for Differentiation of Bourgeoisie and Petty Bourgeoisie

	ECONOMIC CRITERIA			POLITICAL CRITERIA			IDEOLOGICAL CRITERIA	
	Legal Owner-ship	Econo-mic Owner-ship	Posses-sion	Direct Pro-ducer	Dom-ina-tion	Sub-ordi-nation	Dom-ina-tion	Sub-ordi-nation
Traditional Entrepreneurial Capitalists	+	+	+	-	+	-	+	-
Top Corporate Executives	-	+	+	-	+	-	+	-
Managers	--	-	+	-	+	-	+	--
Heads of State Apparatuses	-	--	-	-	+	-	+	..
Traditional Petty Bourgeoisie	+	+	+	+	-	+	+	+

remain unitary parts of capital as such. Thus, occupying any such position is sufficient to define the manager as bourgeois. This is an arbitrary solution. It is equally plausible to argue that exclusion from economic ownership defines non-capitalists in capitalist society, and thus managers who are "mere" possessors of the means of production should be excluded from the bourgeoisie. A third possibility—which will be developed more fully below—is to argue that there are positions in the social division of labour which are *objectively contradictory*. Managers who are excluded from any economic ownership would constitute such a category, even if they retain partial possession of the means of production.

A second problem with Poulantzas's analysis of the bourgeoisie is that he tends to regard economic ownership and possession as all-or-nothing categories. A position either does or does not have real economic control of the means of production (economic ownership), or does or does not have the capacity to put those means of production into operation (possession). In fact, many managerial positions must be characterized as having limited forms of both ownership and possession. Some managers may have substantial control over one small segment of the total production process; others may have fairly limited control over a broader range of the production process. While it is clear that an agent whose control is so attenuated that he/she merely executes decisions made from above should be excluded from the bourgeoisie, there is considerable ambiguity how middle-level managers of various sorts should be treated. Poulantzas's apparent solution is to argue that "In all cases, therefore, the managers are an integral section of the bourgeois class".[47] Again, an alternative solution is to treat contradictory cases as contradictory cases rather than to collapse them artificially into one class category or another.

An Alternative Conceptualization of Class Boundaries

Perhaps the most serious general criticism of Poulantzas's perspective centres on his treatment of ambiguous positions within the class structure. In his analysis of the working class, *any* deviation at all from the pure working-class criteria in Chart 1 is sufficient for exclusion from the proletariat; in his analysis of the bourgeoisie, on the other hand, it is necessary to deviate on *all* criteria in order to be excluded from the capitalist class. In neither case is the possibility allowed that positions within the social division of labour can be objectively contradictory.[48]

Contradictory Locations within Class Relations

An alternative way of dealing with such ambiguities in the class structure is to regard some positions as occupying *objectively contradictory locations within class relations*. Rather than eradicating these contradictions by artificially classifying

47. Ibid., p. 180.

48. Poulantzas at one point does suggest the possibilities of ambiguous cases when he writes: "The mental/manual labour division is reproduced as a tendency, in the sense that it does not provide a typological classification into rigid compartments for this or that particular agent, and that what matters for us here is its social functioning in the existence and reproduction of social classes." (Ibid., p. 256.) This theme, however, is never developed or given any theoretical specificity in its own right. At most, Poulantzas suggests that there may be some ambiguity in the application of a particular criterion for class position, but not that there may be ambiguities created by contradictions among criteria.

every position within the social division of labour unam-
biguously into one class or another, contradictory locations need
to be studied in their own right. This will be the primary objective of the rest of this chapter.[49] (In a sense, of course, all class
positions are "contradictory locations", in that class relations
are intrinsically antagonistic, contradictory social relations.
The point is that certain positions in the class structure constitute doubly contradictory locations: they represent positions
which are torn between the basic contradictory class relations of
capitalist society. Rather than refer to these positions with a
cumbersome expression such as "contradictory locations within
the basic contradictory class relations", I will for convenience
simply refer to them as "contradictory class locations".)

So far, our discussion of class structure has centred around
the elaboration of various criteria for class. This has perhaps
been somewhat misleading. When the word "criteria" is used,
there is usually an implication that the purpose of the analysis
is the construction of formal, abstract typologies. Ambiguities
in the class structure then appear as classification problems in
the typology, as failures of analytical imagination rather than
as objective characteristics of the society itself. The concept of
contradictory locations within class relations, however, does not
refer to problems of pigeon-holing people within an abstract
typology; rather it refers to objective contradictions among the
real processes of class relations. To fully grasp the nature of the
class structure of capitalist societies, therefore, we need first to
understand the various processes which constitute class relations, analyse their historical transformation in the course of
capitalist development, and then examine the ways in which
the differentiation of these various processes has generated a
number of contradictory locations within the class structures of
advanced capitalist societies.

To anticipate the conclusion of the analysis, three clusters of

49. Carchedi's analysis (op. cit. and "Reproduction of Social Classes at the
Level of Production Relations", *Economy and Society*, Vol. IV, No. 4, pp.
362–417) of the new middle classes bears a certain resemblance to the present
discussion of contradictory locations within class relations. Carchedi defines the
new middle classes as positions which perform both the "global function of
capital" and the "function of the collective worker" and thus "are only iden-
tifiable in terms of contradiction". For a discussion and critique of Carchedi's
analysis, see Wright, "Class Structure . . .", op. cit. appendix to chapter 2.

positions within the social division of labour can be characterized as occupying contradictory locations within class relations (see Fig. 2.1): 1. *managers and supervisors* occupy a contradictory location between the bourgeoisie and the proletariat; 2. certain categories of *semi-autonomous employees* who retain relatively high levels of control over their immediate labour process occupy a contradictory location between the working class and the petty bourgeoisie; 3. *small employers* occupy a contradictory location between the bourgeoisie and the petty bourgeoisie. Our first task is to analyse how these contradictory locations emerge out of the dynamics of class relations in advanced capitalist society.

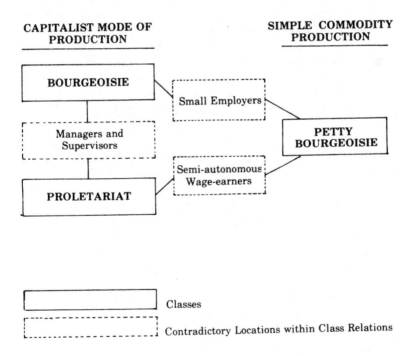

Figure 2.1   The Relationship of Contradictory Class Positions to Class Forces in Capitalist Society

The Processes of Class Relations

Three interconnected structural changes in the course of capitalist development can help us to unravel the social processes underlying class relations in advanced capitalism:[50] the progressive loss of control over the labour process on the part of the direct producers; the elaboration of complex authority hierarchies within capitalist enterprises and bureaucracies; and the differentiation of various functions originally embodied in the entrepreneurial capitalist.[51] Since each of these developments has been thoroughly studied elsewhere, I will only briefly review them here in order to give more substance to the social processes used in the rest of the analysis.

1. *Loss of control over the labour process by workers.* The saga of the progressive dispossession of the direct producers in the course of capitalist development has been told many times. The point that needs stressing here is that the loss of control over the labour process is not an all-or-nothing phenomenon, but has occurred gradually over a long period of time and exists in varying degrees even today. In the earliest capitalist production process, the direct producers generally maintained considerable control over the labour process. Often, especially in cottage industries, they even owned all or part of their immediate means of production. Such a situation made it much easier for the direct producers to control the pace of their labour and the length of their working day, thus making it more difficult for capitalists to raise the rate of exploitation. The net result was that workers' control over their own labour acted as a serious constraint on the accumulation process in early capitalism.[52]

Much of the history of class struggle between capitalists and workers, especially in the 19th century, can be seen as a

50. See ibid., chapter 2 for a considerably more elaborate discussion of these processes of class relations.

51. The point of studying these three historical transformations is less to understand their historical origins as such, than to use structural re-orderings of the capitalist system as a way of gaining insights into the social processes underlying class relations in contemporary capitalism. The epistemological assumption is that a number of distinct social processes are congealed in the class relation between the proletariat and the bourgeoisie and that an analysis of the historical transformations of that class relation is a way of gaining knowledge about the underlying processes themselves.

52. See Chapter 3, p. 170.

struggle over the terms of the control of the labour process.[53] As Stephen Marglin has argued, one of the major impulses for the creation of factories was the desire to undermine worker control.[54] At a minimum factory owners had much greater control over the length of the working day, and generally over other aspects of the labour process as well.

Once workers were gathered within factories, the assault on their remaining control of the labour process continued in the form of technical innovations which fragmented the production process and progressively "deskilled" the labour force.[55] Capitalists could force workers to work in the factory for ten hours by the clock, but as long as the worker maintained real autonomy in the labour process it was difficult for the capitalist to be sure of getting anywhere near ten hours of actual labour from the worker. The close supervision of the labour process is much easier when tasks are simple and routinized and their pace is determined by machinery rather than the worker. Thus, capitalists look for innovations which tend to reduce skill levels and reduce the autonomy of workers on the job. The culmination of this process was the mass production assembly line regulated by principles of Taylorism, in which the worker lost all autonomy and became virtually a human component of machinery itself.

The reverse tendency also exists within capitalism. As technology changes, new skills are needed and new categories of jobs are created in which the worker may have greater immediate control over the labour process. Furthermore, in recent decades the crude scientific management advocated by Taylor has been replaced at least partially in some corporations by "human relations" approaches to the problem of worker productivity. One part of such new approaches is, in principle, the "enrichment" of jobs and the enlargement of the sphere of decision-making under the control of the worker.

Both of these counter-tendencies to the general process of deskilling and the erosion of worker autonomy in the labour

53. See especially Katherine Stone, "The Origins of Job Structures in the Steel Industry", *Review of Radical Political Economics*, Vol. 6, No. 2, Summer 1974.

54. "What Do Bosses Do?", *Review of Radical Political Economics*, Vol. 6, No. 2, 1974.

55. See Harry Braverman, *Labour and Monopoly Capitalism*, New York 1974.

process, however, still reflect the salience of control over the labour process as a dimension of class relations. While new skills are continually being created, it is also true that there is constant pressure to reduce the skill levels needed to perform a given task. Thus, for example, when computers were first being developed, the actual operators of computer hardware tended to be engineers. Gradually over the past twenty years this job has been "deskilled" until, at present, computer operators are technicians with only one or two years of post-high school training.

As for the various experiments with worker participation, such enlarged autonomy is almost always confined within very narrow limits and is always seen as a way of getting workers to work more productively. That is, control is relinquished—and generally peripheral control at that—only when it is more than compensated for by increasing production. Thus, in a report to the Conference Board[56] entitled "Job Design for Motivation", Harold Rush writes: "The current emphasis [in job design] is on gaining internal motivation from the employee so that he performs his tasks with more dedication and commitment, as contrasted with coercion, robot-style control, and machine-like pacing.... The design and redesign of jobs may be said to have a single purpose, though it is a purpose with a double edge: to increase both employee motivation and productivity."[57]

Greater worker control of the labour process, or what is often called "worker participation", is one important form of this redesigning of jobs to increase productivity. In a second Conference Board report entitled "Worker Participation: New Voices in Management", John Roach writes: "A Conference Board survey of top level executives in 50 countries indicates that participation concepts are winning increased acceptance as approaches to improving productivity, motivating job satisfaction, and resolving labour-management problems both

56. The Conference Board is a nonprofit business research organization which is, in its own words, "an institution for scientific research in the fields of business economics and business management. Its sole purpose is to promote prosperity and security by assisting in the effective operation and sound development of voluntary productive enterprise." Members of the Conference Board are drawn from the top executives of the largest corporations in the United States and generally the views of the Conference Board can be interpreted as reflecting the "vanguard" position of the American capitalist class.

57. Harold Rush, "Job Design for Motivation: Experiments in Job Enlargement and Job Enrichment", *Conference Board Report* No. 515, New York 1971.

within and outside traditional collective bargaining processes. Indeed, responses from the international panel suggest that a widening emphasis on participation is adding a broad new dimension to the operation of free enterprise in the Western World. That is not to say that management has decided it should share any of its board-room prerogatives with unions, works councils, or other worker representatives. On the contrary, the general mood of the 143 executives cooperating in the Board's survey is that management must resist attempts to usurp its ultimate authority to make the big decisions."[58]

Far from contradicting the importance of control of the labour process as a dimension of class relations, the sporadic trends towards increased worker participation reveal the underlying logic of this dimension. Capital tries to extract as much actual labour out of the worker during the work day as possible (this would hardly be denied by any capitalist). Control over the labour process is a basic means of accomplishing this. Under certain historical conditions, for example when a large proportion of the industrial work force are newly proletarianized petty bourgeois (artisans, peasants, etc.) with little experience of factory discipline and without proper work habits, strict and despotic control of the labour process may be the most effective structure of control from the capitalist point of view. Under contemporary conditions, a partial relaxation of direct control may accomplish the same end.[59] In any event, social relations of control over the labour process remain a basic dimension of class relations.

2. *The differentiation of the functions of capital.* No development in capitalist social relations has been used more often as "proof"

58. John Roach, "Worker Participation: New Voices in Management" *Conference Board Report* No. 564, New York 1973.

59. This is not to suggest that the capitalist simply decides what structure of control of the labour process is most advantageous for increasing the rate of exploitation, and then proceeds to adopt that form of control. In the 19th century there was often considerable resistance on the part of craft labour to efforts at deepening capitalist control over the labour process, and at the present many of the experiments in enlarged worker participation, especially in Europe, have been the result of pressures from workers rather than initiatives from capitalists. Control of the labour process is a constant object of class struggle (or perhaps more precisely: it is a dimension of class struggle), and the actual patterns of control which emerge should be seen as the outcome of such struggle and not simply manipulative devices used by capitalists.

that Marx's image of class structure is outmoded than the so-called "separation of ownership and control" in the modern corporation. Of course, no one can deny the considerable growth of managerial hierarchies in the modern corporation and the general decline of the traditional family-owned firm in favour of the joint-stock company (although, as Zeitlin forcefully argues, there are considerable data to indicate that the proponents of the "managerial revolution" thesis have grossly exaggerated these changes).[60] The issue is not whether professional managers play a bigger role in running corporations today than 100 years ago, but how such positions should be structurally interpreted in terms of a theory of class relations.

The apparent separation of ownership and control in the large corporation hides a complex process involving a whole series of structural transformations and differentiations. Two such transformations are of particular importance for our discussion: the functional differentiation between economic ownership and possession, and the partial dissociation between legal ownership and economic ownership. In the 19th century, all three of these dimensions of ownership were embodied in the entrepreneurial capitalist. As part of the process of the concentration and centralization of capital, these three dimensions of ownership have tended to become at least partially differentiated.

The partial separation of economic ownership (control over the flow of investments into production, or more concretely, control over *what* is produced) from possession (control over the production process, or control over *how* things are produced) is a consequence of the concentration and centralization of capital within the accumulation process. Increasing concentration and centralization has encouraged the differentiation of economic ownership and possession for two reasons: first, and most obviously, as the scale of both ownership and production increases, it becomes less and less practical for the same individuals to be equally involved in both functions. Competitive pressures will tend to push capitalists to hire professional managers to deal with specific aspects of production and eventually to help coordinate the production process as a whole. Secondly, as

60. Maurice Zeitlin, "Corporate Ownership and Control: the Large Corporation and the Capitalist Class", *American Journal of Sociology*, Vol. 79, 1974.

Poulantzas has emphasized, there is a tendency in monopoly capitalism for the concentration and centralization of economic ownership to develop more rapidly than the concentration and centralization of possession, i.e. for a diverse collection of production processes to be formally united under a single economic ownership. In such circumstances it becomes impossible for the two functions of capital—ownership and possession—to be completely united in a single position.

Capitalist development has also been characterized by a gradual dissociation between formal legal ownership and real economic ownership. This is the famous phenomenon of the dispersion of stock ownership in the large corporation. The fact of such dispersion has been the core datum used by supporters of the managerial revolution thesis to argue that the control of the corporation has moved from property owners to professional managers. Marxists have generally drawn quite different conclusions. Building on the arguments of Hilferding, De Vroey writes: "Concerning the second aspect of the separation of ownership and control, i.e., the dissociation between legal ownership and ownership as a relation of production, the Marxist interpretation is as follows: the dispersion of stock among a large number of small owners is accepted as a matter of fact, and explained as a means to mobilize the ever increasing amount of capital needed for accumulation. But rather than seeing the dispersion of stock as an obstacle to concentrated control, Marxism interprets it in exactly the opposite way: as a means for reinforcing the actual control of big stockholders, who thus succeed in commanding an amount of funds out of proportion to their actual ownership. Paradoxically, dispersion of stock thus favors the centralization of capital."[61] For the managerial revolution proponents to prove their case, therefore, it is not enough to show that stock is widely dispersed. They must show that real economic ownership is in the hands of managers, i.e., that they actually control the accumulation process as a whole. The emphasis on economic ownership as opposed to formal legal ownership should not be taken to imply that legal title to stocks and other forms of property is irrelevant to understanding class relations. On the contrary: as long as capitalist relations of

61. Michael DeVroey, "The Separation of Ownership and Control in Large Corporations", *The Review of Radical Political Economics*, Vol. 7, No. 2, 1975.

production remain embedded in the legal superstructure of private property, formal legal ownership is in general a *necessary* condition for economic ownership. The point of the distinction between economic and legal ownership is that formal title is not a *sufficient* condition for actual participation in the control of the investment and accumulation process.[62]

3. *The development of complex hierarchies.* The same process of concentration and centralization of capital that generates the basic differentiation of economic ownership and possession, also generates various forms of internal differentiation within each of these dimensions of ownership. First let us look at relations of possession. Relations of possession concern the direction and control of the capitalist production process. Such direction involves two analytically separable aspects: first, control of the physical means of production; second, control of labour. Even in the earliest capitalist enterprise, there was some structural differentiation between these two aspects. Foremen were typically excluded from any real control of the physical means of production, yet played an important role in the supervision of workers. As the capitalist enterprise expanded, additional layers of supervision were added, leading eventually to the complex hierarchy of social control within the monopoly corporation. Capitalist development has also produced an elaborate hierarchy within the other aspect of possession, control over the physical means of production. At the highest levels of the hierarchy, top managers control the entire apparatus of production.[63] Below them, various middle levels of management

62. The debate on the relationship between legal ownership and real economic ownership becomes especially important in the analysis of class relations in societies where all property is legally owned by the State (such as the USSR or China). The most vigorous defenders of the thesis that legal ownership is of entirely secondary significance tend to be those who wish to demonstrate that such countries are essentially capitalist. I will not address the questions of class in such state-owned economies. In the West, legal ownership cannot be relegated to a purely epiphenomenal status. Legal title to property remains the essential vehicle for controlling resources in capitalist societies and thus shaping the entire accumulation process. Not all individuals who own stock are part of the bourgeoisie, but all occupants of bourgeois class locations own substantial quantities of stock (or other forms of property in the means of production).

63. "Level" refers principally to the scope of control attached to a particular position, rather than the formal location within an organizational hierarchy (although the two would generally tend to coincide). The word "control" in this

participate in the control of segments of the production process. At the bottom, certain categories of workers maintain some real control over their immediate production process (i.e. over *how* they do their jobs).

A similar line of reasoning can be developed for economic ownership. In the earliest capitalist enterprise, economic ownership was not organized hierarchically. A single figure was essentially responsible for the entire accumulation process. In the modern corporation, however, different levels of economic ownership can be distinguished. Full economic ownership refers to participation in the control of the overall investment and accumulation process. Typically, the highest executives in the corporation and certain members of the board of directors would occupy this position. Under most circumstances, full economic ownership implies a substantial level of formal legal ownership as well. Below this level there are executives and managers who participate in decisions concerning investments in either sub-units of the total production process (e.g. branches) or partial aspects of the entire investment process (e.g. marketing). Finally, minimal economic ownership involves control over *what* one produces in one's immediate labour process, even though one has no control over what is produced in the production process as a whole.[64] These various hierarchical levels within the relations of economic ownership and relations of possession are summarized in Table 2.7.

On the basis of this brief sketch of historical developments

---

context should not be taken to imply that the *individual* who occupies a particular social position controls the means of production as an individual. Rather the word designates a social relationship between the position and the means of production. To say that top managers "control the entire apparatus of production" does not mean that any one individual by him/herself controls the entire apparatus, but rather that the individual occupies a position which participates in the control of the entire apparatus of production.

64. Such residual economic ownership constitutes genuine ownership to the extent that genuine control over the disposition of resources—what is produced—exists. Of course, in most corporate settings such minimal ownership is highly constrained by higher level ownership relations, both in the sense that the range of possible uses of resources is limited by higher up decisions and in the sense that the magnitude of resources available for use may be strictly determined from above. When such control over what is produced becomes so marginal as to be irrelevant to the overall accumulation process, then it ceases to make sense to talk about even residual forms of economic ownership.

Table 2.7 Hierarchical Levels within Ownership Relations

	Relations of Economic Ownership (control over *what* is produced)	Relations of Possession (control over *how* things are produced)		Legal Ownership
		Control of means of production	Control over labour power	
Full control	Control over the overall investment and accumulation process	Control over the entire apparatus of production	Control over the entire supervisory hierarchy	Sufficient stock to ensure influence on investments and accumulation
Partial control	Participation in decisions concerning either sub-units of the total production process or partial aspects of the entire investment process	Control over one segment of total production process	Control over one segment of the supervisory hierarchy	Sufficient stock to ensure financial stake in profits of corporation (stock is a significant part of income)
Minimal control	Control over *what* one produces in one's immediate labour process	Control over one's immediate instruments of production; over *how* one does one's own job	Control over the direct producers, over immediate subordinates but not part of the hierarchy as such	Marginal stock ownership (stock is an insignificant part of income)
No control	Complete exclusion from participation in decisions about what to produce	Negligible control over any aspect of the means of production	No ability to invoke sanctions on other workers	No stock ownership

within capitalist relations of production, it is possible to isolate three central processes underlying the basic capital-labour relationship: control over the physical means of production; control over labour power; control over investments and resource allocation. The first two of these comprise what Poulantzas has called possession; the third is essentially the same as economic ownership. Again, it must be stressed that these three processes are the real stuff of class relations in capitalist society; they are not merely analytic dimensions derived from *a priori* reasoning.[65]

The fundamental class antagonism between workers and capitalists can be viewed as a polarization on each of these three underlying processes or dimensions: capitalists control the accumulation process, decide how the physical means of production are to be used, and control the authority structure within the labour process. Workers, in contrast, are excluded from the control over authority relations, the physical means of production, and the investment process. These two combinations of the three processes of class relations constitute the two basic antagonistic class locations within the capitalist mode of production.

When the capitalist system is analysed at the highest level of abstraction—the level of the pure capitalist mode of production—these are the only class positions defined by capitalist relations of production.[66] When we move to the next lower level

65. The non-arbitrariness of the choice of these three dimensions of class relations is reflected in their correspondence to the three elements in the formal value equations of Marxist political economy (total value = C + V + S). The control over the physical means of production represents relations of control over constant capital; control over labour implies relations of control over variable capital; and control over investments and accumulation implies relations of control over surplus value. (This correspondence was suggested by Michael Soref).

66. There is a strong tradition within Marxism which limits the definition of classes to this most abstract level. Such simple polarization views of class insist that except for the residues of classes from pre-capitalist modes of production, all positions within capitalist society fall either within the capitalist class or the working class. Typically, in such analyses all wage-earners are considered workers. The basic weakness of simple polarization views of the class structure is that they assume that the simplicity of class relations at the level of abstraction of the mode of production can be directly translated into a corresponding simplicity at the level of concrete societies. The added complexities of concrete social structures are taken to be of purely secondary importance. They may contribute to divisions within classes, but they in principle can have

of abstraction—what is generally called the level of the "social formation"—other class positions appear.

They appear, first of all, because real capitalist societies always contain subordinate modes of production other than the capitalist mode of production itself. In particular, simple commodity production (i.e., production organized for the market by independent self-employed producers who employ no workers) has always existed within capitalist societies. Within simple commodity production, the petty bourgeoisie is defined as having economic ownership and possession of the means of production, but having no control over labour power (since no labour power is employed). The relationship of the petty bourgeoisie to the polarized class positions of the capitalist mode of production is illustrated in Table 2.8.

A second way in which additional class positions appear when we leave the abstraction of the pure capitalist mode of production is that the three processes which constitute capitalist social relations of production do not always perfectly coincide. This non-coincidence of the dimensions of class relations defines the contradictory locations within class relations.

The Analysis of Contradictory Locations within Class Relations

We will explore two different kinds of contradictory locations: 1. contradictory locations between the bourgeoisie and the proletariat, i.e. locations defined by contradictory combinations of the three processes underlying class relations within the capitalist mode of production; 2. contradictory locations between the petty bourgeoisie and both the proletariat and the bourgeoisie, i.e. locations situated between the capitalist mode of production and simple commodity production.[67] Table 2.9

---

no effects on the criteria for class boundaries. This is a fundamentally incorrect way of understanding the relationship between abstract and concrete levels of analysis. Abstract relations do not obliterate the importance of concrete complexities, but rather render them theoretically intelligible. As we will see below, contradictory class locations can be understood only with reference to the basic polarized class relations of the capitalist mode of production, and yet they cannot be reduced to those polarized class positions.

67. We will not discuss contradictory locations that occur because an individual simultaneously occupies two class positions within social relations of

Table 2.8 Unambiguous Locations within Class Relations

| | PROCESSES UNDERLYING CLASS RELATIONS | | |
| | *Economic Ownership* | *Possession* | |
	Control over investments and the accumulation process	Control over physical means of production	Control over the labour power of others
Bourgeoisie	+	+	+
Proletariat	−	−	−
Petty bourgeoisie	+	+	−

+ Full Control   − No Control   (See Table 2.7 for precise definitions)

presents the basic relationship between the unambiguous locations illustrated in Table 2.8 and the contradictory locations. In addition to the three social processes discussed above, this chart also contains three juridical categories: legal ownership of property, legal status as the employer of labour power, and legal status as a seller of labour power. These three juridical processes have been included because they so often are treated as the determinants of class position. It must be kept in mind in referring to them that the juridical criteria are of strictly secondary importance; the fundamental issue remains the patterns of contradictory locations defined by the three substantive processes of class relations.

Contradictory Locations Between the Proletariat and the Bourgeoisie
One thing is immediately obvious from Table 2.9. The contradictory quality of a particular location within class relations is a variable rather than all-or-nothing characteristic. Certain

---

production. For example, a craftsman who works in a factory on weekdays may operate as a self-employed petty-bourgeois artisan on weekends and evenings. While such dual class membership may be important in certain historical circumstances, it does not pose the same kind of analytical problem as positions which are themselves located in a contradictory way within class relations.

Table 2.9 Contradictory Locations Within Class Relations

| | Substantive social processes comprising class relations | | | Juridical categories of class relations | | |
| | Economic Ownership | Possession | | Legal Ownership | | Wage Labour |
	Control over investments, resources	Control over the physical means of production	Control over the labour power of others	Legal ownership of property (capital, stocks, real estate etc.)	Legal status of being the employer of labour power	Sale of one's own labour power
Bourgeoisie						
Traditional capitalist	+	+	+	+	+	–
Top corporate executive	+	+	+	Partial	–	Minimal
Contradictory location between the proletariat and the bourgeoisie						
Top managers	Partial	Partial	+	Minimal	–	Partial
Middle managers	Minimal	Minimal	Partial	–	–	+
Technocrats	Minimal/–	–	Minimal	–	–	+
Foremen/line supervisors	–	–	Minimal	–	–	+
Proletariat	–	–	–	–	–	+
Contradictory location between the proletariat and the petty bourgeoisie						
Semi-autonomous employees	Minimal	Minimal	–	–	–	+
Petty bourgeoisie	+	+	–	+	–	–
Contradictory location between the petty bourgeoisie and the bourgeoisie						
Small employers	+	Minimal	Minimal	+	Minimal	–

Full control   Partial: Attenuated control   Minimal: Residual control   – No control
(See Table 2.7 for precise definitions)

positions can be thought of as occupying a contradictory location around the boundary of the proletariat; others as occupying a contradictory location around the boundary of the bourgeoisie.

The contradictory location closest to the working class is that of foremen and line supervisors. Foremen typically have little real control over the physical means of production, and while they do exercise control over labour power, this frequently does not extend much beyond being the formal transmission belt for orders from above. It is difficult to say whether during the course of capitalist development over the past century, the class location of foremen has moved closer to or further from the working class. On the one hand, the early foreman often participated directly in the production process alongside workers and even defended workers against arbitrary treatment by the boss. On the other hand, the foreman in the nineteenth-century factory often had much greater personal discretion and personal power than today. In the nineteenth century, authority within the capitalist factory was typically organized in much the same way as an army. There was a simple chain of command and the authority at each level was absolute with respect to the level below. Such a system Marx aptly termed "factory despotism", and foremen in such a factory had at least the potential of being petty despots. As the capitalist enterprise grew in scale and complexity, the authority structure gradually became more bureaucratized. As Weber would put it, foremen increasingly became the administrators of impersonal rules rather than the dispensers of personal fiats.

Richard Edwards, in a study of work norms in bureaucratically structured capitalist organizations, describes this shift in authority relations as follows: "What distinguishes modern enterprises from their earlier and cruder prototypes—and in particular, what distinguishes bureaucratic organization from simple hierarchy—is that in bureaucratically organized enterprises, the exercise of power becomes *institutionalized*. External, arbitrary, personal commands from the boss are replaced by established rules and procedures: 'rule of law' replaces 'rule of personal command'. Work activities become directed by rules. Supervisors at all levels, no longer directing the worker's activities by personal instruction, merely enforce the rules and evaluate (reward or penalize) their sub-ordinates according to pre-established criteria for adequate work performance. More and more, the work structure is designed so that administrative control can replace executive control."[68] The development of the capitalist enterprise has thus pushed foremen in two opposing directions: they have moved further from workers by becoming less involved in direct pro-duction, and they have moved closer to workers by gradually having their personal power bureaucratized. Superficially at least, it would seem that the first of these tendencies probably dominated during the first part of this century, while the second tendency probably dominates today. In any event, when the control of supervisors over labour power becomes so attenuated that the supervisor lacks even the capacity to invoke negative sanctions, then the position really merges with the working class proper and should no longer be thought of as a con-tradictory location. This would be the case, for example, of the chief of a work team who has certain special responsibilities for coordinating activities of others in the team, but lacks any real power over them.

At the other end of the contradictory location between work-ers and capitalists, top managers occupy a contradictory loca-tion at the boundary of the bourgeoisie. While top managers are generally characterized by limited participation in economic ownership, they differ little from the bourgeoisie in terms of relations of possession. Again, at the very top of the managerial hierarchy, corporate executives essentially merge with the capitalist class itself.

The most contradictory locations between the bourgeoisie and the proletariat are occupied by middle managers and what can loosely be termed "technocrats". Technocrat in this context refers to technicians and professionals of various sorts within the corporate hierarchy who tend to have a limited degree of autonomy over their own work (*minimal* control over what they produce and how they produce it) and a limited control over subordinates, but who are not in command of pieces of the productive apparatus. Middle managers, on the other hand, control various pieces of the labour process; they have control

68. *Alienation and Inequality: Capitalist Relations of Production in Business Enterprises*, Ph.D. Dissertation, Department of Economics, Harvard, p. 102.

not only over immediate subordinates but over part of the authority hierarchy itself. Both middle managers and techno-crats have, in Harry Braverman's words, one foot in the bourgeoisie and one foot in the proletariat. In discussing new technical occupations and middle management, Braverman writes: "If we are to call this a 'new middle class', however, as many have done, we must do so with certain reservations. The old middle class occupied that position by virtue of its place outside the polar class structure; it possessed the attributes of neither capitalist nor worker; it played no direct role in the capital accumulation process, whether on one side or the other. This 'new middle class', by contrast, occupies its intermediate position not because it is outside the process of increasing capi-tal, but because, as part of this process, it takes its charac-teristics from *both sides*. Not only does it receive its petty share of the prerogatives and rewards of capital, but it also bears the mark of the proletarian condition."[69] Unlike line supervisors and foremen on the one hand, and top managers on the other, middle managers and technocrats do not have a clear class pole to which they are attached. The contradictory quality of their class location is much more intense than in the other cases we have discussed, and as a result it is much more difficult to assess the general stance they will take within class struggle.

Contradictory Locations between the Petty Bourgeoisie and Other Classes

The analysis of the contradictory locations between the petty bourgeoisie and other classes poses a somewhat different prob-lem from the contradictory locations between the bourgeoisie and the proletariat, since it involves locations between different modes of production rather than within a single mode of pro-duction.

The contradictory location between the petty bourgeoisie and the bourgeoisie is conceptually simpler than between the petty bourgeoisie and the proletariat. The distinctive feature of capitalist production is the appropriation of surplus-value through the exploitation of workers in the labour process. In simple commodity production, on the other hand, there is no exploitation; whatever surplus is produced is generated by the

69. Braverman, *Labor and Monopoly Capital*, p. 467.

petty-bourgeois producer and his/her family. In general, of course, the surplus is likely to be very small and thus little if any accumulation is likely to occur. When a petty-bourgeois producer employs a single helper, there is an immediate change in the social relations of production, for the labour of a worker can now be exploited. Still, the surplus-value appropriated from a single employee is likely to be very small; most importantly, it is likely to be less than the surplus product generated by the petty-bourgeois producer him/herself. This is especially likely since frequently in petty-bourgeois production a considerable amount of labour is contributed by unpaid family members. As additional employees are added, the proportion of the total surplus product that is generated by the petty-bourgeois family declines. At some point it becomes less than half of the total surplus product, and eventually becomes a small fraction of the total surplus. At that point, the petty-bourgeois producer becomes firmly a small capitalist. There is no *a priori* basis for deciding how many employees are necessary to become a small capitalist. This number would vary considerably for different technologies employed in production and for different historical periods. In any event, between such a small capitalist and the pure petty-bourgeois producer lies the contradictory location between the capitalist class and the petty-bourgeoisie.

The contradictory location between the petty bourgeoisie and the proletariat can perhaps best be understood by returning to the historic process of proletarianization of the petty bourgeoisie. The central dynamic underlying this transformation was the need of capital to increase its control over the labour process. Each step of the transformation involved a deeper penetration of capitalist domination into the labouring activity of direct producers, until in the classic form of scientific management, the direct producer has no control whatsoever over his/her work. This process is constantly being re-enacted within capitalism; it is not a process which was somehow completed at the beginning of this century.

Today there are still categories of employees who have a certain degree of control over their own immediate conditions of work, over their immediate labour process. In such instances, the labour process has not been completely proletarianized. Thus, even though such employees work for the self-expansion of capital and even though they have lost the legal status of being self-employed, they can still be viewed as occupying residual islands of petty-bourgeois relations of production within the capitalist mode of production itself. In their immediate work environment, they maintain the work process of the independent artisan while still being employed by capital as wage labourers. They control *how* they do their work, and have at least some control over *what* they produce. A good example of this is a researcher in a laboratory or a professor in an elite university. Such positions may not really involve control over other people's labour power, yet have considerable immediate control over conditions of work (i.e. research). More generally, many white-collar technical employees and certain highly skilled craftsmen have at least a limited form of this autonomy in their immediate labour process. Such minimal control over the physical means of production by employees outside of the authority hierarchy constitutes the basic contradictory location between the petty bourgeoisie and the proletariat.

While there is some debate on the question, it seem likely that in the course of capitalist development over the past fifty years, this particular kind of contradictory location has been somewhat reduced. It is certainly true that white-collar employees have increased as a proportion of the labour force, but as Braverman has forcefully shown, this expansion of white-collar employment has been combined with a constant proletarianization of the working conditions of white-collar labour. It remains to be shown whether the net effect of these two tendencies—the expansion of white-collar employment and the proletarianization of white-collar work—has increased or decreased the contradictory locations between the working class and the petty bourgeoisie. At any rate, it seems almost certain that the large majority of white-collar employees, especially clerical and secretarial employees, have—at most— trivial autonomy on the job and thus should be placed within the working class itself.

How much autonomy is really necessary to define a position as occupying the contradictory location between the working class and the petty bourgeoisie? Surely the criterion of absolutely any autonomy whatsoever is too broad. While the historical data on the labour process are rather meagre, it is unlikely that more than a small fraction of the working class was ever characterized by the classic image of the fully proletarianized worker, totally under the control of the capitalist through a minutely subdivided labour process governed by principles of scientific management. Most workers, most of the time, have been able to maintain at least some residual control over their immediate labour process. Similarly, it would be inappropriate to restrict the concept of "semi-autonomy" to positions which, like university professors, have extremely high levels of control over the pace of work, the scheduling of work, the content of work, etc. Clearly, then, a certain amount of arbitrariness will inevitably enter into any attempt rigorously to define the semi-autonomous employee class location.[70]

Provisionally, the minimum criterion for semi-autonomy which I will adopt is that such positions must involve at least some control both over what is produced (minimal economic ownership) as well as how it is produced (minimal possession). This means that positions such as laboratory technicians would not be included in the semi-autonomous category since such positions would generally not involve any control over what kind of experiments were done in the lab, even though a technician might have very considerable control over other conditions of work (pace, breaks, techniques used, etc.). A research scientist, on the other hand, would often not simply have autonomy over how he/she performed an experiment, but over what experiments were performed. Research scientists, therefore, would be firmly within the semi-autonomous employee category.[71]

70. A similar problem exists with the other contradictory locations. How many employees are necessary to transform a small employer (the contradictory location between the petty bourgeoisie and the bourgeoisie) into a proper capitalist? How residual must the authority of a foreman be before he/she should be considered a worker? How much participation in investment decisions is necessary before a top manager should be thought of as part of the bourgeoisie itself? In every case, therefore, there will be ambiguous locations right at the boundaries of polarized classes, and a certain arbitrariness will occur whenever formal criteria are applied to such positions. The semi-autonomous employee category, however, poses additional problems because of the ambiguities in the very concept of "autonomy".

71. There is an important relationship between Poulantzas's discussion of mental labour and this discussion of semi-autonomous employees. Poulantzas defines mental labour as labour which involves "secret knowledge" of the production process, in the sense of having knowledge about the organization and

Several other contradictory locations could be discussed. For example, the owners of fast food and gas station franchises could be seen as occupying a contradictory location between the petty bourgeoisie or small employers and managers. While they maintain some of the characteristics of self-employed independent producers, they also become much more like functionaries for large capitalist corporations. Professors with large research grants which enable them directly to hire research assistants, secretaries, etc., could be thought of as occupying a contradictory location between the semi-autonomous employees and small employers. Other special cases could be given, but the most important contradictory locations are the ones discussed above.

The Size of Contradictory Locations
On the basis of the same data we used to analyse the size of the working class using Poulantzas's criteria, we can make some rough estimates of the size of the various contradictory locations within class relations. The results are presented in Figure 2.2. The criteria used to operationalize the high and low estimates for each category are given in Table 2.10.

Unfortunately, the survey that was available did not contain any precise information on the autonomy of workers in the sense we are using that concept. The survey did, however, contain a number of questions on subjective evaluations of job characteristics. Respondents in the survey were asked to indicate whether a series of job descriptions characterized their own job "a lot", "somewhat", "a little" or "not at all". Two of these descriptions bear on the question of job autonomy:

"A job that allows you a lot of freedom as to how you do your work."

"A job that allows you to make a lot of decisions on your own."

These questions are obviously subjective, since it was left up

---

coordination of the production process as a whole. Poulantzas also emphasizes that to be mental labour (in his sense of the term) it is not enough to simply have such knowledge; it is necessary to actually use it within the production process (see footnote 17 above). Semi-autonomous employees are, in these terms, employees with such knowledge of the production process as a whole, who have the capacity to use such knowledge on their jobs. This is what it means to have minimal control over what is produced and how it is produced.

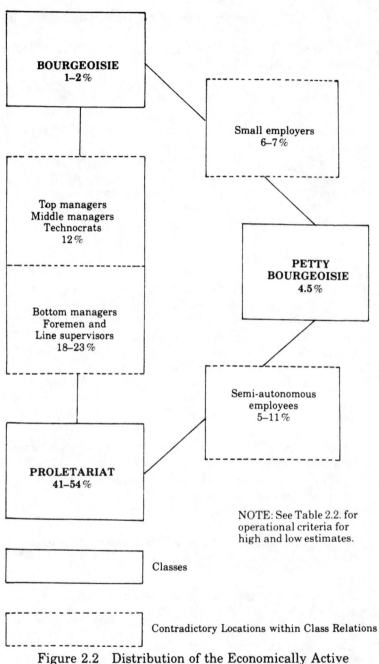

BOURGEOISIE
1–2%

Small employers
6–7%

Top managers
Middle managers
Technocrats
12%

Bottom managers
Foremen and
Line supervisors
18–23%

PETTY
BOURGEOISIE
4.5%

Semi-autonomous
employees
5–11%

PROLETARIAT
41–54%

NOTE: See Table 2.2. for
operational criteria for
high and low estimates.

Classes

Contradictory Locations within Class Relations

Figure 2.2   Distribution of the Economically Active
Population into Contradictory Class Locations (1969)

to each respondent to define what "a lot" means, what "freedom" means, what "decisions" means, and so on. The fact that 46 per cent of the respondents say that having a lot of freedom characterizes their job "a lot", and 49 per cent say that making a lot of decisions describes their job "a lot" reflects the subjective quality of the questions. For the purposes of the present analysis, I will assume that individuals within positions which are genuinely semi-autonomous will answer "a lot" to *both* of these subjective job descriptions. The high estimate of the contradictory location between the proletariat and the petty bourgeoisie (11 per cent of the economically active population) includes all non-supervisory employees who score high on both of these descriptions. The low estimate adds information about the respondent's occupation to this subjective criterion of job autonomy. The U.S. Department of Labour has constructed a "Dictionary of Occupational Titles" (D.O.T.) which codes all occupations in terms of the typical relationship to data, things and people which characterizes that occupation. The low estimate of the semi-autonomous employee category (5 per cent of the economically active population) includes all non-supervisory employees who scored high on the subjective autonomy questions and whose occupation is classified as having a complex relation to data and things in the D.O.T. (see Table 2.10 for more detailed explanation). Because of the extreme vagueness of the subjective autonomy question, this low estimate is probably closer to the correct proportion.

The figures for the contradictory location between the working class and the bourgeoisie are also only rough estimates. Since all we know is whether or not the respondent supervises people, we have certainly included some positions which involve virtually no real control over labour power and thus should belong to the working class proper. We have also included some top executives in the contradictory location who should really have been placed in the bourgeoisie. In any event, this latter problem involves a very small proportion of the total population, perhaps 1–2 per cent of all managers. No questions were asked in the survey which enable us accurately to distinguish between top managers, middle managers and technocrats, and line supervisors and foremen. We can use occupational titles to make some crude estimates. We will assume that all super-

Table 2.10   Criteria Used in High and Low Estimates for Sizes of Classes

	High estimate	Low estimate
Semi-autonomous Employees	All non-supervisory employees who score high on both questions concerning subjective autonomy.[a]	Those non-supervisory employees who score high on the subjective autonomy questions and whose occupation is classified as having a complex relation to data and things by DOT classification[b]
Small Employers	Less than 50 workers	Less than 10 workers
Managers/Supervisors Top/middle managers	Professionals, technicians and managers (by occupational title) who say they supervise people on their job	
Bottom managers/ supervisors	All supervisors not classified as top/middle managers	Excludes operatives and labourers
Workers	All non-supervisory employees plus semi-autonomous employees whose occupations are classified as non-complex by the DOT, plus supervisors whose occupations are operatives or labourers	Non-supervisory employees who score low on either subjective autonomy question

[a] Jobs which the respondent claims are characterized "a lot" by *both* of the following descriptions:
 1) "a job that allows a lot of freedom as to how you do your work"
 2) "a job that allows you to make a lot of decisions on your own"

[b] The Dictionary of Occupational Titles codes occupations in terms of their relationship to data and to things in the following way:
 relationship to things: 0. setting up; 1. precision working; 2. operating-controlling; 3. driving-operating; 4. manipulating; 5. tending; 6. feeding-offbearing; 7. handling; 8. no significant relationship to things.
 relationship to data: 0. synthesizing; 1. coordinating; 2. analysing; 3. compiling; 4. computing; 5. copying; 6. comparing; 7–8. no significant relationship to data.
 An individual whose occupation scored 0–2 on data and 0–2 or 8 on things, or who scored 0–2 on things and 7–8 on data, was classified as having a "complex" job.

visors who say that they are professionals, managers or technicians are probably technocrats, middle managers or top managers. All the rest we will assume are line supervisors or foremen. The high estimate for this bottom category includes all supervisors who are not classified in the top-middle management position; the low estimate excludes operatives and labourers, most of whom are probably heads of work teams rather than actual foremen. On the basis of these estimates, approximately 12 per cent of the economically active population falls into the middle manager/top manager contradictory location between the working class and the bourgeoisie, while somewhere between 18 per cent and 23 per cent occupy the contradictory location at the boundary of the working class. If we take ten employees as the cut-off point for small capitalists, then the contradictory location between the petty bourgeoisie and the bourgeoisie consists of about 6 per cent of the population. If we take fifty employees as the cut-off, then this increases to 7 per cent.

Overall, on the basis of these statistics, the working class (i.e. non-supervisory, non-autonomous employees) in the United States consists of between 41 and 54 per cent of the economically active population. At the boundaries of the working class are another 25–35 per cent of the population, depending upon which estimates are used. The total potential class basis for a socialist movement, consisting of the working class and those contradictory locations closest to the working class, is thus probably somewhere between 60 per cent and 70 per cent of the population.

Class Interests and the Definition of Class Positions

To briefly recapitulate the argument so far, we have analysed the class relations of capitalist society in terms of three processes underlying social relations of production: control of labour power, control of the physical means of production and control of investments and resources. The central class forces of capitalist society—the bourgeoisie and the proletariat—can be understood as representing polar class positions within each of these three processes. The petty bourgeoisie, on the other hand, is defined by the second and the third of these processes within simple commodity production. We then defined contradictory locations within class relations as situations in which these three processes did not perfectly correspond to the basic class forces within the capitalist mode of production or to the petty bourgeoisie in simple commodity production. This led to the analysis of three contradictory locations: managers and supervisors occupy a contradictory location between the bourgeoisie and the proletariat; small employers occupy such a position between the bourgeoisie and the petty bourgeoisie; and semi-autonomous employees occupy a contradictory location between the petty bourgeoisie and the proletariat.

Thus far, no mention has been made of positions in the social structure which are not directly defined by the social relations of production and would thus not be explicitly encompassed by the criteria so far elaborated. Such positions would include housewives, students, pensioners, people permanently on welfare. If one wanted to adopt a fairly narrow conception of relations of *production*, the class location of people employed in the administrative, repressive and ideological apparatuses of the state would also not be directly defined by the criteria discussed above. What then is the relationship of such positions to the structural categories defined directly by the social relations of production? In order to answer this question it is necessary to introduce another distinction into the discussion: the distinction between *fundamental* and *immediate* class interests.

Immediate and Fundamental Class Interests

It is important to be quite clear about how we will use the term "interests" before we discuss the distinction between immediate and fundamental levels of class interests. To make a claim about objective class interests is to make a claim about *potential* objectives of class actors.[72] It makes no sense at all to talk about "interests" which can *never* become actual objectives of real struggles. Not all potential objectives of class actors, however, can be considered class interests. We therefore need to be able to

72. To talk about the objectives of the class struggle is very similar to talking about the *subjective motives* or the class *consciousness* of class actors. In general, I prefer to use the expression "objectives" since it does not have the psychologistic overtones of either subjective motives or consciousness. Nevertheless, to talk about real objectives of struggle is to talk about a certain constellation of subjective motives/consciousness in the actors.

distinguish between objective *class* interests and other kinds of interests (potential objectives). Class interests in capitalist society are those potential objectives which become actual objectives of struggle in the absence of the mystifications and distortions of capitalist relations. Class interests, therefore, are in a sense hypotheses: they are hypotheses about the objectives of struggles which would occur if the actors in the struggle had a scientifically correct understanding of their situations. To make the claim that socialism is in the "interests" of the working class is not simply to make an ahistorical, moralistic claim that workers ought to be in favour of socialism, nor to make a normative claim that they would be "better off" in a socialist society, but rather to claim that if workers had a scientific understanding of the contradictions of capitalism, they would in fact engage in struggles for socialism.[73] In these terms, the very definition of class is systematically linked to the concept of class struggle: to define a position as located within the working class is to say that such a position can potentially sustain socialist objectives in class struggles.

Within this general conception of class interests it is possible to distinguish between what can be termed immediate and fundamental interests. Immediate class interests constitute interests within a given structure of social relations; fundamental interests centre on interests which call into question the structure of social relations itself.[74] That is, immediate

---

73. This is a somewhat oversimplified account of interests. Mystification is not the only factor which obstructs the translation of objective interests into subjective motives within the class struggle. The repressiveness of the state may equally block the organization of struggle around various class interests. The critical point is that to posit class interests is to posit actual subjective orientations towards struggle which would emerge in the absence of such impediments. It should also be noted that while this concept of interests does involve an implicit notion of the rationality of class actors (under specified objective conditions), it has little to do with the utilitarian notions of people as rational, utility-maximizing *individuals*. There is no claim that subjective motives will emerge because individuals *qua* individuals personally have a scientific understanding of their class situation. *Class* interests can only be defined in terms of the potential subjective motives of collectivities, not simply individuals.

74. The distinction between immediate and fundamental interests is not necessarily equivalent to a temporal distinction between short-run and long-run interests. While it is often the case that struggles over the very structure of society are "long-run" struggles, the critical issue is what the objective of struggle is, not the time horizon for that struggle.

interests are interests defined within a given mode of production (i.e. interests which take the mode of production as a given), while fundamental interests are defined between modes of production (i.e., they call into question the mode of production itself). The immediate economic interests of the working class, for example, are defined largely by market relations. Struggles for wages, better living conditions, better education opportunities and so forth all constitute struggles for objectives defined within the basic structure of capitalism. Struggles for socialism, on the other hand, challenge the premises of capitalist relations and reflect the fundamental interests of the working class.[75]

Immediate interests are not "false" interests; they are "incomplete" interests. The struggle over wages reflects a correct understanding by workers of their immediate conditions of existence within capitalism; the *restriction* of struggles to questions of wages, however, reflects an incomplete understanding of the nature of capitalist society as a whole, for it fails to grasp the possibility of transcending the entire system of capitalist exploitation through socialism.

Immediate and fundamental interests do not exist apart from each other; they are dialectically linked. On the one hand, because immediate interests are real, because they impinge directly on the day-to-day existence of workers in capitalist society, it is utopian to conceive of class struggle organized around fundamental interests which does not as well deal with immediate interests. On the other hand, the working class is much more divided at the level of immediate interests than at the level of fundamental interests. Skilled workers are generally in much more favourable market conditions than

75. Because of the manifest conflicts generated by market relations, many sociologists have taken the market to be the central basis for class differentiation. This is especially true for Max Weber who defines classes primarily in terms of market position: "But always this is the generic connotation of the concept of class: that the kind of chance in the market is the decisive moment which presents a common condition for the individual's fate. 'Class situation' is, in this sense, ultimately 'market situation'." (*Economy and Society*, ed. by Guenther Roth, New York: 1968, p. 928.) This general stance has been extended by Anthony Giddens (*Class Structure of the Advanced Societies*, London 1973), who explicitly defines "middle" classes in terms of a market capacity rooted in the possession of educational skills. In all such treatments, classes are defined primarily in terms of immediate interests at the economic level.

unskilled workers and thus often have different immediate interests from other workers. Because of labour market segmentation, male workers may have different immediate interests from female workers, black workers from white workers. Because immediate interests divide the working class, and because they do not directly call into question the structure of capitalist relations, the durability of capitalism depends, in part, on the extent to which struggles over fundamental interests are displaced into struggles over immediate interests.

This contradiction between the immediate and fundamental interests of the working class pervades debates on the left: socialist struggles must take seriously immediate interests, and yet struggles over immediate interests tend to undermine socialist struggles. This contradiction cannot be wished away; it is inherent in the class relations of capitalist society itself. Only in a revolutionary situation do the struggles over immediate and fundamental interests begin fully to coincide (indeed, this might be part of the definition of a revolutionary situation: a situation in which the struggle for objectives within the dominant mode of production directly reinforces struggles over the mode of production).[76]

The Class Location of Positions not Directly Determined by Production Relations

With this understanding of the distinction between immediate and fundamental interests, we can now approach the problem of the class location of various positions in the social structure which are not directly determined by production relations. As a general proposition, the class location of such positions is determined by their relationship to the fundamental interests of classes defined within the social relations of production. Let us see what this means for a number of specific categories of positions defined outside of production relations.

76. One way of interpreting André Gorz's notion of "non-reformist reforms" is to view them as reforms at the level of immediate interests which, even in non-revolutionary situations, tend to reinforce struggles over fundamental interests. This does not mean that there is no tension between such reforms and fundamental interests; but it does imply that within the range of possible reforms compatible with capitalist social relations, some are much more coincident with fundamental interests of the working class than others.

1. *Housewives.* A variety of strategies have been adopted to deal with the class location of housewives. In some accounts, domestic production is treated as a subsidiary mode of production in its own right, in which the male occupies the position of exploiter and the female, the position of exploited. In other accounts, household production is treated as the final state of capitalist production itself, and the housewife as an unpaid worker who is indirectly subordinated to capital.[77]

A much more straightforward way of dealing with this question is to examine the fundamental interests of housewife positions. In particular, in what sense do the fundamental *class* interests of the housewife of a worker differ from those of the worker himself? One might want to claim that she has different interests as a woman, but do her class interests differ in any meaningful way? Does she have any less of a fundamental interest in socialism? Unless one is willing to argue that working class housewives have different interests with respect to socialism, then it is clear that they fall within the working class. This does not in any way imply that the sexual division of labour is unimportant, that women are not oppressed within that division of labour, but simply that the sexual division of labour does not create a division of fundamental *class* interests between husbands and their housewives.[78]

2. *Students.* Like housewives, students are not directly engaged in production relations. The class locations of students, therefore, must be defined by the class location into which they will move upon the completion of their studies. Student positions, in

---

77. For a review of alternative strategies of a class analysis of housewives, see Terry Fee, *Review of Radical Political Economics*, Summer 1976.

78. This treatment of the class location of housewives is sometimes viewed as sexist, since it assigns the class position of the housewife on the basis of the class location of the husband. If we treat the family as the essential unit of analysis, and ask: how is the family articulated with production relations, then it is clear that the class location of the housewife is not defined via her husband but via the family unit of which they both are a part. It is, indeed, a reflection of the sexism of capitalist society that the division of labour within such a family unit often sends the man out to work and leaves the woman in the home. But it is not sexist to identify the class location of the woman in terms of the way in which the family is inserted into capitalist relations of production. The only way of identifying how the family is so inserted is then to examine the class location of the husband.

this sense, should be thought of as pre-class positions, as positions which are linked with greater or lesser certainty to specific class destinies. Daniel Bertaux has suggested that the appropriate way of dealing with such positions is as parts of class-*trajectories*: a life-time structure of positions through which an individual passes in the course of a work career.[79] Student slots constitute the first stage of such trajectories, and their class location must be defined by the class content of the trajectory as a whole. It is the fundamental class interests of such trajectories, rather than the class *origins* of the student which defines their class location.

3. *Pensioners.* Pensioners pose the opposite problem from students. They occupy post-class locations rather than pre-class locations. But like students, their class can only be understood in terms of the trajectories of class positions to which they are linked.

4. *The unemployed; welfare recipients.* Temporarily unemployed people—the reserve army of the unemployed—pose no special problem for a class analysis. Like students and pensioners, they are tied to trajectories of class positions, and this defines their basic class location. The category of permanently unemployed, on the other hand, is more problematic. In classical Marxism, such positions were generally identified as "lumpenproletariat", the underclass of society. This is not an entirely satisfactory way of classifying such positions, for it suggests that they have fundamentally opposed interests to the working class, and thus would play at best an ambivalent role in socialist struggles.

79. Daniel Bertaux, *Destins Personnels et Structures de Classe*, Paris 1977. In a personal correspondence, Bertaux has suggested that all class positions should be understood as trajectories rather than "empty places". This implies that there is a certain indeterminacy in a given individual's class location at any moment in time, since with few exceptions, a given slot may be linked to multiple potential trajectories. One of the critical aspects of a class structure, in these terms, is the degree of such indeterminacy, how it is spread out over the life-cycle, how it is distributed in the population. It must be noted that this is not a simple recasting of the old problem of social mobility (although there is a certain relationship to the problem of mobility). Rather, the argument is that many job changes which look like mobility are not mobility at all, but merely different phases of a single trajectory. The only genuine mobility would be situations in which individuals move from one trajectory to another.

94

At the level of immediate interests, to be sure, there is certainly a tremendous gulf between the working class and the permanently unemployed, at least in the United States, since welfare payments come directly out of taxes and workers see those taxes as coming out of their own labour. At the level of fundamental interests, the question becomes much more ambiguous. If we adopted a purely normative stance towards interests, then it would be easy to say that the permanently unemployed would undoubtedly "benefit" from socialism. But the same could be said of feudal peasants, slaves, and even many small shopkeepers; yet such positions would not thereby fall into the working class.[80] The question is not whether on the basis of ahistorical, utilitarian criteria an individual who is permanently unemployed would benefit from socialism, but whether socialism is a potential objective of struggle for such positions. That is, are those positions linked to capitalist relations of production in such a way that they potentially produce socialist working class consciousness? I cannot adequately answer this question. While it is certainly the case that the conditions of the permanently unemployed can engender an anti-capitalist consciousness, it is less clear whether they would systematically generate or sustain a socialist consciousness. As a purely provisional solution to this problem, the permanently unemployed can be considered a marginalized segment of the working class.

5. *Employees in political and ideological apparatuses*. The final category of positions not directly defined by production relations are positions located entirely within what has traditionally been called the "superstructure": policemen, preachers, professors, etc. How can we understand the fundamental class interests of such positions? In order to answer this question, it is necessary to expand our discussion of class interests from purely economic class interests (socialist vs. capitalist organization of

80. The vaguer concept of "the people" or sometimes "the masses" is sometimes used to include all oppressed classes which, at least in a utilitarian-economic sense, would benefit from a socialist transformation. The working class, however, is clearly a narrower concept, defined by a specific structural location within capitalist society. That structural location does not merely give workers a material benefit from socialism, but provides the structural suppport for a socialist consciousness (i.e., for the historical emergence of the subjective interest in a socialist transformation).

production) to political and ideological class interests (socialist vs. capitalist organization of the state and ideology). Once this is done, we can analyse the relationship between different locations within the political and ideological apparatuses to these interests.

The fundamental interest of the capitalist class at the political and ideological level is to prevent the working class from acquiring state power and ideological hegemony. In different periods of capitalist development this implies different concrete class objectives, but throughout the history of capitalism it has implied the maintenance of hierarchical and bureaucratic structures within the political and ideological apparatuses.[81] Such bureaucratic structures are essential in protecting the capitalist state from potential working class domination.

The fundamental interests of the working class at the political and ideological level are, in a dialectical manner, to obtain state power and establish ideological hegemony. This implies a qualitative restructuring of the capitalist state—what is polemically referred to as "smashing" the state—in ways which allow the working class as a class to exercise state power. While the precise contours of such a reorganization are impossible to specify in advance, the minimum requirement is that they be radically democratic and antibureaucratic.

Different positions within the bureaucratic structures of the political and ideological apparatuses of capitalist society clearly have different relationships to these fundamental bourgeois and proletarian class interests. Schematically, positions within the political and ideological apparatuses can be grouped into three functional categories in terms of these antagonistic class interests:

a. *bourgeois positions* involving control over the creation of state policies in the political apparatuses and the production of ideology in the ideological apparatuses. Examples would include the top bureaucratic positions in the state, churches, universities, and other such institutions.

b. *contradictory locations* involving the execution of state policies and the dissemination of ideology. Examples would include a beat policeman and a high school teacher.

81. See Chapter 4 for a detailed discussion of the centrality of bureaucratic structures for bourgeois political domination.

c. *proletarian positions* involving complete exclusion from either the creation or execution of state policies and ideology. Examples would include a clerk or janitor in a police station and a typist in a school.[82]

In the analysis of positions within the ideological apparatuses, the central issue is the social relations of control over the apparatuses of ideological production *per se*, not simply the participation in the production of ideology. A news reporter, for example, is to a greater or lesser extent involved in producing ideology, but is generally completely excluded from the control over the news apparatus as a whole, and would thus not occupy the bourgeois position within the news media. In these terms, it would be possible further to elaborate this schema of class locations within the ideological apparatuses by introducing the notion of petty bourgeois positions (self-employed, independent intellectuals who control their process of ideological production) and "semi-autonomous" positions (positions which have some control over their immediate production of ideology, but do not control the apparatus of ideological production at all). A novelist might fall into the former category, an assistant professor into the latter. For present purposes, however, I will use the simpler schema of bourgeois, contradictory locations and proletarian positions within the ideological apparatuses.[83]

Extended Definitions of Classes

On the basis of this discussion of fundamental class interests, we can now give a more elaborate definition of classes within capitalist society. The working class can be defined as those positions which:

82. In practice, these three levels within the political and ideological apparatuses can be operationalized in much the same way that the social relations of production at the economic level were operationalized. That is, the working class position in both cases involves exclusion from control over resources, physical means of production/administration, and labour power. The contradictory location involves exclusion from any basic control over resources, but generally does involve some amount of control over physical means of production/administration and labour of others. Finally the bourgeois position in both the political/ideological apparatuses and the economy involves substantial amounts of control over resources, physical means of production/administration and labour.

83. While it is fairly easy to define a petty-bourgeois position at the ideolog-

(a) occupy the working class position within the social relations of production, i.e., wage labour which is excluded from control over money capital, physical capital and labour power; or,

(b) are linked directly to the working class through immediate family or class trajectories; or,

(c) occupy working class positions within political and ideological apparatuses, i.e., positions which are excluded from either the creation or execution of state policy and ideology.

In a complementary manner, the bourgeois class can be defined as those positions which:

(a) occupy the bourgeois position within the social relations of production, i.e., positions of control over money capital, physical capital and labour power; or,

(b) are linked directly to the bourgeoisie through families or class trajectories; or,

(c) occupy bourgeois positions within the political and ideological apparatuses, i.e., positions which involve the control over the creation of state policy and the production of ideology.

Finally, contradictory class locations between the bourgeoisie and the proletariat can be defined as those positions which:

(a) occupy a contradictory location within the social relations of production, i.e., positions which involve a non-coincidence of relations of control over money capital, physical capital and labour power; or,

(b) are linked directly to contradictory locations through families or class trajectories; or,

(c) occupy a contradictory location within the political and ideological apparatuses, i.e., execute but do not create state policy, or disseminate but do not control the production of bourgeois ideology.

Class Structure and Class Struggle

It is all very well and good to clarify the structure of positions defined by social relations of production and to link these to

---

ical level (independent intellectuals), it is much less clear how to define a petty bourgeois location at the political level. This suggests, possibly, a critical difference between political and ideological levels of social structures: the political level is much more tightly organized within the framework of capitalist relations than is the ideological.

other positions in the social structure. Marxism, however, is not primarily a theory of class structure; it is above all a theory of class struggle. It is therefore essential to analyse the relationship between class struggle and class structure, in particular between contradictory class locations and class struggle.

We have already briefly touched on part of this question in our discussion of class interests. Fundamental interests, it will be recalled, were ultimately defined by the potential objectives of class struggle (objectives which call into question the mode of production itself). But how should we conceptualize the ways in which class structure actually shapes class struggle? To deal with this question we need to introduce one final distinction into the discussion: the distinction between class *interests* and class *capacities*.

Class Interests and Class Capacities

At the heart of Marx's analysis of class relations is the thesis that the working class not only has an interest in socialism, but also has the capacity to struggle for and to organize a socialist society. This is precisely what distinguishes "scientific socialism" from various forms of "utopian socialism". Scientific socialism does not simply posit a moral imperative for a socialist society, but also identifies the social agents capable of creating such a society.

How then can we understand theoretically this notion of class capacity, of the capacity of a class to realize its class interests? Class capacities are defined by the *social relations within a class* which to a greater or lesser extent unite the agents of that class into a class formation. Class interests were analysed in the previous section as the potential objectives of classes within the class struggle. Class interests were, in these terms, the link between class structure (i.e., the structure of social relations *between* classes) and class struggle. Similarly, class capacities constitute the link between class formation (i.e., the structure of social relations *within* classes) and the class struggle: capacities constitute the potential basis for the realization of class interests within the class struggle.[84]

84. Throughout this discussion, the actual structure of social relations within a class will be referred to as "class formation"; the consequences of those social

The diverse social relations which objectively link together the agents within a common class location can be divided into two general categories: those links which are generated directly by the structural developments of capitalist society, and those links which are constituted by the conscious organization of the members of that class. The first of these can be called the *structural capacities* of a class, the second, the *organizational capacities* of a class.

The structural capacity of the working class which has received the most attention by Marxists can be termed the capacity of the *collective worker*. The collective worker is a concept which taps the fundamental changes in the labour process which have occurred in the course of capitalist development. The story has been told many times. In the earliest stages of capitalism workers were dispersed in cottage industries or very small shops in which each individual worker was responsible for the fabrication of an entire commodity. As capitalism expanded and developed, workers became increasingly concentrated in large factories in which a very complex division of labour has created considerable interdependence among individual workers. Commodities are no longer produced by individual workers but by the "collective worker". As a result, the objective links among workers within the labour process—their structural capacity within production—have been strengthened and deepened. Marx for one felt that this development was of decisive importance for enabling the working class to struggle effectively against capital and eventually to revolutionize capitalist society.[85]

---

relations for class struggle will be referred to by the expression "class capacities". This use of the term "class formation" is quite similar to that employed by Adam Przeworski in his paper "The Process of Class Formation from Karl Kautsky's *The Class Struggle* to Recent Debates", *Politics and Society* (forthcoming), 1977. Przeworski argues that class formation is a continual process of the organization, disorganization and reorganization of classes. But what is a "formed" class or a class organization if not a structure of social relations within a class which generates a capacity for the struggle over class objectives?

85. To say that the collective worker constitutes the structural capacity of the working class within production does not imply that workers within highly collective, industrial labour processes will necessarily be the most militant or radical in a given period. There are obviously many other factors which determine actual activity within the class struggle aside from the capacity for

The capitalist class, of course, is not oblivious to the implications of the growing concentration of labour within the production process. As Katherine Stone has so effectively demonstrated in the case of the steel industry in the United States, the capitalist class has consciously attempted to undermine the solidarity created by the social relations among workers within production through the creation of job hierarchies, structures of privileges and promotions, etc.[86] To the extent that such strategies weaken the social relations among workers within production, they undermine the structural capacity of the working class (in a sense job hierarchies and the like can be thought of as constituting a structural incapacity of the working class).

The structural capacity of the working class is not determined only within the production process. One can also talk about the structural capacity (and incapacity) of the working class which is rooted in community, i.e., the social relations among workers outside of production. Under certain circumstances, such community based linkages may be at least as important as social relations among workers within production. The kind of class solidarity which emerges in mining towns is probably a good example of this. Ethnic solidarity may also, under certain circumstances, serve to reinforce the class-based social relations within the community.[87]

The relationship between the structural capacity of workers within production and within community is extremely impor-

---

struggle. The fact that in the 19th century many of the most intense class struggles were waged by craft labour resisting proletarianization certainly demonstrates that it is impossible to make a simple equation between the collective worker and actual struggles. The point is not that the structural capacities of classes necessarily predict class *behaviour* within the class struggle, but rather that they condition the possibilities for successfully realizing class interests within those struggles.

86. "The Origins of Job Structures in the Steel Industry", cited above.

87. Al Gedicks shows how in the copper mining communities of Northern Michigan at the turn of the century, community and ethnic solidarity served to reinforce the social relations among workers generated within production: the result was an extremely militant and cohesive movement among miners in the period. "Ethnicity, Class Solidarity and Labor Radicalism among Finnish Immigrants in Michigan Copper Country", *Politics and Society*, Vol. 6, No. 4, 1976, and *The Radical Finns of Northern Minnesota: A Study in the Development of Working-Class Politics*, Ph.D Dissertation, Department of Sociology, University of Wisconsin, 1978.

tant. It can be argued that while capitalist development in the United States over the past century has led to an increasing concentration and differentiation of labour within production, with an accompanying increase in the structural capacity of the working class within production, there has been a corresponding dispersion and disintegration of working class communities. Suburbanization, increasing home-ownership (at least until recent years), geographical mobility, and other factors have all contributed to a loosening of ties among workers outside of production, and thus to a weakening of the non-production based structural capacity of the working class.[88]

The structural capacities of classes can be thought of as structuring the possibilities for the self-organization of classes.[89] The organizational capacities of classes, on the other hand, constitute the actual linkages among members of a class created by and through consciously directed class organizations. Unions, for example, constitute an organizational structure of social relations among workers consciously directed towards the realization of immediate economic interests. The strength and forms of unions depend, in part at least, on the development of the underlying structural capacities of the working class (the collective worker), and thus we can treat the structural capacities as shaping, or setting limits upon, the organizational capacities.

Organizational capacities play a pivotal role in understanding class struggle and social change. As Przeworski has argued, the class struggle is in the first instance a struggle over the very existence of organized classes before it is a struggle between organized classes.[90] To the extent that the working class can be prevented from transforming structural capacities into organizational capacities, the capitalist class is capable of

88. See Daniel Luria, *Suburbanization, Home-ownership and Working-Class Consciousness*, Ph.D. Dissertation, Department of Economics, University of Massachusetts, 1976.

89. Marx's famous analysis of peasants as a "sack of potatoes" in *The Eighteenth Brumaire of Louis Bonaparte* represents an analysis of the relationship between structural and organizational capacities of classes. Marx argues that the physical isolation of peasants—their structural incapacity—makes it impossible for them to form themselves into a class—that is, to develop a viable organizational class capacity.

90. "The Process of Class Formation from Karl Kautsky's *The Class Struggle* to Recent Debates."

containing the pervasive contradictions of capitalism; to the extent the working class is able to forge enduring organizational capacities around fundamental interests, the very existence of capitalism is potentially threatened.[91]

Class Structure, Class Formation and Class Struggle

We are now in a position to introduce the concept of class struggle into the analysis. Class struggle will be conceived as the complex social processes which dialectically link class interests to class capacities. This relationship is symbolically represented in Figure 2.3, using the modes of determination discussed in Chapter 1. While the diagram should be read as a dialectical totality, nevertheless it will be useful to go through each of the connections in the diagram in turn.

1. *The relationship of class structure to class struggle.* The class structure sets the broadest limits of variation on class struggle in at least two senses. First, the class structure defines the *potential* actors in the class struggle (for example, without peasants it is impossible to have land seizures as a form of class struggle). Secondly, the class structure defines the range of potential *objectives* of class struggle (for example, until the emergence of large-scale industrial capitalism, nationalization as an objective of the class struggle was not a viable possibility).

2. *The relationship of class formation to class struggle.* A given class structure determines only the broadest possible limits of variation of class struggle. A wide variety of social processes

91. Poulantzas's well-known analysis of the dual functions of the capitalist state—to disorganize the working class and organize the bourgeoisie—can be interpreted in terms of the relationship between structural capacities and organizational capacities of classes. The critical problem that the capitalist class faces with respect to the working class, Poulantzas argues, is the potential organization of the working class created by the internal developmental tendencies of capitalism. It is essential, therefore, that mechanisms be established which prevent the structural capacities of the working class from being transformed into organizational capacities. Many of the characteristics of the capitalist state accomplish just this. The creation of the juridical citizen, the individualized process of political participation, the organization of political conflict around commodity relations rather than production relations, and so on, all serve to atomize the working class and (partially) block the translation of structural into organizational capacities.

function as selective forces on class struggle within those limits. Class capacities constitute one of the most decisive selection determinations of class struggle. The underlying structural capacities of classes and the specific organizational forms shaped by those structural capacities have a tremendous impact on forms of class struggle. The form of economic class struggle, for example, is heavily influenced by the forms of trade unionism (organizational class capacity of the working class at the economic level). When unions are organized by competing political tendencies (communist unions vs. socialist unions vs. christian unions), trade union struggles are much more likely to be directed at the state and coordinated with party struggles, rather than simply directed at the immediate capitalists involved in a conflict. When unions are organized on an industrial basis as in certain sectors in the United States, on the other hand, union activity is likely to be much more focused on the immediate employer. Perhaps an even more telling example of the relationship of class capacity to class struggle concerns the political organizational capacity of the working class. The organization of the working class through electoral parties has a pervasive impact on class struggle. Under most conditions, this has resulted in a systematic displacement of class struggles from fundamental interests to immediate interests, since parliamentary competition pushes parties to advocate in practice only those programmes which are compatible with the overall reproduction of capitalism. In the final chapter of this book we will discuss whether such displacement is an inevitable consequence of parliamentary politics, but the historical record of such displacement is certainly impressive.

3. *The relationship of class struggle to class structure and class formation.* Class struggle is not a "dependent variable" shaped by external causes; rather, it enters into the very process by which it is itself determined. Specifically, both the class structure and the organizational capacities of classes are objects of class struggle and are transformed by class struggle. The entire process of primitive accumulation in early capitalism should be viewed as class struggle over class structure: the emerging capitalist class attempting to expand the size of the proletariat through various means (enclosures, immigration, poor laws,

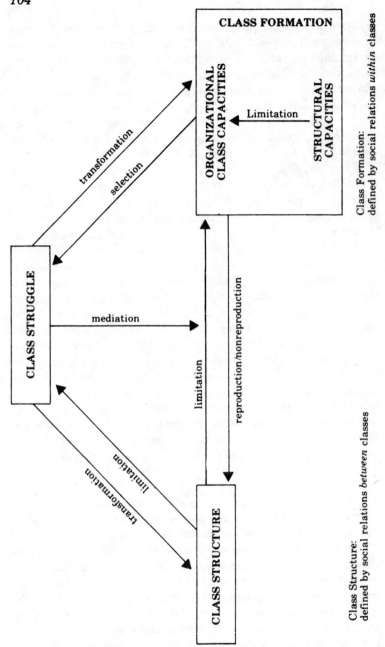

Figure 2.3 Model of Determination of Class Structure, Class
Formation and Class Struggle

etc.); the threatened urban and rural petty bourgeoisie attempting to resist such proletarianization. Similarly, organizational capacities are objects of class struggle. The fights for union rights and the franchise were the earliest forms of such struggles by the working class; the struggles for workers' councils and neighbourhood councils in advanced capitalism are contemporary forms. In each of these cases the organizational capacity for the working class to engage in struggle is itself transformed by class struggle.

4. *The interrelationship of class structure and class formation.* Just as class structure sets objective limits of variation on forms of class struggle, so it sets limits of variation on the forms of class capacities. What is particularly important in this relationship, however, is the role of class capacities in reproducing/nonreproducing the class structure itself. Not all forms of class capacity which are structurally possible in capitalism are reproductive of capitalist class relations. To the extent that working class organizational capacities are organized around fundamental interests, those capacities are likely to become non-reproductive of the class structure itself. If the working class is to be organized at all, it is thus critical to the capitalist class that it be organized around immediate interests. Many of the characteristics of the capitalist state can be seen as accomplishing precisely this (see footnote 91).

5. *Class struggle as mediating the relationship between class structure and class formation.* The ways in which class struggle mediates the relationship between class structure and class capacities are of the utmost importance. A given class structure does not generate a unique configuration of class capacities. Class struggle enters into the determination of class capacities in two ways. One has already been mentioned: class struggle directly transforms existing class capacities. But class struggle also mediates the very way in which class structure affects class capacities.

What precisely does this mean? Class structure is defined by the social relations between classes, class capacities by the social relations within classes. When we say that class structure establishes limits on class capacities, what we mean is that it establishes limits on the ways in which social relations are formed among positions within the class structure. One way of looking at this process is to imagine that every position in the class structure has a certain probability of being organized into a given class formation. The concept of "limits", in these terms, refers to the patterns of these probabilities as they are determined directly by the class structure. Of particular importance is the fact that many positions in the class structure have essentially a zero-probability of being mapped into certain class formations: bourgeois positions, for example, cannot be organized into working class trade unions or revolutionary socialist parties.[92] In these terms, contradictory locations within class relations can be viewed as those positions which have the least determinate probabilities of being organized into given class formations. They are characterized by multiple potential mappings into class formations, which reflect the objective contradictory character of the class interests of such positions.

To say that class struggle mediates this process of mapping class positions into class formations means that class struggle can alter the very probabilities of given positions being mapped into given class formations. In the case of the working class and the bourgeoisie, this process of mediation determines, above all, the extent to which they will be organized as classes in the first place. As Przeworski stresses, all classes are in a constant process of organization, disorganization and reorganization. It is conditions of class struggle which determine the extent to which a given structure of class relations will produce a high level of class organization or disorganization.[93]

92. This does not mean, of course, that individuals who occupy bourgeois class locations cannot support trade unions or, for that matter, join revolutionary socialist parties. Engels is a classic example of a bourgeois who, as an individual, played an important role in working class organizations. But the position itself cannot be mapped into trade unions or working class parties. When Engels died, there was no reason whatsoever for the next incumbent of his bourgeois class location to be tied to the working class. When an industrial worker dies, there are systematic social forces which link the next incumbent of the same position to working class organizations. It is important throughout this discussion to remember that the analysis refers to the forging of social relations between positions, not simply between individuals. Both processes are important, but the logic of positions has an analytical priority over the analysis of individual relations within those positions.

93. It is important to be clear about the distinction between mediation and transformation. Both involve processes by which class struggle shapes class

A good example of this process of mediation is the process of class mobilization in Portugal in 1974–1976. In the post-Caetano period, class struggle entered into the process of class formation in all of the ways indicated in Figure 2.3. Through the appropriation of land in the south, the nationalization of certain important industries and the occupations of many factories, the class structure of Portugal was directly transformed, although in limited ways, by the class struggles beginning in 1974. Class struggle also directly transformed class formation, especially through the dismantling of the old state apparatus, the legalization of parties of the left, etc. But perhaps most significantly, class struggle mediated the relationship between class structure and class formation. The new forms of class struggle established a political climate which radicalized certain segments of the petty bourgeoisie and of the working class. The shift in the balance of class forces and the relative disorganization of the bourgeoisie meant that more people were drawn into working class organizations. In the terms of our discussion, the changed conditions of class struggle meant that the same basic class structure generated different objective limits on class formation: different positions within the class structure could be mobilized into class organizations, the class capacity of the working class could be strengthened beyond what had been possible under earlier conditions, and the interests around which those class organizations were mobilized could move away from purely immediate interests towards fundamental interests. This changed situation of class formation in turn changed the selective forces operating on class struggle.

The processes of mediation by class struggle are especially important for the class formation of contradictory locations: class struggle plays a decisive role in determining how such positions are empirically organized or disorganized into classes.

---

capacities, but the logics of the two are quite different. In transformation, class capacities are a direct object of class struggle, and existing class organizations are transformed in the course of those struggles. Mediation, on the other hand, concerns the ways in which class struggle affects the relationship between class structure and class formation. In a sense, in the process of mediation, class struggle operates as a contextual process which shapes the conditions of class formation, whereas in processes of transformation, class struggle directly impinges on class formation.

Depending upon the conditions of class struggle, for example, semi-autonomous employees may be formed into petty bourgeois class organizations (professional associations) or into working class organizations (trade unions) or, for that matter, they may remain completely unformed into classes altogether. Because contradictory locations have contradictory class interests, they are objectively torn between class forces within the class struggle and can potentially be organized into more than one class capacity. Class struggle itself therefore determines to a large extent the degree to which the complexities of the class structure are reproduced at the level of class formation.

The central message from the model of determination in Figure 2.3 is that it is essential to analyse the complex dialectical relationships between class structure, class formation and class struggle in any analysis of classes. While decoding the class structure may be the appropriate starting point of the analysis, it is impossible to deduce any political lessons simply from the analysis of class positions. An adequate political understanding of the possibilities and constraints present in a given social formation depends upon showing the ways in which class structure establishes limits on class struggle and class formation, the ways in which class struggle transforms both class structure and class formation, and the ways in which class struggle mediates the relationship between class structure and class formation.

Conclusion

Where does all of this leave us in terms of a general analysis of the class structure of advanced capitalist countries? We began this chapter by saying that it mattered both for theory and for politics how the boundary of the working class was defined. We can now indicate somewhat more fully why it matters.

Defining the working class matters because it helps to specify the extent to which the task of building a viable socialist movement hinges on drawing contradictory locations within class relations into working class organizations. The contradictory locations around the boundary of the working class represent positions which do have a real interest in socialism, yet simultaneously gain certain real privileges directly from capitalist relations of production. Somewhere between a quarter and a third of the American labour force falls into these locations near the boundary of the working class. When such contradictory locations are formed into the working class, the contradictory quality of their underlying class interests does not disappear. This implies that to the extent that contradictory locations are mapped into working class organizational capacities, those organizations will have to contend with potential conflicts of interests, and not simply conflicts of immediate interests but of fundamental interests as well. Thus, for example, if workers and semi-autonomous employees are organized into some form of factory councils, the conflict of interest is immediately posed between the *individual* autonomy (petty bourgeois autonomy) of the semi-autonomous employees and the collective control of the labour process by the working class. Similarly, if managers are also organized into such working class capacities, then the problem of elitism and authoritarian control is posed. Such conflicts are rooted in the relations of production themselves and thus are of a more fundamental character than conflicts over questions of wages and the like. Since any socialist movement in advanced capitalist societies will inevitably have to attempt to bring such categories into socialist struggles in order to be successful, it is essential that the nature of the conflicting class interests within such a socialist movement not be obscured. Developing a rigorous concept of the working class is necessary if the contours of fundamental class interests engaged in struggles for socialism are to be understood.

Defining the working class also matters because it makes it possible to distinguish immediate from fundamental interests, and to link those interests to the formation of class capacities. One of the central issues at stake in class struggles within capitalist society is the extent to which manifest social conflicts revolve around immediate interests or fundamental interests. Part of the impressive durability of capitalist systems can be attributed to the capacity of capitalism to displace conflicts from the fundamental to the immediate level, and one of the central tasks of any serious socialist movement is to reorient those conflicts back towards fundamental interests.

The difficulty of such a task is that immediate interests are real; they are not merely mystifications, false consciousness. A viable socialist movement cannot deny the importance of immediate interests, but must adopt strategies which attempt to join immediate and fundamental interests in such a way that the organizational capacities of the working class are strengthened rather than weakened in the process. Revolutions occur not when the masses of the people are willing to abandon all immediate interests for the prospect of realizing fundamental interests, but when the struggle for immediate interests begins to coincide with the struggle for fundamental interests.

3

Historical Transformations of Capitalist Crisis Tendencies

Introduction

The last chapter ended with a discussion of the complex ways in which class struggle mediates the relationship between class structure and class formation. That discussion was incomplete in one crucial respect. While the model of determination does show the dialectical logic of the analysis of class relations, that model remains indeterminate in a basic sense. There are no "laws of motion," no tendencies of development or dynamics of systematic structural change. Class struggle is said to transform class structure, but such a transformation is completely directionless. The whole schema thus so far remains suspended abstractly in thin air: a logic of historical materialism without history.

The next problem is thus to discover why it is that the structural transformations mediated by class struggle are not random—why they assume a given direction of development. The solution to this problem lies in deciphering the logic of the capitalist accumulation process, specifically by revealing the nature of the contradictions within that process and the crises which those contradictions generate. This is not to say that the dynamics of accumulation mechanistically determine a unique path of development, but rather that the accumulation process generates contradictions, the temporary solutions to which push the development of the capitalist system in specific directions. More concretely, the argument which will be developed in this chapter can be summarized as follows:

1. At different stages of capitalist development, the accumulation process faces different dominant constraints or impediments. These impediments are not exogenous factors which interfere with the accumulation process but are generated by the accumulation process itself.

2. In order for capitalist production to continue, these constraints must be overcome. In a fundamental sense capitalists do not have the choice of passively accepting the impediments to accumulation. As individuals, capitalists must attempt to overcome these impediments in order to survive in a competitive world; as a class, capitalists must strive to remove the impediments to accumulation in order to contain the class struggle.

3. The systemic solutions to the dominant impediments at a given stage of capitalist development generate the new impediments which constrain the accumulation process in the subsequent stage. It is in this sense that the impediments to accumulation can be considered *contradictions* in accumulation rather than merely obstacles to accumulation. They are contradictions because the "solutions" to a particular impediment become themselves impediments to accumulation.

4. The current world-wide capitalist economic crisis can be (tentatively) understood as part of a transition from one pattern of constraints on accumulation, characterized by Keynesian solutions, to a new set of emergent constraints which were in part caused by those very Keynesian strategies in earlier crises and which are no longer amenable to Keynesian solutions.

The chapter will be divided into three sections. Part I will briefly discuss the meaning of accumulation and the reasons why accumulation is such an integral part of capitalist society. Much of this discussion will involve a somewhat painstaking exposition of the basic concepts of Marxist political economy. Such a discussion of basic concepts is necessary both to make the conceptual apparatus of the argument accessible to readers relatively unfamiliar with the Marxist categories, and because many of the debates over the theory of accumulation are rooted in differing conceptualizations of the basic categories. I hope that by making my particular formulations of these concepts quite clear it will be easier for any weaknesses in the more substantive parts of the chapter to be criticized. In part II, this conceptual apparatus will be used to examine the underlying logic of several potential constraints on the accumulation process. Finally, in part III, these potential constraints on accumulation will be systematically related to the general stages of capitalist development. The chapter will conclude with a more speculative discussion of likely developments in the immediate future.

I. The Meaning of Accumulation

At some stage early in every Marxist textbook of political economy it is stressed that "capital" is not a *thing*, but a *social relation*, and an antagonistic social relation at that. But frequently, after this proclamation is made, the accumulation of capital is substantively treated as the accumulation of things, of the machinery, buildings, raw materials, and so forth that are usually grouped under the rubric "constant capital". This is fundamentally incorrect from a Marxist point of view: capital accumulation must be understood *as the reproduction of capitalist social relations on an ever-expanding scale through the conversion of surplus value into new constant and variable capital.* Before explaining this statement, it will be helpful very briefly to define two of its constituent elements: *capitalist social relations*, and *surplus value*.

1. Capitalist social relations.[1] All class societies, whether capitalist or not, can be understood as consisting of two broad categories of people: direct producers, the men and women who produce the goods and services which allow the society to continue; and non-producers—those who live off the production of others. Corresponding to this distinction between classes is an analytic distinction between two categories of labour of the direct producers: "necessary labour" and "surplus labour".

---

1. Depending upon the problem under study, capitalist social relations can be analysed at several different levels of abstraction. In the previous chapter, we analysed these social relations largely at the level of the social formation, since we were particularly interested in the complexities of class relations that are created by the interpenetration of diverse modes of production in concrete societies. In the present chapter we are primarily interested in analysing the laws of motion and contradictions of capitalism as a mode of production, and thus it will be more appropriate to analyse capitalist social relations at a higher level of abstraction, at the level of the mode of production itself.

Necessary labour constitutes the expenditure of human activity for production of the means of livelihood of the direct producers. *Surplus labour* represents the human activity which produces a surplus beyond the requirements of simply reproducing the direct producers themselves, a surplus which is appropriated by the non-producing classes.

These categories of direct producers and non-producers, necessary and surplus labour, pertain to all class societies. What fundamentally distinguishes one kind of class society from another are the types of social relations between the direct producers and non-producers, and the social mechanisms by which surplus labour is extracted from the direct producers. The characteristic social relations in a capitalist society involve on the one hand propertyless workers who own neither the means of production nor the products of production and are thus forced to sell their labour power—their capacity to produce goods and services—in order to survive, and on the other hand capitalists who own the means of production and purchase labour power on the labour market for the purpose of setting those means of production in motion. The essential social mechanism by which surplus labour is extracted from the direct producers is the creation of *surplus value* in the process of production.

2. *Surplus value*. Much of the Marxist analysis of capitalism revolves around the concept of surplus value, and thus it is important to make this concept as clear as possible. In order to do this it is first necessary to define briefly a number of other concepts.

a. *commodity*: A commodity is something which is produced for exchange rather than simply for its direct use. Whereas in all societies the objects of production must be in some sense useful (or have "use value"), in a capitalist society production in general is primarily organized around exchange.

b. *labour power*: Labour power is a special kind of commodity—human productive capacity sold on a labour market for use in the production of other commodities.

c. *value*: If one wants to analyse the mechanisms by which the social product is divided among the various classes of society, it is necessary to have units for measuring different quantities of products. The most obvious metric, of course, is simply the price of commodities. This has been in practice the solution to the problem for most economists. But using price as the metric for comparing quantities of products raises the question: what is it that the money attached to a commodity is measuring? What is the theoretical content of the quantitative dimension of the social product that prices tap? If the answer is not to be totally circular, some sort of value theory—i.e., a theory of what constitutes the quantitative dimensions of commodities—is necessary.[2]

In principle it is possible to measure the total quantity of the social product in any number of ways. One could weigh the total social product and state that so many tons went to the working class, so many tons to the capitalist class. One could calculate the total amount of energy from all sources that went to produce the social product as a measure of the total "machine activity" embodied in commodities. Or, one could measure the total number of hours of human labour that directly and indirectly went to produce the social product. All of these represent some kind of quantitative "value" of the social product. Obviously, for different purposes, different measures of value might be more or less appropriate.

The premise of the labour theory of value is that *if one is interested in understanding the relationship of class forces to social production, then a measure of value based on hours of human labour embodied in commodities is the most useful.* There are two basic justifications for this claim. First, if one is interested in social relations, in understanding dynamics, then a measure of value that directly taps social activity—labour time in production—is attractive. Secondly, it can be shown that the embodied labour time in commodities bears a systematic relationship to the ratios at which commodities exchange.[3] This

2. Much of what has come to be known as the "Cambridge capital controversy" concerns the problem of whether or not prices can be considered an acceptable metric of physical capital (or other commodities).

3. See Meghnad Desai, *Marxian Economic Theory*, London 1974, pp. 41–76, and Shinzaburo Koshimura, *Theory of Capital Reproduction and Accumulation*, Ontario 1975, pp. 64–94. The relationship of values (embodied labour times) of commodities to actual exchange ratios among commodities (relative prices) involves two transformations: 1) the transformation of the value of the inputs into the prices of the inputs, or what is usually called the "prices of production"; and 2) the transformation of the prices of production into the concrete market

does not mean that other theories of value cannot also predict exchange ratios. Piero Sraffa has shown, for example, that relative prices can be predicted from a value theory based on a "standard commodity" rather than embodied labour times.[4] The point is that only the labour theory of value provides a link between the *quantitative* ratios at which commodities exchange and the qualitative social relations which underlie the production process.

Because of the relationship of embodied labour time to the ratios at which commodities exchange, labour time is generally referred to as the *exchange* value of a commodity (to distinguish it from the use value of the commodity). More precisely, the exchange value of a commodity is defined as the average number of hours of labour of average skill and intensity used directly and indirectly in the production of the commodity, or more succinctly, the socially necessary labour time used to produce the commodity.[5]

The precise logical status of the definition is somewhat ambiguous. For many Marxists, the identification of exchange value with socially necessary labour time is a theoretical pre-

---

prices of commodities. The first of these is the object of the debates over what is called the "transformation problem". A variety of solutions to the transformation problem have been proposed. In the present context it is not necessary to choose between them: all solutions involve a systematic relationship between embodied labour times and prices of production. The second transformation, of prices of production into market prices, lies outside of value theory proper. There are a myriad number of factors other than embodied labour times—relative scarcities, monopoly power, government price fixing, etc.—which enter into the determination of concrete relative prices. The point is that embodied labour represents the characteristic *of the commodity itself* (as opposed to contingent forces external to the commodity, such as market forces) which influences prices. To the extent that one is interested in the actual market-exchange rates between two individual commodities, value theory will be helpful mainly as an indicator of the strength of these external factors. On the other hand, when one is concerned with the relative magnitudes of large aggregates of commodities and the development of the capitalist system as a whole, then value theory becomes much more powerful since one can assume that many of the external contingent factors cancel each other out.

4. *The Production of Commodities by Commodities*, Cambridge 1960.

5. For a discussion of the problems involved in this definition, see Shane Mage, *The Law of the Falling Tendency of the Rate of Profit*, Ph.D. Dissertation, Columbia 1963; Paul Sweezy, *The Theory of Capitalist Development*, New York 1942; and Bob Rowthorn, "Skilled Labour in the Marxist System", *Bulletin of the Conference of Socialist Economists*, September 1974, pp. 25–45.

mise; for others it is a proposition, deduced from prior assumptions. Martin Nicolaus's discussion of surplus value is a good example of the view that embodied labour time is not merely a definition of exchange value. "Marx brings up the central problem of the theory of capitalism and proceeds to solve it. How is it, he asks, that at the end of the production process the capitalist has a commodity which is worth more than the elements that went into it? He pays the price of machinery, raw materials and the price of labour, yet the product is worth more than all three together. What, in other words, is the source of the surplus value (*Mehrwert*) which the capitalist appropriates? The problem is insoluble, Marx writes, so long as 'labour' is considered a commodity like any other commodity (as it was, specifically, in the *Manifesto*). If labour were such a commodity, then capitalist production would be: price of machinery + price of raw materials + price of labour = price of product. Where then is the capitalist's profit? If we evade the question by saying that the capitalist fixes an arbitrary profit percentage and simply adds it to the price of the product, as high as the market will bear, then it appears that the buyer of the commodity is the source of the capitalist's profit. Yet what the capitalist gains in this way, the buyer loses, and it is impossible to see how an aggregate surplus could arise out of such transactions. Marx rejected this mercantilist theory, according to which one nation could get richer only by cheating another in commerce. This theory is overcome, and the problem of surplus value is solved, when one realizes that the worker sells the capitalist not 'labour', but labour *power* (*Arbeitskraft*). Although its price varies with supply and demand, this specific commodity has the exceptional quality of being able to produce more value than is necessary to reproduce it".[6]

The difficulty with this treatment of value is that one can quite easily conceive of other commodities which can in fact produce a "value" greater than their own costs of reproduction. As Braverman points out: "An ox too will have this capacity, and grind out more corn that it will eat if kept to the task by training and compulsion."[7] The reason why an Ox theory of

6. Martin Nicolaus, "Proletariat and Middle Class in Marx", *Studies on the Left*, No. 7, 1967, pp. 266–267.

7. *Labour and Monopoly Capital*, p. 56.

value or a machine theory of value is less adequate than the labour theory of value is because we are interested in revealing the relationship of human social activity to the distribution and appropriation of the social product, not the relationship of ox activity or machine activity to distribution.

How then can the labour theory of value help us to understand the mechanisms by which the social product is expropriated from the working class by the capitalist class? As a first approximation, the division of the social product between the working class and the capitalist class can be viewed as the outcome of two social processes: the exchange relationship between labour *power* and *capital*, and the production relation between *labour* and *capital*.[8] In the exchange relation, the worker sells a particular kind of commodity to the capitalist: labour power, i.e., the capacity to work. Like all commodities, the value of this commodity is defined by the socially necessary labour time that goes into its production and reproduction. The magnitude of these reproductive costs is in turn determined by various technical considerations (training costs, transportation costs, etc.) as well as by class struggles over wages (what Marx called the "historical and moral elements" in the value of labour power). The point in the present context is that however these reproductive costs are determined, when the worker sells his/her labour power to the capitalist it appears that an exchange of equivalents has occurred: the worker sells the commodity labour power to the capitalist and receives in return a wage more or less equal to the value of the commodity. This is the realm of "freedom, equality, property and Bentham" and the class relations underlying distribution remain opaque.

It is at the level of production relations that the class character of the distribution of the social product is revealed. In production the capacity to work—labour power—is transformed into actual labour, actual new value embodied in commodities. From the point of view of workers, this means that part of each

8. This is somewhat of an oversimplification. Other social processes—in particular taxation, budget policies by the state and monopoly pricing—can also potentially influence the distribution of the social product (i.e. the appropriation of the surplus product by the capitalist class). It is clearly a mistake to view exploitation as simply a consequence of the interplay of exchange and production relations, as many Marxists tend to do. This point will be discussed later in this chapter.

day the worker is labouring to provide the means of livelihood of the worker and his/her family, and part of the day the worker creates new value for the capitalist. This new value is called "surplus value". Looked at from the point of view of the capitalist class as a whole, if accumulation is to take place it is essential that the magnitude of the value created by workers be greater than the value of labour power, i.e., greater than the costs of reproducing the working class.[9] The extent to which labour power is transformed into actual labour within the production process is thus of crucial importance to the capitalist class. The whole thrust of "scientific management" at the turn of the century was directed towards this end.[10] While in the past fifty years, as we discussed in Chapter 1, more sophisticated approaches to extracting surplus labour may have replaced crude Taylorism in certain industries, the basic problem facing the capitalist class remains the same: how to generate as large a surplus as possible above the socially necessary reproductive costs of labour power.

As was stated at the outset of this discussion of accumulation, the hallmark of all class societies is the appropriation of surplus labour from the direct producers by the dominant classes. In capitalist societies the central mechanism of appropriation is rooted in the specific pattern of exchange relations and production relations discussed above: labour power is sold freely on the market as a commodity, but is coerced within production to produce more value than its own costs of reproduction.

We are now in a position to explain our definition of capital accumulation as the reproduction of capitalist social relations on an ever-expanding scale through the conversion of surplus value into new constant and variable capital. To understand what is meant by "reproduction on an ever-expanding scale" it is first necessary to understand what reproduction on a static scale (or simple reproduction) means. The traditional Marxist

9. While it is essential for the capitalist class as a whole that the reproductive costs of total labour power be less than the value produced by the working class, this is not necessarily the case for any individual capitalist. The individual capitalist may be able to obtain a share of the total surplus value without generating any surplus value in his/her own production process. This is the case, for example, in banking and other totally "unproductive" spheres of capitalist activity.

10. Braverman, *Labour and Monopoly Capital*, pp. 85–137.

conception of simple reproduction is as follows. Imagine an economy with two sectors, one of which produces the means of production, the other of which produces consumption goods. Within each sector, the total value of the commodities produced can be represented by the traditional Marxist formula

$c + v + s = P$ where:

> P = the total value produced (gross product).
> c = the value of the constant capital (machines, buildings, raw materials) used up in production.
> v = the value of the labour power used up in production, or variable capital. (It is called variable capital because it produces a variable amount of new value—surplus value—in the production process.)
> s = the value of the surplus product produced by the workers
> $v + s$ = the total amount of living labour time used in production (or the value of the net product, i.e., the gross product minus depreciation, raw materials, etc.).

The simple two sector model would then be expressed in the following way:

> sector 1 (production goods):
> $c_1 + v_1 + s_1 = P_1$
> sector 2 (consumption goods):
> $c_2 + v_2 + s_2 = P_2$

Each of the terms in these equations can be considered simultaneously a supply of and a demand for certain commodities, expressed in value terms: P_1 represents the value of the total supply of production goods; P_2 the value of the total supply of consumption goods; v_1 constitutes that part of the total supply of production goods which must be exchanged for consumption goods in order to reproduce the labour power used in the production of production goods; c_1 represents that part of the total supply of production goods which must be used to replace the means of production used up in the production of production goods; etc. The equilibrium condition for simple reproduction is that year after year, the magnitude of each of the terms in these equations remains unchanged. That is, the total amount of constant capital used up in production in both sectors is equal to the total supply of constant capital produced in sector 1, and the total consumption by capitalists and workers is equal to the total production of the consumption goods sector. For this to be true, the entire surplus value (s_1 and s_2) must be consumed by the capitalist class.

Expanded reproduction constitutes the situation in which at least part of the surplus value is used to augment the level of constant and variable capital in production. Part of the supply of production goods represented by s_1 is used to increase the level of constant capital, c_1 and c_2, and part of the supply of consumption goods represented by s_2 is used to increase the level of variable capital, v_1 and v_2. Expanded reproduction thus consists of the accumulation of both constant capital and variable capital, and the *rate* of accumulation can be expressed as $\dfrac{\triangle c + \triangle v}{c + v}$.

Since both $\triangle c$ and $\triangle v$ come out of surplus value, the *value rate of profit*, $\dfrac{s}{c + v}$, is often used to indicate the maximum rate of accumulation possible in a given period.[11] It is because accumu-

11. Technically, the ratio $s/(c+v)$ is the rate of profit only when it is assumed that the turnover time for capital stock is one production period. Since the rate of profit is usually measured on total investment (not merely on raw materials and depreciation and wages, i.e., $c+v$), a more complex expression including the capital stock and turnover rates is necessary if longer turnover times are to be included in the analysis. Since I have seen no evidence to indicate that the added complexity of including capital stock in the analysis changes any of the basic relationships, I will use the simpler model throughout this paper, assuming a one-period turnover of constant capital. (For the problem of the time-dating of capital, see Geoffrey Hodgson, "The Falling Rate of Profit", *New Left Review* no. 84, 1974). It should also be noted that throughout this paper I will make no distinction between profit, interest, and rent as components of surplus value. The expression "profit" will be used to designate the total surplus value.

The reason for saying that $s/c+v$ indicates the maximum "possible" rate of accumulation is that surplus value is used for capitalist consumption (among other things) as well as for expanded reproduction. To the extent that the capitalist class has some discretion over the proportion of surplus value reinvested as new capital, it is not necessarily true that an increase in the rate of profit will immediately produce an increase in actual accumulation, and vice-versa.

lation involves an expansion both of the means of production controlled by capitalists and of the size of the working class that it constitutes "the reproduction of capitalist social relations on an ever-expanding scale".

One final issue needs at least brief discussion before we turn to the analysis of the contradictions and impediments in the accumulation process. Why is accumulation so important for the survival of capitalism? Is a stagnant, no-growth, non-accumulating capitalism a viable possibility? The example of the British economy in recent years certainly indicates the possibility of there being a capitalist system in which little accumulation takes place over an extended period of time. Marxists have generally tended to discount the possibility of a return to an economy of simple reproduction under the conditions of advanced capitalism. Paul Mattick, for example, has written: "A non-accumulating capitalism is only a temporary possibility; it is a capitalism in crisis. For capitalist production is conceivable only in terms of accumulation."[12] As will become clear in the rest of the paper, I do not think that a non-accumulating capitalism is an impossibility or that it necessarily leads to economic and social breakdown. But I do think that a non-accumulating capitalism is a precarious capitalism, and that a variety of repressive social mechanisms have to be created or expanded in order to cope with such a situation. This precariousness can be understood at the level of both "capital in general" and "many capitals".[13] At the level of capital in general, of the capitalist system understood as the essential confrontation of capital and labour, accumulation plays a vital role in containing and channelling the class struggle. Accumulation

12. *Marx and Keynes*, Boston 1969, p. 60.
13. The distinction in the analysis of capitalism between "capital in general" and "many capitals" must not be confused with the common distinction in economics between macro-economics and micro-economics. The micro vs macro distinction refers to the *unit of analysis* under examination: the behaviour of individual firms and consumers in the former case, of the economic system as a whole in the latter. In contrast, the distinction between capital in general and many capitals refers to the *level of abstraction* of the analysis. In the analysis of "capital in general", the capitalist system has been stripped to its barest, simplest essence: the confrontation of capital and labour. The analysis of "many capitals" does not shift the unit of analysis from system to individual, but rather adds complexity to the analysis of the system as such through the discussion of market structures, competition, diverse technologies, etc. To say that the analy-

underpins much of the ideological legitimation of the in-equalities of capitalist society. The ever-expanding pie enables the standard of living of the working class to increase slowly without threatening relations of production. At the same time it helps to legitimate the vastly higher standard of living of the capitalist class. A prolonged period of non-accumulation (let alone disaccumulation) would seriously undermine such legitimations and would lead to a considerable intensification of class conflict.

At the level of many capitals, non-accumulation would con-siderably intensify competition on both a national and an inter-national scale. In a period of general economic growth, the expansion of individual capitals occurs partially because each captialist tries to increase his share of the market at the expense of other capitalists, and partially because the total size of the market is increasing. In a period of non-accumulation, the latter of these disappears, and all individual expansion takes the form of a zero-sum game. Marx describes such a situation elegantly: "So long as everything goes well, competition affects a practical brotherhood of the capitalist class as we have seen in the case of the average rate of profit, so that each shares in the common loot in proportion to the magnitude of his share of investment. But as soon as it is no longer a question of sharing profits but of sharing losses, everyone tries to reduce his own share to a minimum and load as much as possible upon the shoulders of some other competitor . . . competition then transforms itself into a fight of hostile brothers. The antagonism of the interests of the individual capitalists and those of the capitalist class as a whole then makes itself felt as previously the identity of these interests impressed itself practically as competition."[14]

---

sis of many capitals is at a lower level of abstraction than the analysis of capital in general does not imply that these added complexities are unimportant or that they cannot change the dynamics of the capitalist system in fundamental ways. The method of beginning with the simplest, most abstract conceptualization of capitalism and then moving to the more concrete does not mean that the propositions derived at the most abstract level are unaffected by forces that are analysed at more concrete levels. But this method does mean that the more concrete complexities introduced in the analysis of many capitals acquire their theoretical specificity in terms of their relationship to the analysis of capital in general.

14. *Capital,* Vol. III, New York 1967, p. 253.

Such an intensification of class conflict and capitalist competition does not, however, necessarily imply the end of capitalism. Contradictions can increase and social systems can muddle through, especially if new institutional arrangements are created in the attempt to contain those contradictions. The point of an analysis of contradictions in and impediments to the accumulation process is not to prove the inevitability of the collapse of capitalism, but to understand the kinds of adaptations and institutional reorderings that are likely to be attempted in the efforts to counteract those contradictions. Such an understanding is crucial to the development of a viable socialist politics.

II. Impediments and Contradictions in the Accumulation Process

There has been considerable debate among Marxist political economists over the nature of the essential contradictions in the accumulation process which push the capitalist system towards economic crisis. The contemporary debates on crisis have generally focused on one of four critical impediments to accumulation: 1) the rising organic composition of capital;[15] 2) the problem of realizing surplus value, and in particular problems of underconsumption in capitalist society;[16] 3) a low or falling rate of exploitation resulting from rises in wages;[17] and 4) the contradictory role of the state in accumulation.[18]

In this section we will examine the underlying assumptions

15. See Paul Mattick, *Marx and Keynes*; David Yaffe, "The Marxian Theory of Crisis, Capital and the State", *Economy and Society*, Vol. 2, 1973; Mario Cogoy, "The Fall in the Rate of Profit and the Theory of Accumulation", *Bulletin of the Conference of Socialist Economists*, Winter 1973; Shane Mage, *The Law of the Falling Tendency of the Rate of Profit* (cit).

16. Paul Sweezy, *The Theory of Capitalist Development*, New York 1942; Paul Baran and Paul Sweezy, *Monopoly Capital*, New York 1966; Joseph Gillman, *Prosperity in Crisis*, New York 1965.

17. Andrew Glyn and Bob Sutcliffe, *British Capitalism, Workers and the Profits Squeeze*, London 1972.

18. Mario Cogoy, "Les Théories Néo-Marxistes, Marx et l'Accumulation du Capital", *Les Temps Modernes*, September–October 1972; David Yaffe, "The Marxian Theory of Crisis, Capital and the State" (cit); James O'Connor, *The Fiscal Crisis of the State*, New York 1973; Claus Offe, "Structural Problems of the Capitalist State" and "The Theory of the Capitalist State and the Problem of Policy Formation" (cit).

and logic of each of these positions. In the following section I will argue that the four interpretations of crisis are not fundamentally incompatible if they are interpreted in an historical perspective as tapping the changing contradictions of accumulation at different periods of capitalist development.

Two brief comments are necessary before discussing these alternative perspectives on crisis. First, the discussion will focus on economic *crisis*, not simply business *cycles*. While the two kinds of disturbances in economic relations are obviously related, they have a different theoretical status: a crisis implies that in order for accumulation to continue some sort of restructuring of the accumulation process is necessary; a cycle merely implies that there has been some sort of disturbance in accumulation which can be alleviated without any basic structural changes. A given impediment to accumulation, such as the rising organic composition of capital, can function as either a crisis mechanism or a cyclical mechanism, depending upon how it is linked to the total process of accumulation. Indeed, one of the themes which we will explore is how certain factors historically shift from being basic structural obstacles to being cyclical mechanisms and vice versa.[19]

Second, most of the discussion of these four impediments to accumulation will be based on the value categories discussed in section I above. It is important to stress that such a value analysis does not exhaust Marxist work on economic crisis. A complete understanding of crisis would also involve an analysis of monetary instability, credit imbalances and other problems strictly in the sphere of circulation. These issues will not be included in the present discussion, since, while such problems are important, it is a theoretical priority to analyse the impedi-

19. Because our concern is with crisis mechanisms, I will not systematically discuss the so-called "disproportionality" theories of crisis, i.e. conceptions of crisis which see the disruption of accumulation as rooted in imbalances between the various sectors of capitalist production, these imbalances themselves being generated by the "anarchy" of capitalist production. While such disproportionalities undoubtedly do occur, it is difficult to make a case that they constitute basic structural obstacles to accumulation which require basic restructuring of the accumulation process. Disproportionalities resulting from the chronically disorganized condition of capitalism are a constant feature of capitalist production and distribution, and while they may aggravate crisis tendencies, they do not themselves constitute a fundamental crisis mechanism in the sense discussed in this paper.

126

ments to accumulation in terms of contradictions in the sphere of production. It is on these contradictions that the present analysis will be focused.

1. The Organic Composition of Capital and the Falling Rate of Profit

As discussed in part I, it is a fundamental premise of Marxist political economy that only living labour can produce surplus value, and thus profits. The rate of profit, however, is based not merely on labour costs of the capitalist (v) but on all capital costs (c + v). Therefore, the reasoning goes, if it should happen in the course of capitalist development that the value of the dead labour used in production should grow much more rapidly than the living labour, there will be a tendency, all other things being equal, for the rate of profit to decline. This constitutes the basic logic for studying the relationship between changes in the productive forces of capitalist society—the technology broadly conceived—and the rate of profit. The "organic composition of capital" is a ratio that is designed to reflect the salient aspects of technology that impinge on the rate of profit. The most useful simple expression for this is the ratio of dead labour (constant capital) to living labour in production:[20]

20. This expression is not the traditional way that Marxists have defined the organic composition of capital. The usual practice has been to regard the ratio c/v as the organic composition of capital. This has been the usage of economists such as Sweezy, Dobb, Mattick, and Gillman. This expression constitutes the ratio of dead to living capital and is generally treated by these writers as reflecting in value terms what in bourgeois economics is called the capital-intensity of the technology. A number of recent authors—Mario Cogoy, Shane Mage and David Laibman—have argued that the ratio c/v is not an adequate measure of capital intensity, since the level of v depends in part upon the rate of exploitation and not merely on the relative amounts of constant capital and human labour in production. The ratio of dead labour to living labour in production, c/v+s, has therefore been substituted for the ratio of constant capital to variable capital. While Marx himself is somewhat ambiguous in his own usage of the various expressions, it is possible to interpret a number of important passages in *Capital* as indicating that his notion of the organic composition of capital is best represented by this ratio. (See especially Marx's discussion at the beginning of section 1 of chapter XXV in Vol. I of *Capital*, "The General Law of Capitalist Accumulation". For a discussion of this section of *Capital*, see Cogoy "The Fall in the Rate of Profit", pp. 56–57.) In practical terms it is not terribly important which ratio is used. None of the significant results which we will derive below are substantially different if c/v is used instead of c/v+s. Nevertheless, since the ratio of dead to living labour in production is a closer reflection of the technical relations of production, we will adopt it throughout this discussion.

$$Q = \frac{c}{v + s}$$

One other expression, the rate of exploitation (also called the rate of surplus value), will be important in the discussion of the falling rate of profit. The rate of exploitation is defined as the ratio of the unpaid to the paid portions of the working day (see the discussion of surplus value above), or, alternatively, the ratio of surplus value to variable capital:

$$e = \frac{s}{v}$$

One note of caution before we proceed further. It is very important not to interpret the rate of surplus value, s/v, as an expression simply reflecting the state of class struggle, and the organic composition of capital as an expression simply reflecting the nature of the technology. Both ratios are affected by both class struggle and technology, although in different ways. The average level of productivity in the society, especially in the wage goods sector, has a direct bearing on the rate of surplus value; and the class struggle has a direct bearing on the length of the working day and the intensity of work, and thus on the denominator of the organic composition of capital. While we will interpret the organic composition of capital as *reflecting* technical relations, this does not imply that it is a purely technical coefficient.

Using the expression $Q = \frac{c}{v+s}$ for the organic composition of capital, and $e = \frac{s}{v}$ for the rate of exploitation, we can write the rate of profit as:

$$r = \frac{s}{c + v} = \frac{s/(v + s)}{\frac{c}{v+s} + \frac{v}{v+s}} = \frac{e/(1+e)}{Q + 1/(1 + e)} = \frac{e}{Q(1+e) + 1} \quad (1)$$

This function is graphed in Figure 3.1 (for convenience in this graph, the reciprocal of the rate of exploitation is used).

Equation (1) and Figure 3.1 will help us to explain the theory of the falling tendency of the rate of profit. There are six propositions in the argument:

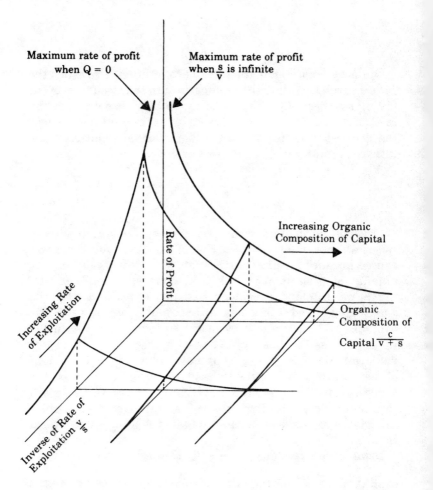

Note: In this figure, intersections of vertical planes parallel to the exploitation/ rate of profit plane with the profit surface represent the rate of profit as a function of exploitation for fixed levels of the organic composition of capital. Intersections of vertical planes parallel to the organic composition/rate of profit plane represent the rate of profit as a function of the organic composition of capital for fixed rates of exploitation. The intersection of a horizontal plane with the profit surface represents the locus of points with a common rate of profit.

Figure 3.1   The Rate of Profit as a Function of

$$\frac{c}{v+s} \quad \text{and} \quad \frac{v}{s}$$

1) There are forces intrinsic to the process of capital accumulation which tend to raise the level of the organic composition of capital.

2) As the organic composition of capital rises, there is a tendency for the rate of profit to fall *unless* the rate of exploitation increases sufficiently to counter-balance the rise in the organic composition of capital (or unless some other counteracting force intervenes).

3) In the long run, rises in the rate of exploitation cannot completely counteract the rising organic composition of capital, and thus there will be a definite tendency for the rate of profit to decline.

4) When the decline in the rate of profit becomes sufficiently serious and can no longer be compensated for by the existing rate of exploitation, an economic crisis occurs: the least profitable capitals disappear as businesses go bankrupt; and capitalists increasingly withhold investments because there are no profitable outlets. Aggregate demand, which is fundamentally derived from the rate of accumulation, therefore declines with the result that the crisis takes on the *appearance* of a crisis of overproduction of commodities. Whereas under-consumptionists (see below, subsection 2) argue that the crisis is caused by an overproduction of commodities, by an overproduction of surplus value, the theory of the falling rate of profit argues the exact opposite. "Because *not enough* (surplus value) has been produced, capital cannot expand at a rate which would allow for the full realization of *what has been* produced. The relative scarcity of surplus-labour in the production process appears as an absolute abundance of commodities in circulation."[21]

5) These conditions of crisis, however, serve the function of restoring conditions favourable for subsequent profitable accumulation. Several mechanisms accomplish this: a) unproductive capital is eliminated from the market, thus leaving the remaining capital at a higher level of productivity; b) in addition, when individual capitals go bankrupt they are forced to sell their existing constant capital at prices below real exchange values. The devaluation of capital means that in the aggregate the numerator in the organic composition of capital declines,

21. Mattick, *Marx and Keynes*, p. 79.

thus raising the rate of profit; c) finally, workers are thrown out of work, the reserve army of the unemployed swells, and capitalists can push wages below their value, thus increasing the rate of exploitation. Once these processes have advanced sufficiently to restore an acceptable rate of profit, accumulation resumes and the crisis ends.

6) While the crisis tendency of capitalist society takes the form of periodic business cycles, there is also an overarching tendency for cycles to become progressively more severe. Each successive crisis occurs at a higher level of accumulation and thus a higher level of the organic composition of capital. The problems of restoring conditions for renewed profitable accumulation thus tend to become more difficult in each successive crisis.[22]

With slight variations, these six propositions are all held by proponents of the theory of the falling tendency of the rate of profit. The first three constitute the heart of the theory, for if it can be demonstrated that there is a tendency for the rate of profit to fall, the particular conception of how this in turn produces economic crisis and how economic crisis itself restores conditions of renewed accumulation follows fairly naturally. We will therefore concentrate our attention on the first three propositions.

The second and third of these can be dealt with purely formally in terms of equation (1). It is immediately obvious from equation (1) that for any fixed value of the rate of exploitation, the rate of profit becomes simply a function of the inverse of the organic composition of capital. Thus, if Q rises and e remains constant, the rate of profit will necessarily fall. The second proposition in the argument therefore follows immediately from the definitions of r, Q, and e.

The validity of the third proposition is less obvious. While it is clear that if the organic composition were to rise to infinity even an infinite rate of exploitation could not counteract the fall in the rate of profit, this limiting case is not very helpful for understanding the movements of the rate of profit in the real world. What we would like to know is the extent to which a rise in the organic composition of capital will constrain the accumu-

22. Mattick, *Marx and Keynes*, p. 69.

lation process at *any* arbitrary level of Q, and not just in the limiting case where Q is infinite. One way of examining this problem is to ask if the extent to which the rate of exploitation can function as a counteracting force is itself affected by rises in the organic composition of capital. It is easy to show using elementary calculus that as the organic composition of capital rises, the rate of profit becomes progressively less sensitive to changes in the rate of exploitation.[23] Thus, not only does a high organic composition of capital produce a lower possible profit, but it also makes changes in the rate of exploitation less useful as a strategy for bolstering the rate of profit. Furthermore, the higher the rate of exploitation already is, the less sensitive will the rate of profit be to subsequent changes in the rate of exploitation. Thus, *if* in fact there is a secular rise in the organic composition of capital, then, even if the rate of exploitation also increases it becomes progressively less likely that it will be able to counteract completely the rising organic composition of capital. It is, therefore, quite reasonable to regard rises in the organic composition of capital as a significant impediment to the accumulation process, and equally reasonable to assume that if it does tend to rise, complementary rises in the rate of exploitation will not be able to counteract the fall in the rate of profit in the long run.

The first proposition in the argument is the most problematic. Neither the empirical demonstrations of a general tendency for the organic composition of capital to rise over time, nor the theoretical arguments marshalled in its support, have been particularly convincing. It is unquestionably true that in *physical* terms the amount of machines, raw materials, buildings,

23. Using the definition of the rate of profit in equation (1), take partial derivatives with respect to the rate of exploitation:

$$r = \frac{e}{Q(e+1) + 1}$$

$$\frac{\partial r}{\partial e} = \frac{[Q(e + 1) + 1] - Qe}{[Q(e+1) + 1]^2} = \frac{Q + 1}{[Q(e + 1) + 1]^2}$$

Since Q appears in the denominator at a higher power than in the numerator, equation (2) indicates that as the organic composition of capital rises, a given change in the rate of exploitation will produce a smaller change in the rate of profit.

etc., per worker has vastly increased with capitalist development. But the organic composition of capital is a *value* concept, and it is far from obvious that the value of constant capital per worker has risen or has a tendency to rise, especially in the later stages of capitalist development.

For the value of constant capital per worker to rise there must be a net excess of labour-saving technological innovations (innovations which substitute machinery for labour power) over constant *capital-saving* innovations (innovations which substitute cheap machines—machines that require relatively little socially necessary labour time to produce—for expensive machines). When Marx wrote *Capital*, this was a fairly plausible assumption to make. Although Marx did recognize the possibility that increasing productivity in the capital goods sector of the economy might result in a "cheapening of the elements of constant capital",[24] he regarded this as at most a transient counter-tendency to a generally rising organic composition of capital. In Marx's view, progressive introduction of labour-saving technologies was an intrinsic part of the accumulation process.

Two arguments have been urged as to why labour-saving innovations should on balance outweigh constant-capital-saving innovations. The first emphasizes the relationship between labour-saving innovations and the labour market. Assume for the moment accumulation without any net direction to technical innovations (i.e. there is a rough balance between labour and capital saving innovations). Under these conditions, the expansion of capital will eventually exhaust the available supply of workers, since the working population is finite. Yaffe argues: "On the one hand we have capital as 'value in process', as value attempting to expand itself without limit, and on the other we have population, the limited basis of that expansion."[25] There may, of course, be periods in which there is a relative abundance of available exploitable labour, periods with a large reserve army of the unemployed. During such periods there would not be especially strong pressures for specifically labour-saving innovations. But eventually, as capital expands, it will confront the limit of exploitable labour power,

24. *Capital*, Vol. III, p. 236
25. "The Marxian Theory of Crisiś, Capital and the State", p. 195.

and thus further expansion will require labour-saving, not constant-capital-saving, innovations. Each individual capitalist will experience this situation as a "tight" labour market with rising wage costs and will thus look for new machines which will displace labour. The aggregate effect of such individual decisions will be a rise in the organic composition of capital.

The basic weakness in this argument is the assumption that the "normal" condition for capitalist development is a limited supply of labour. While it is undoubtedly true that there have been periods when there were general shortages of labour, it is equally plausible to characterize the "normal" state of capitalism as one of an overabundance of exploitable labour. This is especially true if the pool of exploitable labour is seen on a world scale rather than simply a national scale. When capitalists face tight labour markets they are as likely to deal with the problem through the importation of masses of foreign labour as they are through the introduction of new technologies. This is hardly to deny that labour-saving innovations are important, but merely to say that it is difficult to explain them strictly in terms of the "limited size of exploitable labour power".

The second argument for why there should be a systematic tendency for labour-saving innovations to outweigh constant-capital-saving innovations places more stress on class struggle in general than on the limits of the labour market. There is one fundamental difference between machines and workers. Machines do not resist capitalist domination. Capitalists seek to replace workers with machines not simply because of the technological advantages that may result from the innovation, but because workers organize to resist exploitation. The intensity of that resistance may vary with the tightness of the labour market, but it is class struggle rather than the labour market as such which is the crucial pressure for labour-saving innovations.

This is certainly a compelling argument. There is a sense in which, for the *individual* capitalist, the perfect factory would be one that was totally automated, which the owner could simply turn on in the morning and turn off at night.[26] The question,

26. While the 100% automated factory might be a fantasy of the individual capitalist, it would clearly be a disaster for the capitalist class, since without labour in production there would be no surplus value, and thus no profits. It is

then, is whether or not there are other systemic pressures faced by capitalists which would tend to generate capital-saving innovations, potentially in excess of labour-saving innovations. No one, of course, denies that such capital-saving innovations occur. Indeed, the existence of such innovations was one of the "counter-tendencies" to the rising organic composition of capital discussed by Marx. The question, however, is whether such innovations are systematically produced within capitalism. As Yaffe argues: "Unless such inventions are continually re-occurring the general tendency of the organic composition to rise would reappear . . . To give any more significance to such inventions it has to be shown that, *necessarily*, they must continually re-occur."[27]

Real capitalists are under constant pressure to innovate because of competition with other capitalists, not simply class struggle with workers, and in the competitive struggle it does not matter whether costs are cut by savings on labour or on constant capital.[28] In fact, a strong argument can be made which suggests that in advanced capitalist economies, there should be a tendency for an increase to occur in the pressures for capital-saving innovations relative to labour-saving technological innovations. In earlier periods of capitalist development, when mechanization was first occurring, the introduction of machines necessarily implied the substitution of machines for workers. Once an industry is fully mechanized, however, all innovations tend to take the form of machines replacing machines. Even if such machines do in fact still replace workers, there is no reason

precisely this contradiction between the imperatives facing the individual capitalist and the requirements of the capitalist system which, in the classic Marxist view, lies at the heart of the rising organic composition of capital and the resulting crisis tendencies in capitalist society.

27. "The Marxian Theory of Crisis, Capital and the State", p. 198.

28. Yaffe insists that all of the essential characteristics of the laws of motion of capital and the resulting crisis mechanisms can be derived strictly at the level of "capital in general". Thus, he argues it is unnecessary (even irrelevant) to examine questions of competition among capitalists. At the level of abstraction of capital in general, Yaffe is quite right that the only coherent pressure for technological change comes from the basic capital-labour antagonism. But, unless Yaffe can show that in principle the more "abstract" pressure inevitably carries greater concrete weight in determining the balance between labour-saving and capital-saving innovations, there is no a priori reason to assume that capital saving innovations will be an insignificant social reality.

why they should not also be cheaper machines. In the competitive struggle among the producers of machines, after all, there will be attempts to expand markets by producing less expensive machines (i.e., machines that take less total labour to produce) as well as more productive machines (i.e., machines which produce more output per total labour input).[29]

Furthermore, it might also be expected that as constant capital increases as a proportion of total costs (i.e., as the *value* composition of capital, c/v, rises), individual capitalists will tend to be more concerned about saving on constant capital. A capitalist in a high technology industry in which vast amounts of constant capital are used per worker is likely to be less concerned about cutting labour costs, than about cutting costs of machinery, energy, raw materials, etc. A plausible model for the rate of increase in the organic composition of capital could postulate that, all other things being equal, the *net* rate of labour-saving innovations over capital-saving innovations is inversely related to c/v (or directly related to the proportion of labour costs in production). Thus, as the organic composition of capital rose, it would tend to rise at a slower and slower rate, perhaps even asymptotically approaching some high, relatively stable level.

Finally, even if it should happen that in highly mechanized industries the organic composition of capital continues to rise, the aggregate social level of the organic composition might remain constant if there were a relatively faster rate of growth in unmechanized sectors of the economy. The enormous growth of "service sector" employment, which is typically highly labour-intensive, could counterbalance the continuing growth

29. Perhaps the most startling example of such constant-capital-saving innovations in recent years is the production of miniature electronic calculators and computers. Even the most complex pocket calculators cost a fraction of the mechanical calculators which they replaced. While it is always somewhat problematic to make a judgement about values from prices, the old mechanical calculators certainly embodied much more labour than the new electronic calculators. While they have undoubtedly resulted in replacing some living labour as well, the savings in constant capital are clearly much greater. As a result, in labour processes involving calculators, the introduction of miniaturized printed circuits has considerably lowered the organic composition of capital.

in capital intensity in the industrial sector.[30] The tendency for the competitive labour-intensive sector of the economy to grow in a symbiotic relation with the monopoly sector would also tend to counter to some degree the rise in the *aggregate* organic composition.[31]

All of these pieces of suggestive reasoning indicate that while a thorough model predicting the relative proportions of labour-saving and capital-saving innovations has yet to be worked out, there is no a priori reason to assume a general preponderance of labour-saving innovations in a developed capitalist economy.

The empirical evidence is at best indecisive on the question of whether or not the organic composition of capital has risen, done nothing, or even fallen. Since national income accounts are not figured in terms of embodied labour times, and since data on capital invested includes many entries that Marxists would not even consider capital, it is of course highly problematic how data on the organic composition could be reliably gathered. Even as strong a proponent of the rising organic composition thesis as Cogoy has to admit that the meagre data which support his views are as equivocal as the data which oppose them.[32]

If the theoretical basis is weak for assuming there is a tendency for the organic composition to rise, and if the empirical evidence is non-existent, why bother with the theory at all? There are several reasons. First, while there is considerable dispute about the relevance of the theory of the rising organic composition of capital to late 20th century capitalism, there is general agreement among Marxists that it was a significant characteristic of 19th century capitalism. As we will see in section III of this chapter, the theory of the rising organic com-

---

30. For the moment I am ignoring the thorny question of the distinction between productive and unproductive labour and how these categories relate to the organic composition of capital. Clearly, if the service sector is categorically considered unproductive labour, then it would not in any sense offset the rising organic composition in the industrial, productive sector of the economy. The point here is that the social aggregate organic composition may be the result of a complex pattern of relative changes in the size of high-capital-intensity and low-capital-intensity sectors, rather than being merely the result of the growth of the organic composition in already high-capital-intensity sectors of the economy.

31. See O'Connor, *The Fiscal Crisis of the State*, Chapter 2.

32. "Les Théories Néo-Marxistes", p. 63.

position of capital is essential for a historical understanding of the development of capitalist accumulation.

Second, even if it is true that there is no consistent long term tendency for the organic composition of capital to rise, the organic composition still acts as a real constraint on the accumulation process. The results we discussed above indicate that when an economy is in a situation of relatively high organic composition of capital, the rate of profit becomes less sensitive to increases in the rate of exploitation. This means that if the rate of profit were to decline because of some factor other than the organic composition of capital (for example, the growth of unproductive expenditures), the system would be more rigid because of the high organic composition. No one has argued that the organic composition of capital has fallen to any great extent in the past several decades, and thus one can say that it still acts as an impediment to accumulation, even though it may not be the great dynamic source of crisis that its defenders claim.

Finally, even if a secular rise in the organic composition of capital is not the general cause of capitalist crisis, a destruction of values and a corresponding temporary fall in the organic composition of capital may be a crucial part of the solution to cyclical crises. The movement of the organic composition of capital over the past century could be hypothesized to look something like Figure 3.2.[33] Sometime during the first quarter of the 20th century, according to this hypothesis, a relatively stable, fairly high level of organic composition of capital was reached. Since that time, the organic composition of capital has dropped considerably during periods of crisis, and then risen back to this stable level during periods of prosperity as post-crisis un-devaluated constant capital replaced the cheap, devaluated capital acquired during the crisis. A fall in the organic composition of capital can be a solution of crisis without a rise in the organic composition being the fundamental cause of crisis. Under these assumptions, if it should happen that institutional changes in the economy—in particular, growth of government subsidies of inefficient monopolistic firms—should

33. See David Levine's argument in *Accumulation and Technical Change in Marxian Economics*, Unpublished Ph.D. dissertation, Yale University, 1973. Its implications will be more fully discussed when we place the theory of the crises in a more historical perspective in Part III.

block the fall in capital values during a crisis, then it would be expected that a serious "crisis of crisis management" might occur. The issue will be more fully discussed in section III below.

2. Underconsumptionist Theories of Economic Crisis

Marx very explicitly states in the *Grundrisse* that the inherent tendency for the rate of profit to fall is "the most important law of modern political economy and the most essential for understanding the most difficult relationships. It is the most important law from the historical standpoint."[34] But he also makes a number of statements which some Marxists have taken to indicate that Marx supported an underconsumptionist view of crisis. "The ultimate reason for all real crisis", Marx writes in *Capital*, Vol. III, "always remains the poverty and restricted consumption of the masses as opposed to the drive of capitalist production to develop the productive forces as though only the absolute consuming power of society constituted their limit."[35]

As often happens in debates among Marxists, the dispute between the two positions has frequently taken the form of competing exegeses of passages from *Capital*. On that score it seems to me that the proponents of the falling rate of profit probably have the upper hand. While Marx did see the underconsumption of the masses as a chronic state in capitalist society, it only became a factor in crisis given the dynamics of accumulation and the problem of the rising organic composition of capital. Engels states this position very clearly: "The underconsumption of the masses, the restriction of the consumption of the masses to what is necessary for their maintenance and reproduction, is not a new phenomenon. It has existed as long as there have been exploiting and exploited classes. . . The underconsumption of the masses is a necessary condition of all forms of society based on exploitation, consequently also of the capitalist form; but it is the capitalist form of production which first gives rise to crises. The underconsumption of the masses is therefore also a prerequisite condition for crises, and plays in them a role which has long been recognized. But it tells us just as little why crises exist today as why they did not exist

34. *Grundrisse,* Penguin/NLR 1973, p. 748.
35. Moscow, 1962, p. 472–3.

before."[36] A correct exegesis of Marx, however, does not necessarily make a correct interpretation of the world. The cogency of underconsumptionist views must be assessed on the strength of their logical status, not on their formal agreement or disagreement with Marx's own work.

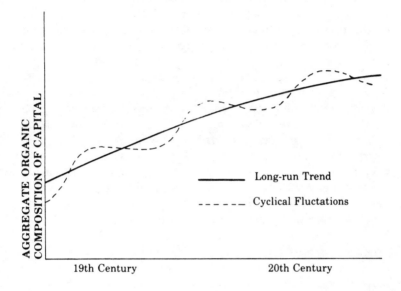

Figure 3.2   Hypothesized Trend in the Organic Composition
of Capital

One of the initial problems in assessing the underconsumptionist logic is that most writings from the underconsumptionist perspective fail to lay out the assumptions and structure of the argument in as coherent a way as the falling-rate-of-profit theorists. The following account of underconsumptionist theory is thus not taken directly from any one defender of the perspective. It is rather my own construction of what I feel a coherent Marxist underconsumptionist theory would be.

36. *Anti-Dühring*, Moscow 1959, p. 395.

A Marxist theory of underconsumption contains four basic propositions:

1) There is a general tendency in capitalist society for the absolute level of surplus value to rise. In addition, with increases in productivity, there is a tendency for the rate of surplus value to increase as well.[37]

2) There is an intrinsic contradiction in capitalist society between the conditions of production of surplus value and the conditions of the realization of surplus value. For realization *not* to be a problem, the growth in aggregate demand must occur at the same rate as the growth in surplus value. This is always problematic in capitalist society since individual capitalists always try to minimize their wage bills and thus restrict the development of effective demand on the part of workers. The result is that there will be a tendency for the growth of demand to lag behind the growth of surplus value unless new sources of aggregate demand can be created (e.g., through increases in government spending, increases in foreign markets, increases in consumer credit, and increases in the rate of accumulation itself.) In the absence of such new sources of demand, part of the surplus value will remain unrealized.

3) The inability of capitalists to realize the full value of the produced surplus value is experienced by capitalists as a fall in the actual rate of profit. This leads to a reduction of investment, bankruptcies, unemployment, etc. Such crisis conditions are resolved when some exogenous source of new demand—such as the state—steps in and restores conditions of profitable realization of surplus.

4) While underconsumptionist tendencies are present at all stages of capitalist development, they become especially acute, and become the source of serious economic crisis, only in the monopoly stage of capitalism. Monopoly power greatly augments the tendency for surplus value to rise, and thus the tendency for underconsumption to occur.

---

37. Note that this proposition states merely that there is a *tendency* for the rate of exploitation to rise with increases in productivity. Like all tendencies there may be counteracting forces which blunt, or even reverse, the tendency itself. In particular, to the extent that wage struggles raise the real wage more or less in step with labour productivity, the tendency for the rate of surplus value to rise will decrease.

There is relatively little disagreement over the first of these propositions. With some exceptions most Marxists feel that with increasing productivity, the *value* of wage goods tends to fall and that thus, although the standard of living of workers may even rise in real terms, the value of labour power will also tend to decline. This results in an increase in the rate of surplus value and, with expanded reproduction of capital, an increase in the mass of surplus value as well. While the underconsumptionists and the falling-rate-of-profit theorists disagree vehemently on the relationship of monopoly to a rising rate of surplus value, they agree on the general proposition that it tends to rise.

On the second proposition there is no such agreement. The falling-rate-of-profit theorists insist that realization problems are a consequence rather than a cause of the fall in the rate of profit. Cogoy makes perhaps the most categorical statement of this view when he argues (in a somewhat cryptic way): "Since total demand under capitalism represents accumulation (demand for subsistence goods represents accumulation, that is accumulation of variable capital), the organic composition determines which part of the total demand consists of demands for subsistence and which for means of production. Thus a falling-off of demand must stem from capital, and capital discontinues its demand only when the profits fall. Thus logically, we can only deduce the over-production of commodities from the fall in the rate of profit and not vice versa."[38]

If all aggregate demand is derived from accumulation, and if capitalists are constantly striving to maximize the rate of accumulation, then clearly the only reason there can ever be an effective demand inadequate for absorbing all of the produced surplus value would be that something happened to the rate of accumulation. This is precisely what the theory of the rising organic composition of capital attempts to demonstrate.

The problem with Cogoy's reasoning, and that of similar critics of underconsumption theories, is that aggregate demand in capitalist society is not simply derived from accumulation. Especially under monopoly conditions, a sizable part of total demand does not come directly from accumulation but from such non-accumulating sources as capitalist personal consumption, much of state expenses, and so on. From the point of

38. "Les Théories Néo-Marxistes", p. 64.

view of the rising-organic-composition theorists this would change nothing fundamental about the problem. Since the rising organic composition of capital creates a problem of inadequate surplus value, such "unproductive expenses"[39] (often called luxury expenses or waste expenditures) would merely exacerbate the problem whose root cause lay in the production process. But things become quite otherwise if we drop the assumption of a rising organic composition of capital.

To analyse the underconsumption problem it is useful to introduce a distinction between potential profits and actual profits. Potential profits are those that would occur in the absence of any realization problems. In terms of our previous discussion, potential profits constitute the surface on Figure 3.1 and the value expression in equation (1). Actual profits will always be less than or equal to such potential profits. The underconsumption argument is an analysis of why there are *tendencies* for a portion of the surplus to remain unrealized, and thus for actual profits to fall short of potential profits.

If the organic composition of capital is more or less constant and the rate of exploitation is rising, there will necessarily occur a rise in the rate of potential profits in value terms. The question then becomes, what are the equilibrium conditions such that all of this increasing surplus will be realized? That is, what total demand must be forthcoming so that the entire surplus product in value terms will be sold? From the basic value equation we have the total supply of commodities:

$$\text{Supply} = c + v + s$$

and the total demand for commodities:

$$\text{Demand} = c + v + \triangle c + \triangle v + U = c + v + I + U,$$

where $\triangle c$ and $\triangle v$ are the demand for additional constant and variable capital or new investment (I) (i.e., the demand derived from accumulation), and U is the demand for unproductive expenditures. The equilibrium condition is therefore:

$$c + v + s = c + v + \triangle c + \triangle v + U$$

39. It must be stressed that the expression "unproductive" is being used in a non-normative sense. An expenditure is unproductive in capitalist society if it does not contribute directly or indirectly to the production of value and surplus value. Some of these expenditures might in fact be "productive" in terms of meeting human needs, but they are not productive in terms of the functioning of a capitalist economy.

or simply:

$$s = \triangle c + \triangle v + U = I + U. \tag{3}$$

Dividing each side of this equation by total capital, c + v, we have:

$$\frac{s}{c + v} = \frac{I}{c + v} + \frac{U}{c + v}. \tag{4}$$

In this equation, the left hand side is simply the potential profit rate, r; I/c+v is the rate of investment, I' (or the rate of accumulation) and U/c+v can be considered the rate of unproductive utilization of resources, U'.

Differentiating both sides of the equation with respect to t, we get:

$$\frac{dr}{dt} = \frac{dI'}{dt} + \frac{dU'}{dt} \tag{5}$$

What can we say about the relative magnitudes of these various terms? Given the assumption of a stable organic composition of capital and a rising rate of surplus value, we know that dr/dt must be positive. Can we say anything general about the relationship between the other two terms? With the assumptions we have made so far, we cannot. But if we are willing to assume that accumulation occurs at a constant rate, then we know that dI'/dt must equal zero. Under this assumption we then know that the requirement for equilibrium is that the rate of unproductive spending must grow at the same rate as the potential rate of profit.

The assumption that accumulation occurs at a constant rather than an ever increasing rate may seem somewhat questionable. In fact, of course, this assumption can be relaxed somewhat and it will still be necessary for the rate of unproductive spending to increase in order for the equilibrium condition to be met (i.e., in order for all of the surplus value produced to be realized). The crucial point is that, unless it is assumed that the *rate* of accumulation increases exactly as fast as increases in the rate of profits,[40] then a growth in the rate of

40. This is in fact the assumption that is made by the falling-rate-of-profit theorists who routinely equate the rate of profit and the rate of accumulation. They argue that since capitalists want to maximize the rate of accumulation, they will necessarily accumulate as much of their profits as possible. Capital-

unproductive expenditures must occur if the equilibrium conditions are to be met.

The tendency towards underconsumption in capitalist society stems fundamentally from the fact that there are no automatic mechanisms which guarantee that the rate of unproductive demand will grow sufficiently fast to fill the gap between the rate of accumulation and the rate of potential profit. The demand for unproductive, wasteful consumption does not grow spontaneously in the same way that demand directly derived from accumulation grows automatically with economic growth. Waste is a social invention, and the maintenance of high levels of wasteful consumption requires conscious planning and intervention. The growth on a massive scale of consumer credit, built-in obsolescence of many consumer durables, the wide range of state interventions in the economy of the Keynesian variety, and so forth, all represent conscious strategies to increase the rate of unproductive demand and thus avoid realization/underconsumption crises.[41] As we will see in section III, these solutions themselves create new problems which the capitalist economy is only beginning to face.

While underconsumptionist tendencies are present at all stages of capitalist development, they have remained largely latent until the monopoly stage. As long as the organic composition of capital did have a tendency to rise, much of the rising surplus was in fact automatically absorbed by the accelerating rate of investment (of accumulation). With the emergence of monopoly capital, however, the situation decisively changes. To begin with, as has already been mentioned, there appears to be a tendency for the organic composition of capital to be relatively stable in the monopoly stage of capitalism, or at least to rise at a much slower rate. Several mechanisms might explain this. The typical productivity bargains worked out between big unions and monopoly capital may have reduced the selective pressures for labour-saving innovations in monopoly capital. Or alter-

---

ists, however, are individually interested in maximizing their rate of profit rather than the aggregate rate of accumulation, and there is no reason to suppose that these two are inevitably equivalent.

41. Any concrete commodity can, of course, represent both accumulation and waste. The distinction being made is an analytical one, not between different categories of concrete commodities.

natively, since monopolies tend to emerge in industries with already high levels of organic composition of capital, (i.e., high barriers to entry), it might be expected that the rate of increase in the organic composition of capital in the period of monopoly capital would tend to be lower (assuming, as we did above, that the rate of labour-saving innovations is inversely proportional to the value composition of capital). Whatever the explanation, this relatively stable organic composition of capital characteristic of developed monopoly capital, will tend to accentuate the problem of rising surplus.

Monopoly capital has a second, and probably more important impact on the tendency towards underconsumption. In a fundamental way, monopoly power transforms the relationship between values and prices. This is an extremely controversial issue and is one of the most heated disputes between the organic composition theorists and the underconsumptionists. The falling rate of profit theorists insist that the structure of market relations can in principle have no fundamental impact on value relations. All that monopoly power can hope to change is the distribution of surplus value from less monopolistic to more monopolistic capitals, but it cannot have any affect on the analysis of capital-in-general.

Sweezy has challenged this view head on. He argues that not only does monopoly power result in a redistribution of value from competitive to monopoly capital, but from wages to surplus value: "Monopoly does not change the total *amount* of value produced—except indirectly to the extent that it affects the total volume of employment—but it does bring about a *redistribution* of value. Marx indicated that this can take two forms: first a transfer of surplus value from competitive to monopolistic capitals; and second, a transfer of value from wages to surplus value."[42]

42. *The Theory of Capitalist Development*, p. 41. The passage from Marx to which Sweezy refers is worth noting: "If a commodity with a monopoly price should enter into the consumption of the labourer, it would increase the wages and thereby reduce the surplus value if the labourer would receive the value of his labour power the same as before. But such a commodity might also depress wages below the value of labour power, of course only to the extent that wages would be higher than the physical minimum of subsistence. In this case the monopoly price would be paid by a deduction from real wages (that is, from the quantity of use values received by the labourer for the same quantity of labour) and from the profit of other capitalists." This is certainly a clear statement that

This means that surplus labour is extracted from the working class through at least two mechanisms during the stage of monopoly capital rather than merely one: in addition to the extraction of surplus value in the labour process itself through the wage contract, surplus value is appropriated in the sphere of circulation through the manipulation of monopoly prices. Why don't workers then organize and force monopoly capital to pay wages equal to the "true" value of labour power? The answer, of course, is that the working class *in the monopoly sector* does precisely this, and by and large wages in the monopoly sector have tended to rise approximately at the same rate as productivity. But workers outside of the monopoly sector of the economy have not been able to raise their wages in a comparable manner. The result is that monopoly sector capitalists in effect extract surplus value from competitive sector workers (and transfer surplus value from competitive sector capitalists) through the mechanism of monopoly pricing. The upshot of all this is that the aggregate rate of surplus value under conditions of monopoly capital rises more rapidly than productivity, and thus the general problem of underconsumption becomes even more acute.

Two general social processes have evolved which at least partially counteract this tendency towards underconsumption in monopoly capitalist society. The first has already been mentioned: the invention and growth of Keynesian policies designed to stimulate aggregate demand through the expansion of unproductive spending, primarily by the state. Such spending has the secondary consequence of bolstering the confidence of investors in the stability of the economy, and thus fostering a higher rate of accumulation. Thus, in equation (5), the growth of dU'/dt becomes a stimulus for the growth of dI'/dt and consequently, for a further reduction in underconsumption pressures.

Second, the growth of collective bargaining may have the effect of reducing the rate of increase in the rate of surplus value itself. In the equilibrium condition in equation (5) this would

monopoly can redistribute value from variable capital to surplus value and thus increase the rate of exploitation. While in Marx's own time the occurrence of monopoly may have been sufficiently rare to make this process of relatively little significance, this is hardly the case at the present time.

mean a reduction in dr/dt and thus a reduced pressure towards underconsumption. Especially in monopoly sector industries, where wages since the war have been fairly closely tied to productivity increases, the gradual rise in the wage has undoubtedly lessened to some extent underconsumption tendencies. The continued growth of monopoly power, however, has at least partially neutralized this counteracting process, since much of the productivity wage increases has in turn been passed on to the working class as a whole in the form of monopoly pricing. As we argued above, this has the effect of further increasing the rate of surplus value for capital as a whole.

The most serious weakness in the underconsumptionist position is that it lacks any theory of the determinants of the actual rate of accumulation. The falling-rate-of-profit theorists have a specific theory of the determinants of the rate of accumulation. In equating the rate of profit with the rate of accumulation, they see a combination of the organic composition of capital and the rate of exploitation as the basic determinant of the actual rate of accumulation. Since they view the organic composition of capital as rising and thus constantly pushing down the rate of profit, the assumption that the rate of profit and the rate of accumulation are equivalent does no damage to their general argument. If anything, the impact of the rising organic composition of capital would be even greater if not all profits were accumulated.

In the underconsumption argument, however, the rate of profit and the rate of accumulation cannot be equated. If they were, there would not be a tendency for underconsumption (i.e., there would be no need for the rate of unproductive spending to increase). Much underconsumptionist writing has, at least implicitly, opted for Keynes' solution to this problem by focusing on the subjective anticipations of profit on the part of capitalists as the key determinant of the rate of accumulation. From a Marxist point of view, this is an inadequate solution. I have not yet seen an elaborated theory of investment and the rate of accumulation by a Marxist underconsumptionist theorist, and thus for the time being the theory remains incomplete.

3. Theories of the Profit Squeeze
Both underconsumptionists and organic-composition-of-capital

theorists maintain that with capitalist development there tends to be a rising rate of surplus value. Where they differ is in their view of the relationship between this rising rate of surplus value and the movements of the rate of profit. The organic-composition theorists insist that changes in technology within the production process itself tend to negate this rise in the rate of surplus and thus produce a fall in profits; underconsumptionists argue that the forces for a rising surplus tend to be stronger than any counterforces, especially under conditions of monopoly capital.

The proponents of the profit squeeze view of crisis agree with the organic composition theorists that the rate of profit tends to fall, but they disagree that this has anything to do with changes in technology, and they disagree with both the organic composition theorists and the underconsumptionists that there is any tendency for the rate of surplus value to rise.

The essential argument of the profit squeeze is very simple: the relative share of the national income going to workers and to capitalists is almost entirely a consequence of their relative strengths in the class struggle. There is therefore no intrinsic reason for wage struggles to be limited, even in the long run, to demands that real wages should rise merely as rapidly as productivity. To the extent that the working class develops a strong enough labour movement to win wage increases in excess of productivity increases, there will be a tendency for the rate of profits to fall (to be "squeezed" by rising wage bills). Such a decline in profits results in a corresponding decline in investments and thus even slower increases in productivity. The end result is economic crisis. Conditions for profitability are restored to the extent that as the reserve army of the unemployed grows during a crisis, the bargaining strength of the working class relative to capitalists declines and thus the profit squeeze is lessened.

The profit squeeze thesis has been used both as an explanation for business cycles and as a theory of structural crisis. Raford Boddy and James Crotty have applied the profit squeeze argument to an analysis of the relationship of macroeconomic state policy to the business cycle. They write:

"Throughout the post-World War II, post-Keynesian period, the profit share of income, indeed the absolute level of profits, has fallen in the latter half of every expansion. Correspondingly, wages and wage share have risen. We view the erosion of profits as the result of successful class struggle waged by labour against capital—struggle that is confined and ultimately reversed by the relaxation of demand and the rise in unemployment engineered by the capitalists and acquiesced in and abetted by the state."[43] Cyclical downturns in the economy are thus portrayed primarily as devices for disciplining the working class.

The most extended attempt to use the profit squeeze argument as the basis of a theory of structural crisis rather than simply business cycles has been made by Andrew Glyn and Bob Sutcliffe in an analysis of the stagnation of British capitalism since the mid-1960s.[44] They argue, contrary to the usual axioms of modern economics that the share of income going to labour and capital has remained constant throughout the century, that if the shares are measured properly, there has been a very definite trend for the share going to labour to increase. Furthermore, they argue that in Britain especially this trend has substantially accelerated since the end of the Second World War, and especially since the mid-1960s. Glyn and Sutcliffe view this rise in the share going to labour as largely the result of the strength of the labour movement. This is especially important given the present international position of British capital. Because of intense international competition and the elimination of most British tariff barriers, British capitalists have a great deal of difficulty passing on wage increases in the form of higher prices, while simultaneously they find themselves less and less able to resist wage demands because of their vulnerability to strikes. Since most of the competition between British monopoly capital and foreign monopoly capital takes the form of struggles over shares of the market, a strike of even moderate length can have a devastating effect on the future prospects of the British capitalist. Whereas traditionally large capitalists have always been able to hold out longer in a strike than their workers, this is less and less the case, especially with

43. "Class Conflict and Macro-Policy: the Political Business Cycle", *Review of Radical Political Economics*, Vol. 7, No. 1, 1975, p. 1.

44. See "The Critical Condition of British Capital", *New Left Review* No. 66, 1971; and *British Capitalism, Workers and the Profit Squeeze*, London 1972.

more substantial strike funds and government welfare programmes providing at least a minimal subsistence to a striking
family. Finally, because of the strength of the union movement,
the increase in unemployment that has accompanied the
deepening crisis has not led to the usual readjustment of wage
rates and a restoration of an adequate rate of exploitation. Thus,
the current crisis of British capitalism is fundamentally deeper
than earlier crises since the normal social mechanisms for
reversing the profit squeeze have been undermined.

The profit squeeze thesis has been sharply criticized, especially by proponents of more orthodox rising organic composition of capital theorists. Perhaps the most general criticism
is that theories of the profit squeeze have adopted what is often
called a "Neo-Ricardian" view of the relationship of profits to
wages.[45] Instead of profits being seen as realized surplus value,
profits are viewed as a deduction from wages. The balance
between wages and profits, therefore, is seen as determined
through struggles at the level of circulation rather than
through dynamics determined at the level of production.

While it is fair enough to argue that theories of the profit
squeeze do tend to de-emphasize class struggles at the level of
production, nevertheless the accusation of neo-Ricardianism is
not entirely appropriate. Marx certainly recognized the role of
class struggle over wages as an essential part of the historical
process by which the value of labour power is established, and
thus as part of the process by which profits are determined. In
Capital, Marx writes: "The fixation of the value of labour power
. . . is only settled by the continuous struggle between capital
and labour, the capitalist constantly tending to reduce wages to
their physical minimum and to extend the working day to its
physical maximum, while the working man constantly presses
in the opposite direction. The matter resolves itself into a question of the relative powers of the combatants."[46]

The rate of profit is a consequence of a plurality of concrete
processes:

45. See especially Ben Fine and Lawrence Harris, "State Expenditure in
Advanced Capitalism—A Critique", *New Left Review* No. 98, 1976, and David
Yaffe, "The Crisis of Profitability, A Critique of the Glyn–Sutcliffe Thesis", *New
Left Review* No. 80, 1973.

46. *Capital*, Vol. II, Chicago 1906, p. 443.

1) class struggles over the standard of living of the working class (real wages);
2) the productivity of labour in the wage goods sector, which determines the value embodied in the standard of living of workers;
3) class struggles over the length of the working day and the intensity of labour, which determine how much total value workers generate in a given day;
4) the organic composition of capital.

The first two of these factors determine the value of labour power. When combined with the third factor, they determine the rate of surplus value (s/v), and when combined with the fourth factor, the value rate of profit $(s/c+v)$.

The profit squeeze theorists may be criticized for focussing too exclusively on the first of these elements and failing to link wage struggles to other aspects of accumulation, but it is hardly a valid criticism that they view struggles over wages as one determinant of the rate of profit.

The question remains, however, whether the empirical case made by the defenders of the profit squeeze is credible. Has the rise in wages of workers in fact tended to "squeeze" profits in recent years? There has been considerable debate on both sides of this issue, and it is clear that the extent to which wages can be viewed as pressing on profits depends heavily on exactly how wages and profits are measured. However, even if we accept the operationalizations offered by Glyn and Sutcliffe or Boddy and Crotty, the empirical basis of the theory still remains very problematic. The essential difficulty lies in the relationship between the share of national income going to wages and the basic categories of Marxist value analysis. To explain this issue requires a brief discussion of the very tricky concept of "unproductive labour".

While there are immense difficulties in rigorously operationalizing the distinction between productive and unproductive labour, it is certainly clear that not all labour power is employed productively in capitalist societies, i.e., not all labour actually produces surplus value. The wages of unproductive workers impinge on the rate of profit through a very different logic from the wages of productive workers. There are two ways of expressing this relationship. The most common way of dealing with this issue has been to treat the wages of unproductive labourers as a direct deduction from surplus value. The unproductive worker, in these terms, is treated exactly the same as a private servant who provides a service for capitalists and is hired for the immediate use value of the worker's labour rather than its exchange value. In this conception the value relations are as follows:

$$C + V + S_u + S_a = P$$

where S_u is the proportion of surplus value which must be devoted to pay for unproductive labour, and S_a is the part of surplus value available for accumulation. Increases in S_u directly reduce the effective rate of profit by reducing the numerator in the value rate of profit.

An alternative way of conceptualizing the relationship of unproductive labour to the value equations has been suggested by Mage.[47] Mage argues that unproductive labour should be treated as a special form of constant capital, "living constant capital" if you will. Like the usual forms of constant capital, most unproductive labour is socially necessary for production, it constitutes a fixed overhead cost of production, and it transfers its value (reproductive costs) to the final product, but without creating any new value (surplus value). In these terms, unproductive labour appears in the value equation as:

$$C + C_L + V + S = P$$

where C_L is "living" constant capital. In this representation, increases in unproductive labour reduce the rate of profit by increasing the denominator of the value rate of profit.[48]

Regardless of which of these formulations is adopted, it is clear that if the employment of unproductive labour increases as a proportion of total labour at a faster rate than the increases

47. *The Law of the Falling Tendency of the Rate of Profit.*
48. This second way of representing unproductive labour in the value equations stresses that constant capital, like variable capital, is not a "thing", but a social relationship. Constant capital is no longer defined as the physical inputs into production, but rather as those socially necessary inputs into production, physical and human, which simply transfer their value to the final product without increasing total value. This conceptualization has interesting implications for the analysis of the organic composition of capital. While it might be difficult to demonstrate that $C/v+s$ or c/v has risen dramatically in the past thirty years or so, it is certainly the case that $(C+C_L)/(V+S)$ and $(C+C_L)/V$ have risen.

of productivity of productive labour, then there will be a tendency for the rate of profit to decline. This is especially clear when unproductive labour is seen as a direct deduction from surplus value: every increase in unproductive labour in this formulation immediately reduces the effective rate of profit.

The difficulty, then, with the data of the profit squeeze theorists is that they are incapable of distinguishing between two situations: a) situations in which profits are squeezed because of rising wage costs; and b) situations where profits are squeezed by increasing employment of unproductive labour. The share of national income going to wages includes both of these processes. To the extent, therefore, that there are general tendencies in monopoly capitalism for unproductive labour to increase, the empirical phenomenon of increasing labour shares of national income could have little to do with successful struggles over wages.

The empirical case for the profit squeeze argument thus remains to be proven. Nevertheless, the profit squeeze argument has the considerable merit of emphasizing the central role of class struggle in the accumulation process. Even if it remains to be demonstrated that rising real wages have been the central cause of declining profits, class struggle and class organization can still impinge on the rate of profit in several critical ways. First, the resistance of workers to layoffs due to technological innovations (featherbedding) may act as a brake on the rate of technical innovation and thus on increases in the productivity of labour. Such a slow-down in innovation in turn makes it more difficult for capital to raise the rate of exploitation in response to declines in the rate of profit (whatever the cause of that decline).

Secondly, the strength of working class organizations can act as a political break on inflation, and can thus make it more difficult for capital to compensate for deteriorating profits through price rises. Inflation is a weapon in the class struggle; it is one of the ways by which capital can attempt to lower the value of labour power, and thus raise the rate of exploitation. As Bob Rowthorn has argued, the obstacles to the effective use of inflation as a way of pushing down real wages in Britain are to a great extent political rather than simply economic.[49]

49. "Late Capitalism", *New Left Review*, No. 98, 1976, pp. 76–77.

Finally, the existence of substantial programmes of unemployment insurance and welfare in most advanced capitalist countries have meant that the disciplining effects of the reserve army of the unemployed have been seriously attenuated. A reduction in the rate of exploitation due to wage struggles may not have been the underlying cause of the current economic crisis, but the difficulty in raising the rate of exploitation may be one of the reasons for the persistence of the crisis.

4. State Expenditures and Accumulation

Marxist theories of accumulation and crisis have generally conceptualized state activity as unproductive in a double sense: First, state *revenues* (principally taxes) are seen as coming out of the existing pool of surplus value, and thus increases in state spending necessarily imply less surplus value available for accumulation. Secondly, state *spending* is seen as unproductive since under normal conditions the state does not engage in direct investment in the production of commodities.

In the underconsumptionist model of crisis this unproductive quality of state expenditures constitutes the central mechanism by which crisis is averted or at least minimized; in rising-organic-composition models, the expansion of such unproductive expenditures is seen as a critical factor which exacerbates the inherent crisis tendencies in the system. In both theories, however, state activity is seen as largely unproductive and as absorbing an increasing share of the surplus value produced in the economy.

This traditional conception can be criticized both in terms of its view of the *sources* of state revenue and of its view of the *impact* of state spending.

The view that all taxes constitute a tax on the *existing* pool of surplus value is based on a mechanistic and static interpretation of the meaning of the value of labour power. Since taxation clearly reduces the money wages of workers, the view that all taxes come from surplus value implicitly assumes that prior to taxation wages were above the "true" value of labour power. Taxation then merely appropriates that part of the surplus value which had previously been in the disguised form of an inflated money wage. The implicit logic is that if taxation did not occur, wages would be reduced to the present after-tax level anyway. In other words, if the state did not tax this surplus value it would be available to the capitalist for accumulation. These assumptions are at best dubious, if real wages and taxation are seen as at least partially the outcome of class struggle. Because of the enormous weight of the state's power of legitimation, it is reasonable to assume that many workers are willing to accept a level of taxation on their money incomes greater than a corresponding wage cut that might occur in the absence of such taxes. In this sense taxation actually reduces the value of labour power rather than merely reduces the money wage of labour power to its "true" value. Taxation, of course, cannot itself create *value*, but taxation can increase the part of total value that is appropriated as *surplus value*. Tax exploitation did not die with the feudal mode of production just because wage exploitation became the dominant way that surplus is extracted from workers in capitalist society. Thus, taxation, like monopoly pricing, can potentially expand the rate of surplus value. This is not to say that there are no limits to the extent to which taxes can have this effect, and certainly not that all or even most taxation in fact expands surplus value, but merely that the assumption that all taxation constitutes a drain on existing surplus value is incorrect.[50]

Quite apart from the relationship of taxation to existing surplus value there is the question of the impact of taxation on the subsequent production of surplus value. It is certainly true that with very few exceptions, state production is itself not production for the market and thus the state does not accumulate capital out of any realized profits from its own production. Most state expenditures therefore do not *directly* produce surplus

50. It would be an extremely difficult task to obtain a reasonable estimate of the extent to which actual taxes come out of existing surplus value and the extent to which taxes increase the effective rate of exploitation. An examination of how much money wages tend to increase with increases in the rate of taxation would help to give some indication of the relative proportions. If money wages increase exactly in step with increases in total taxation so that real wages are never reduced by taxes, then it would be reasonable to say that most taxes are taxes on existing surplus. This is an empirical question and I have no basis for predicting a particular *a priori* ratio between surplus absorbing and surplus expanding taxation.

value.[51] But as O'Connor has thoroughly argued, this does not preclude the state from playing an important role in *indirectly* expanding surplus value and accumulation. Many state expenditures have the effect of reducing the reproduction costs of labour power by socializing many expenses that would otherwise have to be paid for by individual capitalists (medical care, training and education, social security, etc.). Furthermore, a great deal of state spending on research and development, transportation infrastructures, communications, etc. have the effect of increasing the level of productivity of capital as a whole, and thus contributing to accumulation. Even in terms of classical, wasteful Keynesian demand-maintenance state interventions, such state spending may have the side effect of increasing capacity utilization and thus increasing productivity. Again, this is not to say that such indirectly productive expenditures are necessarily the dominant mode of state activity, but rather that it is incorrect to see the state's role in the accumulation process as simply being a drag on accumulation.

Given that to some extent taxes as a mechanism of exploitation can expand surplus value and that to some extent state spending can expand accumulation, what is crucial to analyse is not merely the forces which produce a general expansion of state activity, but the extent to which these forces selectively expand the unproductive or (indirectly) productive activities of the state, and the extent to which surplus-expanding or surplus-absorbing taxation tends to grow more rapidly. Little can be said about the latter issue. The current growth of the so-called "tax-payers revolt" in the USA might indicate that the growth of surplus-expanding taxation has reached some sort of limit. Certainly the general battering that the legitimacy of the American state has taken in the last several years would tend to reduce the state's capacity to use taxes as a mechanism for extracting extra surplus value from the working class. At any rate, for the rest of this discussion we will assume that there has not been any major trend one way or the other in the balance between surplus-expanding and surplus-absorbing taxation.

51. This has been well argued by Yaffe and, in a very different context, by Offe: see "The Marxian Theory of Crisis", pp. 216–227, and "Structural Problems of the Capitalist State".

More can be said about the relationship between unproductive state expenditures and indirectly-productive state expenditures. Given the underconsumptionist tendencies inherent in monopoly capitalism, it is obviously necessary for unproductive expenditures to grow more rapidly than productive expenditures. The growth of classical Keynesian make-work and waste programmes, military spending and welfare all reflect this requirement. There are several critical contradictions contained within this role of the state, however, which disrupt the smooth adjustment of unproductive state spending to the needs of monopoly capital.

1) *Contradiction of legitimation and accumulation:* The state does not merely serve the function of facilitating accumulation through demand maintenance; the state also serves a vital legitimation function in capitalist society which helps to stabilize and reproduce the class structure as a whole. The legitimation function directs much state activity towards coopting potential sources of popular discontent by attempting to transform political demands into economic demands. The expansion of Keynesian programmes beginning in the 1930s created a perfect political climate for state spending to expand dramatically such legitimating expenditures. For a long time it appeared that the state in effect could kill two functional birds with one economic policy stone.

The difficulty, however, is that once a demand on the state to provide some social service or meet some social need is granted and becomes institutionalized, it becomes viewed as a right. There is a certain logic to legitimation which means that the political apparatus gets progressively diminishing returns in added legitimation for a given programme over time. Once a programme becomes seen as a right, the continuation of the programme adds little to the legitimacy of the state whereas a cutback in the programme would constitute a source of delegitimation. There is thus not only a tendency for programmes once established to continue, but a constant pressure on programmes to expand, regardless of the requirements of the accumulation process. The hypothesis can therefore be advanced that once Keynesian demand maintenance programmes become bound up with the legitimation functions of the state, there is a tendency for unproductive spending to rise more rapidly than the requirements for realization of surplus value.[52]

2) *State spending and productivity*. The growth of state spending tends to dampen increases in productivity in two respects. First of all, internal to the state itself, the mechanisms for encouraging increases in productivity are much weaker than in the private sector. This is true both because most state activity is fairly shielded from direct market pressures and because many of the activities of the state are intrinsically difficult to rationalize. Secondly, the impact of much state spending on the economy as a whole often tends to constrain productivity increases. Perhaps the clearest example of this is military spending, especially as it is organized in the United States. Corporations which are major suppliers of military hardware are guaranteed a given profit rate by the state (especially in "cost-plus" contracts) and are thus under relatively little pressure to modernize and innovate in the production process. While there are occasional technological "spin-offs" from military spending which may partially counteract this damper on productivity, it seems unlikely that such technological advances completely balance the negative effects. As a result of these two factors, there will be a tendency for the expansion of state activity to act as a brake on productivity increases in a capitalist society.

3) *The weakening of mechanisms of crisis management*. The usual scenario for crisis and recovery is that in a crisis the least productive capitals are wiped out, capital is devalued, and conditions for profitable accumulation are restored. The growth of monopoly capital and especially of the dominant role of the state in regulating the economy tends seriously to weaken this restorative mechanism. This is most obvious in the case of corporations who become locked into production for the state.

52. Military spending has an additional contradictory aspect which under certain circumstances can become extremely important; there is no necessary reason for the imperatives of military spending generated by imperialism to coincide with the imperatives generated by accumulation. In the case of the United States, the Vietnam War in the late 1960s is an example of a period where these two imperatives were quite contradictory. See Clarence Lo, "The Functions of US Military Spendings", *Kapitalistate*, No. 3, 1975.

Partially because of the personal ties between the corporate elite and the state apparatus (especially in the military–industrial nexus) and partially because of the social dislocation that would result from the bankruptcy of a major monopoly corporation, the state finds it very difficult to abandon a major corporation, even if that corporations's productivity declines drastically (witness the enormous subsidies of a notoriously inefficient and unproductive corporation, Lockheed). Even outside those companies which produce mainly for the state, the state is forced to underwrite the low productivity of many sectors of the economy in order to avoid major disruptions (the railroads in the U.S. are a good example).

Keynesian state policies also tend to undermine crisis management mechanisms on the side of labour. As discussed above in the section on theories of the profit squeeze, the expansion of state welfare programmes, unemployment insurance, etc., has weakened the reserve army of labour as a mechanism for disciplining the working class. In periods of underconsumption, such programmes appear as one way of increasing aggregate demand. If it was possible instantly to abolish such programmes as soon as they ceased to be functional for capital, then they would pose little problem. The legitimation costs of such a retrenchment, however, are unacceptable, and while there have certainly been attempts in numerous capitalist countries to cut back on welfare programmes in the current crisis, the basic contours of those programmes have remained intact.

The upshot of these contradictions in the role of the state is that Keynesian policies tend to become progressively more and more out of proportion to the requirements of accumulation. Although those policies originally emerged as a response to the problem of excessive surplus (as portrayed by the underconsumptionist model), the end result is that they begin to act as a drain on the surplus value necessary for accumulation (the image of crisis in the rising organic composition model). That is, in spite of the necessity for waste in the era of monopoly capitalism, there is a tendency for the level of state waste (i.e., unproductive spending) to expand more rapidly than the capacity of the system to produce waste (i.e., through increases in productivity). Because the crisis-solving mechanisms are partially blocked, the result is chronic inflation combined with relatively high levels of unemployment, or what has come to be called "stagflation".

One way of visualizing this argument is in terms of the standard Neoclassical notion of the Phillips Curve. The Phillips Curve represents the possible combinations of rates of unemployment and rates of inflation characteristic of an economy. It is usually represented as defining the trade-offs between unemployment and inflation that face policy makers. The classical form of the Phillips Curve is presented in Figure 3.3.

The premise of traditional Keynesian policies has always been that this trade-off function was itself more or less fixed and that the forces in the economy merely determine where on the curve the economy will fall at a particular moment in time. The task of policy-making was therefore merely to regulate the economy in ways which kept the economy in an acceptable range of the curve. The analysis presented above (which in a somewhat different form some neo-Keynesians have appended to their own conceptualization of the Phillips Curve) suggests that the developments in the economy and the interventions of the state determine not merely where on some ideal Phillips Curve the economy is located, but also the entire shape and location of the trade-off curve itself. Specifically, the theory of disproportionate growth of unproductive spending would argue that there has been a systematic secular deterioration of the terms of the trade-off over the past several decades. Such tendencies have been further exacerbated by the continual growth of monopoly concentration in certain key sectors of the economy, and especially by the growing internationalization of capital.[53] As a result of these forces, one might hypothesize that the Phillips Curve has moved away from the origin, and further-

53. The internationalization of capital means that a given effort by the state to reduce inflation will result in greater increases in unemployment than would otherwise be the case, since such state policies will tend to increase the movements of capital across the national borders (see Alberto Martinelli, "Nation States and Multinationals", *Kapitalistate*, No. 1, 1973). Internationalization will thus tend to push the Phillips Curve away from the origin. It is probably impossible to disaggregate empirically the relative effects of such increasing internationalization of capital and increasing unproductive state spending on the deterioration of the trade-off of inflation and unemployment, since the two empirically tend to move together.

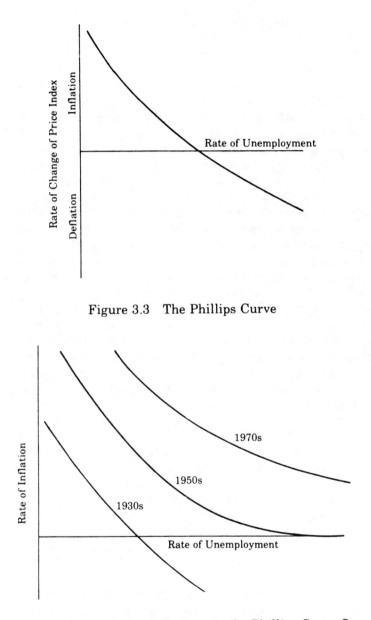

Figure 3.3   The Phillips Curve

Figure 3.4   Hypothesized Changes in the Phillips Curve Over Time

more, that it may not any longer even intersect the horizontal axis at any level of unemployment. This new Phillips Curve is pictured in Figure 3.4. Keynesian policies are totally inadequate to reverse this deterioration of the Phillips trade-off.

The obvious solution to these dilemmas is, of course, for the state to shift the balance of its activities from unproductive to indirectly productive spending. Such indirectly productive expenditures have certainly been steadily growing over the past several decades, although it seems generally at a slower rate than unproductive expenditures. The state is increasingly involved not merely in what Offe calls "allocative" policies (policies which basically redistribute resources already produced or mobilize the production of resources strictly for Keynesian purposes)[54] but in "productive" policies as well (policies which directly impinge on the production process and which contribute to the productivity of the economy). As the productive forces in advanced capitalism have developed highly sophisticated technologies, increasingly interdependent productive processes, increasing requirements for highly specialized technical labour, etc., it has become more and more difficult for individual capitalists to provide all of the requirements for their own expanded reproduction, and thus they have turned to the state for various forms of socialized investments. It might well be thought, therefore, that the solution to the contradictions of Keynesian policies can be simply found in a dramatic expansion of these emergent forms of indirectly productive socialized investments. The problem is that the fundamentally Keynesian politics of the contemporary capitalist state, a politics rooted in pluralist interest-group demands, special interest subsidies, military production, etc., act as a serious constraint on the potential growth of these new productivity-enhancing forms of state intervention. This is at the heart of the "fiscal crisis of the state": the constant pressures from the growth of unproductive spending, which are exceedingly difficult to restrain for the reasons spelled out above, make it highly problematic for the state to finance the new forms of state policy which would help reverse the problem of declining productivity itself. Until such time as new political forces can be

54. See "Structural Problems of the Capitalist State".

mobilized successfully to generate what O'Connor has aptly called a new "social industrial complex",[55] it is difficult to see how this impasse can be overcome.

III. The Development of Capitalism and the Impediments to Accumulation

If these various interpretations are treated as total explanations of crisis tendencies in capitalism, then indeed they are quite incompatible: one cannot, for example, argue that the basic cause of crisis is excessive surplus value (underconsumption thesis) and simultaneously inadequate surplus value (rising organic composition of capital thesis); one cannot posit that the reason for crises is a declining rate of exploitation caused by successful class struggle (profit squeeze) and that at the same time there is a general tendency for the rate of exploitation to rise (underconsumption and rising organic composition perspectives). Either we must reject outright all of these views of crisis but one, or we must adopt a methodological stance which enables us to integrate them within a larger framework.

One strategy for reconciling these various perspectives is to analyse them in terms of the history of capitalist development. Instead of regarding any one crisis mechanism as the panhistorical cause of all economic crises in capitalist society, capitalist development should be viewed as continually transforming the nature of capitalist crisis. To recapitulate the logic of this historical transformation of crisis mechanisms set out at the beginning of this chapter, at each stage of capitalist development there is a characteristic pattern of impediments to the accumulation process. Through a combination of class strategies by the capitalist state and individual strategies by individual capitalists attempting to maximize their profits, these impediments are overcome and the accumulation process continues in new forms. The solutions to the dominant impediments at each level of capitalist development, however, contain within themselves new contradictions which gradually emerge

55. See *The Fiscal Crisis of the State*.

in the subsequent stages.[56] The logic of this dialectical process can be symbolically represented in a model of determination (see Chapter 1 for an explanation). Figure 3.5 illustrates the main contours of this model.

The historically specific articulation of the forces and relations of production—what is traditionally called the "economic base" in Marxist theory—establishes structural limits on the forms of accumulation in a particular period. Furthermore, the forces/relations of production determine the extent to which a given form of accumulation will be reproductive or non-reproductive of those forces/relations of production (i.e. they

56. There is a certain similarity between this conception of the stages of capitalist development and the theory of "long waves" as developed by Ernest Mandel in *Late Capitalism*, London 1975. Although to a certain extent Mandel holds to the traditional Marxist thesis that the ultimate constraint on accumulation is the tendency for the organic composition of capital to rise, he does insist that the dominant contradictions of one phase of capitalist development are not necessarily the same as in another. He stresses that the accumulation process encounters different immediate obstacles in different stages and he tries to show how class struggles mediate the historical readjustments of capitalism. He also argues that the constraints on accumulation encountered at the end of the long waves of capitalist development can only be overcome through fairly radical reorganizations of the mode of accumulation.

In one very critical respect, however, the analysis presented here differs from that of Mandel. For Mandel, the pivotal characteristic of each phase of the history of capitalism, and the decisive transformations which set in motion new long waves of accumulation, centre on technology. Technological revolutions are the essential basis for the structural reorganizations of accumulation, for the liberation of new possibilities of accumulation. As those possibilities become exhausted, accumulation begins to slow down until such time as a new technological revolution occurs. In these terms, the current world economic crisis, Mandel argues, should be seen as a consequence of the petering out of the third technological revolution.

Technology—or, more broadly, the forces or production—is, of course, important, and in a variety of ways contributes to the character of different periods of accumulation. But I do not think that the essential periodization of capitalism should be tied to a periodization of technological change. Nor does the essential structural solution to impediments to accumulation invariably lie in technological revolutions. The social organization of production, the forms of competition and class struggle, can be at least as decisive. It is historically variable which specific kind of structural change will be the most critical to re-establishing conditions for accumulation during periods of crisis. Mandel's work is extremely interesting in pointing out the technical sides of these transformations, but in the end it unwittingly tends to reproduce the monocausal views of crisis which it so correctly rejects. For a similar critique of Mandel, see Bob Rowthorn, "Late Capitalism", *New Left Review*, No. 98, 1976.

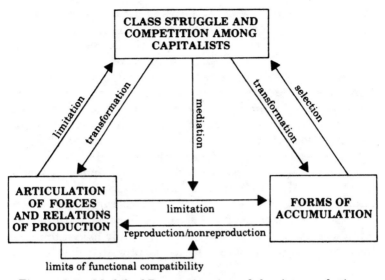

Figure 3.5   Model of Determination of the Accumulation
Process

establish limits of functional compatibility). The critical question, then, is to understand the social processes which tend to
push the forms of accumulation outside those limits of functional compatibility, thus generating structural crises within
the accumulation process.

Class struggle and capitalist competition both directly transform the structure of forces/relations of production and the
forms of accumulation. Of particular importance for understanding crisis tendencies, class struggle and competition continually transform the forces/relations of production. A given
organization of accumulation, therefore, gradually tends to
become less and less reproductive—i.e. as the limits of compatible variation set by the forces/relations of production shift,
a given organization of accumulation moves away from what
could be considered an optimal form of accumulation. Eventually, the form of accumulation may actually cease to fall
within the limits of compatible variation altogether; this is a
situation that can be described as a structural crisis of accumulation. In such situations, typically, the forms of accumulation
are themselves restructured in basic ways, restoring at least a

minimal compatibility of the forms of accumulation with the forces/relations of production. When we speak of "impediments to accumulation" we are referring to the process by which a given form of accumulation progressively becomes non-reproductive. When we speak of "structural solutions" to those impediments, we are referring to the ways in which the accumulation process is transformed to re-establish a compatible relation with the forces/relations of production.[57] It is such structural solutions which define the essential character of the different stages of capitalist development.

Figure 3.6 summarizes the historical development which is generated by the structural relations in Figure 3.5.[58] This figure is, of course, highly oversimplified. The structural "solutions" to a particular impediment to accumulation generally do not eliminate the problem altogether, but merely help it to recede into the background. Every period of capitalist development

57. Two other linkages in Figure 3.4 should be noted. First, class struggle and competition are structurally limited by the forces/relations of production (as discussed in the previous chapter) and selected by the forms of accumulation. This selection relationship is especially important, since it means that the nature of class struggle and the forms of competition among capitalists are shaped by the very process which also becomes non-reproductive for the relations/forces of production. In effect, this means that class struggle and competition respond to a given form of accumulation even when that form of accumulation contradicts the forces/relations of production. This is one aspect of the relationships of determination which tend to push the system towards crisis instead of a stable equilibrium. Secondly, class struggle and competition mediate the relationship between forces/relations of production and the forms of accumulation. The speed at which the obstacles to accumulation emerge, the ways in which they impede further accumulation, the precise forms which they take and the ultimate consequences which they have are all shaped by class struggle and competition. A complete analysis of the accumulation process would have to deal with these complex relations of determination and not simply the ways in which class struggle and competition transform the accumulation process directly.

58. This chart draws heavily from a number of sources. The first three stages come fairly directly from Marx's discussion of primitive accumulation in Part VIII of Vol. I of *Capital*; the shift from stage 3 to stage 4 is quite similar to the analysis by David Levine, especially Part III of his thesis, "The Theory of the Growth of the Capitalist Economy"; the analysis of stage 5 is based largely on the analysis of the *Fiscal Crisis of the State* by James O'Connor; and the analysis of the emergent problems of stage 6 has grown out of the work of Claus Offe. The periodization of emergent forms of imperialism comes primarily from Ernest Mandel's *Late Capitalism* and to a lesser extent from Samir Amin's "Towards a Structural Crisis of World Capitalism", *Socialist Revolution* No. 23, 1975.

contains, if only in residual form, the contradictions characteristic of earlier periods. The same point can be made about the forms of imperialism which emerge in response to given constraints in accumulation. There is no suggestion here that a given form of imperialism occurs uniquely with a given impediment to accumulation; most forms of imperialism—plunder, trade, investment in raw materials, investment in industrial production—occur to a greater or lesser extent in every phase of capitalist development. Different forms of imperialism, however, represent the characteristic response to given crisis conditions within the metropolitan countries and it is this which Figure 3.6 attempts to represent.[59] As will hopefully become clear as we go through each of the stages in the chart, the purpose of the schema is not to present a rigid "stage theory" of capitalist development, but rather to capture the overarching problems and movements of the capitalist system.[60]

59. The discussion of imperialism in Figure 3.6 will be limited in two important ways. First, no attempt will be made to present a comprehensive explanation for imperialism at different periods of capitalist development. Instead, we will focus exclusively on forms of imperialism as responses to crisis tendencies (impediments to accumulation) in the imperialist centres. While such contradictions within accumulation are clearly an important element in any explanation of imperialism, the actual historical development of imperialism is dependent upon many other factors as well. It would be a mistake to reduce imperialism to a mechanism of crisis resolution. Second, imperialism will be discussed only in terms of how it affects the imperialist countries, not how it affects the periphery itself. Of course, in a dialectical manner, the effects of imperialism on the centre are conditioned by the effects of imperialism on the periphery, and a fully elaborated analysis of the contradictions and transformations of capitalism would take this dynamic into consideration. For present purposes, however, I will deal with imperialism in a more limited manner as one of the ways in which the bourgeoisie responds to impediments to accumulation.

60. The chart may give the impression that the particular path of capitalist development and the particular pattern of contradictions which emerge at each stage in the process are rigidly determined. This raises some extremely important questions about the underlying logic of the concept of "contradiction": In what exact sense are the contradictions schematically laid out in the chart "inevitable"? Does the solution to the impediments to accumulation in one period intrinsically and necessarily lead to future impediments? While it is obvious that each of the "solutions" outlined in the chart have certain inherent theoretical limits, it is less obvious that the social forces in capitalist society necessarily push the system towards those limits, and thus transform a structural solution into a contradiction. Why, in other words, does each adaptive

Figure 3.6

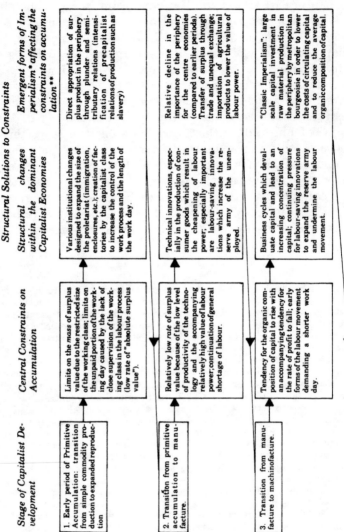

Stage of Capitalist Development	Central Constraints on Accumulation	Structural changes within the dominant Capitalist Economies	Emergent forms of Imperialism* affecting the constraints on accumulation**
1. Early period of Primitive Accumulation: transition from simple commodity production to expanded reproduction	Limits on the *mass* of surplus value due to the restricted size of the working class; limits on the unpaid portion of the working day caused by the lack of close supervision of the working class in the labour process (low rate of "absolute surplus value").	Various institutional changes designed to expand the size of the proletariat (immigration, enclosures, etc.); creation of factories by the capitalist class to increase the control of the work process and the length of the work day.	Direct appropriation of surplus product in the periphery through plunder and semitributary relations (intensification of precapitalist relations of production such as slavery)
2. Transition from primitive accumulation to manufacture.	Relatively low *rate* of surplus value because of the low level of productivity of the technology and the accompanying relatively high value of labour power; continuation of general shortage of labour.	Technical innovations, especially in the production of consumer goods which result in the cheapening of labour power; especially important are labour-saving innovations which increase the reserve army of the unemployed.	Relative decline in the importance of the periphery for the centre economies (compared to earlier periods). Transfer of surplus through trade and unequal exchange; importation of agricultural products to lower the value of labour power.
3. Transition from manufacture to machinofacture.	Tendency for the organic composition of capital to rise with an accompanying tendency for the rate of profit to fall; early forms of the labour movement demanding a shorter work day.	Business cycles which devaluate capital and lead to an increasing concentration of capital; continuing pressure for labour-saving innovations to expand the reserve army and undermine the labour movement.	"Classic Imperialism": large scale capital investment in the periphery by metropolitan bourgeoisie in order to lower the costs of circulating capital and to reduce the average organic composition of capital.

Structural Solutions to Constraints

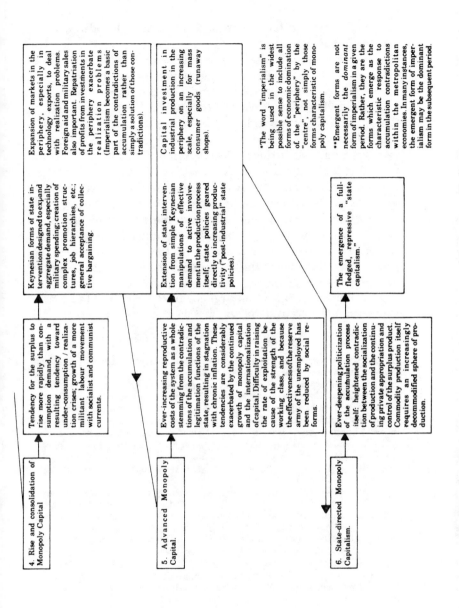

4. Rise and consolidation of Monopoly Capital

Tendency for the surplus to rise more rapidly than consumption demand, with a resulting tendency toward under-consumption / realization crises; growth of a more militant labour movement with socialist and communist currents.

Keynesian forms of state intervention designed to expand aggregate demand, especially military spending; creation of complex promotion structures, job hierarchies, etc.; general acceptance of collective bargaining.

Expansion of markets in the periphery, especially in technology exports, to deal with realization problems. Foreign aid and military sales also important. Repatriation of profits from investments in the periphery exacerbate realization problems (Imperialism becomes a basic part of the contradictions of accumulation rather than simply a solution of those contradictions).

5. Advanced Monopoly Capital.

Ever-increasing reproductive costs of the system as a whole stemming from the contradictions of the accumulation and legitimation functions of the state, resulting in stagnation with chronic inflation. These tendencies are considerably exacerbated by the continued growth of monopoly capital and the internationalization of capital. Difficulty in raising the rate of exploitation because of the strength of the working class, and because the effectiveness of the reserve army of the unemployed has been reduced by social reforms.

Extension of state intervention from simple Keynesian manipulations of effective demand to active involvement in the production process itself; state policies geared directly to increasing productivity ("post-industrial" state policies).

Capital investment in industrial production in the periphery on an increasing scale, especially for mass consumer goods (runaway shops).

6. State-directed Monopoly Capitalism.

Ever-deepening politicization of the accumulation process itself: heightened contradiction between the socialization of production and the continuing private appropriation and control of the surplus product. Commodity production itself requires an increasingly decommodified sphere of production.

The emergence of a full-fledged, repressive "state capitalism."

*The word "imperialism" is being used in the widest possible sense to include all forms of economic domination of the "periphery" by the "centre", not simply those forms characteristic of monopoly capitalism.

**Emergent forms are not necessarily the *dominant* form of imperialism in a given period. Rather, they are the forms which emerge as the characteristic response to accumulation contradictions within the metropolitan economies. In many instances, the emergent form of imperialism may be the dominant form in the subsequent period.

1. The Transition from Simple Commodity Production to Expanded Reproduction

The two crucial constraints on the accumulation process in the early period of primitive accumulation were, on the one hand, the existence of institutional forms of production which made close supervision and control of the work force difficult, and on the other, a relatively small size of the proletariat and thus a limited amount of exploitable labour. The lack of supervision of workers under conditions of cottage industry meant that the capitalist had little control over exactly how much the worker worked per day. It was also often exceedingly easy for the worker to embezzle considerable amounts of raw materials from the capitalist.[61] The result was that the rate of exploitation tended to be low because the effective unpaid portion of the workday was low. In combination with the restricted size of the proletariat, this meant the mass of surplus value available for accumulation tended to be quite low.

As Stephen Marglin has argued, in the English Industrial Revolution the creation of the factory provided the structural

strategy of the capitalist system tend to exhaust itself in time? The simple answer is that none of these adaptive strategies can eliminate the inherent class antagonisms of capitalism. Those class antagonisms make a simple, homeostaic reproduction of the system impossible. The more complex answer is that the forms that class struggle takes are themselves moulded by the dominant adaptive strategies of the system. This is precisely what it means to say that the mode of accumulation "selects" forms of class struggle (i.e. it acts as a force which shapes class struggle within limits set by the underlying structure of class relations). The working class is not simply a passive force, even in its most integrated and contained periods. It adapts its strategies to the "structural solutions" which emerge in the course of capitalist development. In their most class conscious form, these working class strategies are explicitly focused towards exploiting those structural solutions, and pushing them to their limits.

A similar argument can be made about the effects of struggle among capitalists (competition): as solutions to the impediments of accumulation emerge, individual capitalists adopt new forms of competition, new strategies for maximizing their individual accumulation. Since there is no overall planning in capitalist society which coordinates these individual strategies, there is an inherent tendency for these strategies gradually to push towards the limits of the existing structure within which accumulation takes place. There is thus a dialectic between the structural solutions to earlier constraints on accumulation and the forms of class struggle and competition which develop in response to those structural solutions.

61. For an interesting discussion of these issues, see Stephen Marglin, "What do Bosses do?", *Review of Radical Political Economics*, Vol. 66, No. 2, 1974.

solution to the first of these constraints. Workers were brought together under a single roof and closely supervised in their work. They were forced either to work as many hours as the capitalist dictated or not work at all, and thus the amount of surplus labour increased considerably. The creation of factories, however, only heightened the problem of the shortage of free exploitable labour. A variety of state policies such as open immigration, rural depopulation, closing of the poor houses, etc., contributed to the solution of the labour shortage.

The dominant forms of imperialism[62] during the period of primitive accumulation in Western Europe can also be viewed, in part at least, as responses to the central constraints on accumulation. If the ultimate constraint on early capitalist accumulation centred on an inadequate mass of surplus value, the direct appropriation of surplus from the periphery was at least one way of counteracting this constraint. The forms of this direct appropriation ranged from outright plunder, to various forms of tributary relations, to the intensification of pre-capitalist coercive modes of labour control (such as slavery) in agricultural and precious metal production in the periphery for the world market. In all of these cases, a greater mass of surplus value was made available for accumulation than would have been the case simply on the basis of exploitation in the centre.

2. The Transition from Primitive Accumulation to Manufacture

The continual expansion of the proletariat and the factory system characterizes the transition from primitive accumulation to the period of manufacture. In the early period of this transition, the major way in which the rate of exploitation was increased was through the expansion of what is called "absolute surplus value" (i.e., increases in surplus value resulting from the expansion of the working day and the intensity of work). Very quickly, the working day had increased virtually to its biological maximum. In spite of this, however, the actual rate of

62. Throughout this discussion I will be using the expression "imperialism" in the broad sense, covering all forms of economic domination of the periphery by the centre, rather than in the narrow sense of the forms of domination specific to the epoch of monopoly capitalism.

exploitation remained relatively low because of the generally low productivity of technology and the accompanying high value of labour power. Even when the standard of living of the worker was pushed down to bare subsistence, it still took a relatively high proportion of the working day for him/her to reproduce the value of his/her labour power.

The solution to the problem of the relatively low rate of surplus value was the proliferation of technical innovations which drastically cheapened the goods consumed by wage labour, and thus lowered the value of labour power. Since many of these innovations were labour saving, they also had the effect of expanding the reserve army of the unemployed, thus further alleviating the general problem of the shortage of labour that characterized the period.

Imperialism played somewhat less of a role during this period than earlier.[63] Of course, the periphery was still important as a source of raw materials for capitalist production, but this function of imperialism was not primarily a counterforce to crisis tendencies within the centre.

3. The Transition from Manufacture to Machinofacture

The progressive introduction of machines into the production process defines the transition from simple manufacture to what Marx called machinofacture. The earlier tendencies for the expansion of factories, the expansion of the proletariat, and so on, continue, but there is added a constant stream of new innovations in the production process. In addition, in this period the first effective forms of proletarian class organizations emerge. Demands are made both for a shortening of the working day and for rises in real wages. The increasing intensity of class struggle creates considerable additional pressure on capital to introduce labour-saving innovations. The result is that in the period of transition from manufacture to machinofacture there is a very rapidly growing organic composition of capital. Thus, in spite of the increasing rate of surplus value, there was a definite tendency for the rate of profit to fall.

The solution to this impediment to accumulation, as we have discussed above, was contained within the impediment itself.

63. Amin, "Towards a Structural Crisis of World Capitalism", p. 12.

The classic pattern of business cycles, devaluations of capital, elimination of unproductive capitals and increasing concentration and centralization of capital provided the social mechanisms for periodically restructuring capital in ways which restored conditions favourable to accumulation.

The classic forms of imperialism in the second half of the 19th century were also in important ways a response to the impediments to accumulation characteristic of the massive introduction of machine production. In particular, large scale capital investments in raw material production in the periphery (e.g., building of railroads to transport raw materials, capitalization of mining, etc.) helped to counteract the rising organic composition of capital by lowering the cost of circulating capital. Furthermore, since production processes in the periphery were generally characterized by lower organic compositions of capital than in the centre, investments in the periphery helped to reduce the average organic composition of capital.

4. The Rise and Consolidation of Monopoly Capital

As the organic composition of capital continued to rise in the 19th century, and into the 20th century, two things occurred: capital tended to become ever more concentrated and centralized, and the rate of increase in the organic composition of capital (probably) tended to slow down. By sometime in the first quarter of the century it appears that the organic composition of capital more or less stabilized. The rate of exploitation, however, continued to rise both because of general increases in productivity (of both a capital-saving and labour-saving variety) and because of monopoly power itself. The result was that a strong tendency towards realization and underconsumption problems emerged.

One of the consequences of the tendency for surplus value to rise is a systematic stimulus for various forms of speculation since, unless realization problems occur, the prospects for strong future profits seem secure. The contradiction, of course, is that unless some mechanism for the continuous absorption of that surplus is created, serious realization problems will occur. Then, given that such realization problems occur in the context of heavy speculation, the resulting economic crisis will be that much more severe (because of financial failures, collapses of credit systems, etc.). This was the essential scenario of the Great Depression.

Simultaneously with these developments in the accumulation process, the labour movement began to gather considerable strength, especially in the monopolized sectors of the economy. While demands tended to centre on issues of wages and immediate working conditions, the growth of socialist and communist forces within the labour movement, and the experience of the Russian Revolution, made the potential for a more genuinely revolutionary labour movement seem likely.

The great social invention of state sponsored waste, academically legitimated as Keynesianism, constituted the major structural solution to the impediment of underconsumption.[64] Initially, especially in the United States, such programmes of state spending were viewed with considerable suspicion, and it basically took the lesson of the Second World War to make Keynesianism an acceptable tool of crisis management. Keynesianism also helped to counter the threat of labour militancy, since it tended to underwrite the economic orientation of most trade union struggles. The institutionalization of collective bargaining and the proliferation of complex systems of job hierarchies, promotion systems, seniority rights, unemployment insurance, etc. further helped to contain the labour movement within bounds compatible with such Keynesian solutions.[65]

The underconsumption crisis of the 1930s was not dealt with solely in terms of domestic policies. Changes in the international system also clearly played an important role in providing structural solutions to the specific accumulation impediments of the period. Perhaps more significantly, the Second World War provided an immediate antidote to under-

64. Keynesianism is clearly not the only possible response to the structural crises of accumulation characteristic of the rise and consolidation of monopoly capitalism. While it is clearly incorrect to reduce the complex phenomenon of fascism to a solution to economic crisis tendencies, nevertheless, fascism can be interpreted as at least partially a response to the same kinds of accumulation impediments which produced Keynesianism, but under different political and social structural conditions.

65. See Stone, "The Origins of Job Structures in the Steel Industry", and Braverman, *Labour and Monopoly Capital*.

consumption tendencies, both through massive military spending and through the destruction of great quantities of capital.
After the war, the hegemonic position of the United States made
it much easier to establish a stable system for international
trade and finance (as embodied in the Bretton Woods accords)
which greatly facilitated the expansion of markets and international credit necessary to alleviate underconsumption pressures. The long period of positive trade balances for the United
States after the war certainly reduced realization problems in
the U.S., while the investment requirements of economic recon-
struction after the war in Europe reduced underconsumption
pressures there as well.

The role of imperialism in this period is more ambiguous. The
considerable increase in foreign aid, especially military aid, in
the post-war period, and the expansion of trade with the
periphery, especially in technology, contributed to reducing
realization problems in the U.S. However, American imperialism was hardly limited to trade; American direct investments in the periphery also dramatically increased throughout
the post-war period. To the extent that the surplus value generated through these investments was repatriated to the United
States, such investments would only serve to augment realization problems. Compared to earlier periods, imperialism
thus plays a much more contradictory role with respect to crisis
tendencies during the transition from monopoly capitalism to
advanced monopoly capitalism. While individual capitalists
invest in the periphery because they see the periphery as offer-
ing profitable outlets for capital, the impact on the accumulation process as a whole is to heighten the problem of surplus
absorption.

5. Advanced Monopoly Capitalism
The Keynesian solutions to underconsumption tended at least
initially to dovetail with the political requirements for legitimation. But the initial harmony was shattered as the growth of
unproductive state expenditures tended to expand faster than
the surplus-absorbing requirements of the system. The organizational strength of the working class, especially at the
economic level, further aggravated the situation by making it

difficult for the capitalist class to increase the rate of exploitation sufficiently to compensate for the overexpansion of unproductive expenses. To an important degree, the institutional arrangements which underpinned Keynesian state policies—collective bargaining, economism, welfare policies, unemployment insurance, etc.—all served to make it more difficult to adjust to new circumstances.

All of these difficulties were further aggravated by the continued concentration and centralization of capital on both a national and international scale. As has often been noted, competition under relatively monopolistic conditions is waged less in terms of prices than in terms of advertising, market strategies, and political manoeuvring. There is an internal tendency within monopoly capital itself, therefore, for unproductive activities to increase with concentration and centralization of capital. The internationalization of capital has further complicated these contradictions by undermining the capacity of national governments effectively to regulate their own national economies. The net result of all of these factors has been a serious deterioration in the trade-off between inflation and unemployment, which characterizes the economic crisis of the 1970s.

A variety of structural solutions to the accumulation impediments of advanced monopoly capitalism are now emerging. At the international level, foreign investments in the periphery are increasingly centred in manufacturing rather than simply raw material extraction, agriculture and trade. This is especially the case for relatively labour intensive mass consumption commodities. In the face of the difficulty of increasing the rate of exploitation in the metropolitan countries and the increasing burden of unproductive state spending, a considerable amount of industrial investment is occurring in the periphery. In the case of the United States, in addition to this movement of capital abroad there is considerable movement of industrial capital from the highly unionized Northern states to the less unionized South, again because the obstacles to increasing the rate of exploitation are weaker in those areas.

In terms of domestic state policies, the immediate response to the problem of the ever-expanding reproductive costs of monopoly capitalism relative to the growth in productivity has been an attempt at cutting back many Keynesian policies, especially in welfare programmes, education and various public services. The emergent long-run solution is to move from predominantly Keynesian interventions in the economy to active state involvement in the production process itself. Qualitatively new forms of state intervention are called for. It is no longer enough for the state simply to set the parameters for capitalist production by regulating aggregate demand, interest rates and taxes, and to deal with the social costs generated by the irrationalities of capitalism through police, pollution control and mental hospitals. The state needs to become directly involved in the rationalization of production, the coordination and planning of productivity increases, the destruction of inefficient sectors of production, and so forth.

It is, of course, difficult to give precise descriptions of the forms such new interventions will take. The minimal steps would include direct state participation in the planning and allocating of resources for investments. In the United States this is already being proposed for energy development. Energy production will not be organized through unfettered market mechanisms, but through direct state controls. More pervasive forms of such production interventions would include the state directly organizing the modernization of production processes in heavy industry, either through outright nationalizations or through the creation of various kinds of co-planning boards involving the state and private capital (and perhaps labour and "consumers" as well). Given that in monopoly capitalism the classic mechanisms of advancing productivity—bankruptcies, devaluation of capital, etc.—are too costly politically and too disruptive economically, the state will eventually have to take the responsibility of directly increasing productivity.

In order to accomplish such rationalizations, the state will have to increase its capacity to control and discipline individual capitalists and the working class. In the case of capital, this means above all being able to prevent the flight of capital in the face of increasing state involvement in investments as well as being able completely to eliminate unproductive sectors of capital (especially small and medium capital), in the interests of increasing the productivity of capital as a whole. In the case of the working class, it will be necessary severely to constrain wage and employment demands for an extended period of time, in order to increase the rate of surplus value necessary to pay for such rationalizations of production.

The political obstacles to these new forms of state intervention are very high, especially perhaps in the United States where small and medium capital have considerable political power. Organized labour is also extremely wary of such proposals, fearing that state planning will mean much more systematic controls on wages, reductions of monopoly sector employment through rationalization, and generally a weakening of the bargaining position of unions. In Europe, because of the political strength of socialist and communist parties, it may be easier to initiate these state capitalist programmes. Certainly in the case of Italy, there is widespread feeling that only the Communists would be able to maintain discipline within the working class to be able to initiate major new programmes of economic reorganization and rationalization, necessary for a revival of Italian capitalism. Whether or not such a reorganization could become a first step towards a transition to socialism, is, of course, a hotly debated issue. In any event, such a reorganization is necessary for a restoration of favourable conditions for accumulation.

What new impediments to accumulation are likely to emerge in the next phase of capitalist development? While it is quite problematic to speculate about contradictions in the future, several things seem fairly safe to say. As monopoly capitalism moves towards qualitatively new forms of state involvement in production, towards what might be termed State-directed monopoly capitalism, there will be an ever-deepening politicization of the accumulation process itself. It will become increasingly difficult to apply "neutral" market rationality to production; political criteria will become more and more central to production itself. Although it is almost certain that in the United States few major corporations would be formally nationalized, a greater and greater proportion of production will be *de facto* effectively organized by the state. This does not mean, of course, that commodity production (production for exchange) would disappear, but rather that an increasingly important part of production would be organized outside of the market, and not directly subjected to profit-maximizing criteria. Stated more abstractly—in order to perpetuate commodity production, the state will have to organize a continually growing decommodified sphere of production.[66]

All of this would occur within the continuing context of capitalist social relations and a capitalist state serving the function of reproducing the class structure of capitalist society. The expanded decommodified sphere of production would be strictly constrained by the requirements of reproducing commodity production itself. The new forms of impediments to accumulation would therefore centre on the heightened contradiction between the progressive socialization of the process of production alongside the continuing private appropriation (through commodity production) of the surplus product.

As the state assumes an ever-greater role in the actual organization of production, the ideological legitimations of the "free enterprise system" will tend to become more and more tenuous. As a result, it is likely that the socialist alternative will move more into the centre of American working class politics. Class struggles around the state and around production (which increasingly become the same struggles) will thus tend to become more ideological, more politicized, and ultimately more threatening to the capitalist system. Under such circumstances, it is quite possible to imagine the development of a full-fledged state capitalism in the United States (although dressed in the symbols of private capitalism) which would attempt to contain the glaring contradictions between legitimation and accumulation by means of considerable repression and centralized planning.

There is, however, no automatic reason for a "solution" which is theoretically functional for capitalism to be the solution which historically emerges. Whether or not such a structural

66. For an extended discussion of the contrast between commodified and decommodified state interventions, see Gösta Epsing-Anderson, Roger Friedland and Erik Olin Wright, "Modes of Class Struggle and the Capitalist State". *Kapitalistate*, No. 4–5, 1976. Decommodified state interventions have always been present in the capitalist state. To take perhaps a trivial example, public libraries represent a decommodified way of providing books for the public. What would be qualitatively new about decommodified interventions in advanced capitalism would be involvement in the production of use-values and not simply the distribution of use-values. Many of these ideas have been derived from the work of Claus Offe, see especially, "The Capitalist State and the Problem of Policy Formation".

reordering of monopoly capital will occur depends on the one hand on the cohesiveness of the capitalist class and its capacity to generate a class politics in the interests of capital as a whole, and on the other, on the strength of socialist movements in the working class and their capacity to organize a class politics capable of transforming decommodified production in the service of capital into genuinely socialist production in the service of the working class.

4

Bureaucracy and the State

Our discussion of the historical transformations of the process of accumulation closed with a somewhat speculative discussion of the emergent solutions to the economic stagnation of the 1970s and the new contradictions which those solutions were likely to engender. The central proposition was that the capitalist state was likely to engage in qualitatively deeper forms of intervention into the economy, moving from intervention and planning at the level of market relations towards planning within production itself. Such a transformation in the role of the capitalist state would itself generate new contradictions specifically centred around the politicization of the accumulation process.

Such changes in the forms of state activity in capitalist societies and in the contradictions of accumulation are of crucial importance in any discussion of socialist politics. A number of questions are immediately posed: In what ways do these changes in the role of the state affect the relationship of the capitalist state to class struggle? Do these new contradictions open up new possibilities for the left to use the capitalist state as part of a revolutionary strategy? What implications do these developments have for the classic debate between peaceful, incremental roads to socialism and violent, revolutionary strategies for socialism?

I cannot rigorously answer most of these questions, but I will try to clarify some of the issues involved in answering them. In this chapter I will focus on one specific issue which underscores all of these questions on socialist strategies: the problem of bureaucracy. In particular, I will address the question: how should we understand the relationship between class struggle and the internal structure of the state?[1] We will explore this question by comparing the analyses of bureaucracy and the state of two influential theorists, Max Weber and V. I. Lenin. In the next chapter we will link this discussion of bureaucracy and the capitalist state to the analysis of class formation and accumulation contradictions developed earlier.

In the summer of 1917, in opposite corners of Europe, two essays were written on the nature of the state, bureaucracy, and politics. One, *Parliament and Government in a Reconstructed Germany*, was written by Max Weber; the other, *The State and Revolution*, was written by Vladimir Lenin. In spite of the obvious differences between the two men—one was a liberal German academician, the other a professional Russian revolutionary—they had certain things in common. Both were men of about fifty years of age whose intellectual lives had been decisively shaped by the work of Karl Marx. Both felt that their ideas on the state were strongly out of favour in the ruling circles of their respective countries. Both wrote their essays in the hopes of influencing political developments. In the immediate years following the publications of the essays, attempts were made to put the ideas of both into practice: Lenin's ideas in the attempt to build socialism after the Bolshevik Revolution, and Weber's in the attempt to create a viable parliamentary democracy in the Weimar Republic.

Both essays deal with many of the same questions, though in sharply different ways and leading to radically different conclusions: How can the state apparatus be controlled? Is it possible for the masses to govern and control the state? What is the relationship of representative institutions to the state bureaucracy in capitalist society? What can be done about the ever-increasing appropriation of power by bureaucrats? What are the consequences of socialism for the nature of the state? These are

---

1. While there has been a tremendous growth in Marxist theoretical work on the capitalist state in recent years, relatively little has been explicitly focused on the problem of the internal structures of the state. An especially interesting analysis of this question which explicitly contrasts the internal organization structures of the capitalist state with both the feudal state and the socialist state, is Göran Therborn, *What does the Ruling Class do when it Rules?*, London NLB 1978. For an earlier treatment of similar themes developed within the broad framework of the Frankfurt school, see the work of Claus Offe.

issues that are no less important today than half a century ago and are still matters of intense debate.

In the following section, Weber's argument in *Parliament and Government* will be laid out systematically. In a few places material will be drawn from *Economy and Society* (the bulk of which was written before 1917) to elaborate certain points more fully. This will be followed by a comparable presentation of Lenin's argument in *The State and Revolution*. After both Weber's and Lenin's analyses have been presented, the underlying assumptions of both positions will be compared, and the strengths and weaknesses of the arguments assessed.

Weber's Argument

By 1917 Weber was convinced that German politics were being conducted in a totally irresponsible and incompetent manner. As a German nationalist, he felt that it was crucial to understand the sources of this incompetence, for if it were not corrected, Germany "would be condemned to remain a small and conservative country, perhaps with a fairly good public administration in purely technical respects, but at any rate a provincial people without the opportunity of counting in the arena of world politics—and also without any moral right to it." (1462)[2] After examining the history of German politics in the years since Bismarck, Weber became convinced that "every German policy, irrespective of its goals, is condemned to failure in view of the given constitutional set-up and the nature of our policy machinery, and that this will remain so if conditions do not change." (1384) The critical aspect of this constitutional set-up was the powerlessness of parliament. Weber felt that while significantly strengthening parliamentary institutions would not guarantee a dramatic improvement in the quality of German politics, such a change was essential if there was to be any hope for the future.

This general conclusion concerning the necessity for a strong

2. All pages numbers in paretheses in this section refer to the English language edition of *Economy and Society*, edited by Guenther Roth and Claus Wittich, New York 1968. Citations from pp. 1381–1462 are from Weber's essay "Parliament and Government in a Reconstructed Germany: A Contribution to the Political Critique of Officialdom and Party Politics". All other citations are from the text of *Economy and Society*.

184

parliament was based on a number of propositions about the nature of politics and bureaucracies and the problem of political leadership in "modern" society:

Proposition 1. With the development of capitalism and the increasing complexity of society, the needs for rational administration expand both quantitatively and qualitatively. As a result, both public and private organizations tend to become more and more bureaucratized.[3]

"The decisive reason for the advance of bureaucratic organization", Weber writes, "has always been its purely technical superiority over any other form of organization. The fully developed bureaucratic apparatus compares with other organizations exactly as does the machine with the non-mechanical modes of production. Precision, speed, unambiguity, knowledge of the files, continuity, discretion, unity, strict subordination, reduction of friction and of material and personal costs—these are raised to the optimum point in the strictly bureaucratic administration, and especially in its monocratic form." (973)[4]

3. Weber's formal definition of "bureaucracy" includes the following characteristics:
   (1) [Officials] are personally free and subject to authority only with respect to their impersonal official obligations.
   (2) They are organized in a clearly defined hierarchy of offices.
   (3) Each office has a clearly defined sphere of competence in the legal sense.
   (4) The office is filled by a free contractual relationship. Thus, in principle, there is free selection.
   (5) Candidates are selected on the basis of technical qualifications. In the most rational case, this is tested by examination or guaranteed by diplomas certifying technical training or both. They are *appointed*, not elected.
   (6) They are remunerated by fixed salaries in money.
   (7) The office is treated as the sole, or at least the primary, occupation of the incumbent.
   (8) It constitutes a career. There is a system of "promotion" according to seniority or to achievement or both. Promotion is dependent upon the judgement of superiors.
   (9) The official works entirely separated from ownership of the means of administration and without appropriation of his position.
   (10) He is subject to strict and systematic discipline and control in the conduct of the office. (220–221).
   4. By "monocratic form" or "monocracy" Weber means a bureaucratic organization at the top of which is a single individual rather than a group of individuals (a "collegial body").

Bureaucratic forms of organization increasingly characterize private business corporations, churches, political parties, and other organizations in which rational efficiency is important to success. "This is increasingly so", Weber argues, "the larger the association is, the more complicated its tasks are, and above all, the more its existence depends on power—whether it involves a power struggle on the market, in the electoral arena or on the battlefield." (1399) "The future," Weber concludes, "belongs to bureaucratization." (1401)

Proposition 2. As bureaucratization increases, the power of bureaucrats tends to increase, both with respect to nonbureaucratic organizations and with respect to the nonbureaucratic elements of bureaucracies

"The power of a fully developed bureaucracy", Weber writes, "is always great, under normal conditions, overtowering. The political master always finds himself, vis-à-vis the trained official, in the position of a dilettante facing the expert." (991) This progressively increasing power of bureaucracies and bureaucrats grows out of several interconnected characteristics of bureaucratic organization: (1) the practical effectiveness and increasing indispensability of bureaucratic organizations,[5] (2) the expert technical knowledge controlled by the bureaucrats, and (3) the "administrative secrets" (knowledge about the inner workings of the bureaucracy) controlled by bureaucrats. This last element is especially important. Outsiders are in a weak position not merely because of the technical expertise of the bureaucrats, but because of the bureaucratic control of files, information, and procedures.

Given this constant expansion of bureaucratic power, it is increasingly problematic, Weber argues, whether or not any independent power will be able to control the state bureaucracy. In his discussion of bureaucracy as an ideal type Weber stresses

5. Weber writes: "The rule . . . cannot dispense with or replace the bureaucratic apparatus once it exists . . . [for] if the apparatus stops working, or if its work is interrupted by force, chaos results which is difficult to master by any improvised replacements from among the governed. . . . Increasingly the material fate of the masses depends upon the continuous and correct functioning of the ever more bureaucratic organizations of private capitalism and the idea of replacing them becomes more and more utopian." (988)

that "at the top of a bureaucratic organization there is necessarily an element which is at least not purely bureaucratic. The category of bureaucracy is one applied only to the exercise of control by means of a particular kind of administrative staff." (222) This non-bureaucratic top has an intrinsically political quality since it must deal with the alternative ends that the bureaucracy serves and not merely with the means for accomplishing those ends. With the growing power of the state bureaucracy, Weber argues, there is increasing danger that these political positions will become monopolized by the bureaucrats themselves, resulting in the development of a system of "completely unsupervised office holding". "In view of the growing indispensability of the state bureaucracy and its corresponding increase in power, how can there be any guarantee that any powers will remain which can check or effectively control the tremendous influence of this stratum [bureaucrats]?" (1403) The critical issue in this problem of controlling the bureaucracy is how people are selected to fill these top administrative-political positions, in particular, whether they are bureaucrats selected by behind-the-scenes "unofficial patronage" or professional politicians selected through open, parliamentary struggle.

Proposition 3. If the top administration of the state bureaucracy is in the hands of bureaucrats, then there will be a strong tendency for:
(A) the political direction of the bureaucracy to be irresponsible and ineffective, especially in times of crisis; and
(B) the behind-the-scenes influence of big capitalists in the running of the state bureaucracy to be maximized.

A. "The essence of politics", Weber writes, "is struggle": struggle over ends and the power to accomplish ends. Effective and responsible political leadership consists in knowing how to weigh competing and conflicting ends, how to negotiate compromises "sacrificing the less important for the more important" (1404), how to recruit allies and form coalitions in political battles, and so forth. These skills are arts that require intensive training. For the political direction of the state bureaucracy to be effective it is therefore necessary that the top administrators be thoroughly trained in this art of politics, and furthermore, that mechanisms exist which hold them accountable for the *political* quality of their administration.

The entire structure and ethos of bureaucracy makes the professional bureaucrat unsuited for such a political directorate. While bureaucrats are highly skilled in techniques of rational execution of programmes, they are almost inevitably incompetent in political skills. This incompetence stems from the nature of bureaucratic responsibility: "An official who receives a directive which he considers wrong can and is supposed to object to it. If his superior insists on its execution, it is his duty and even his honour to carry it out as if it corresponded to his innermost conviction, and to demonstrate in this fashion that his sense of duty stands above his personal preference." (1404)

There is little or no scope for the development of political talents within the bureaucratic ranks, and as a result, career bureaucrats generally lack the capacity for real political leadership: "Our officialdom has been brilliant whenever it had to prove its sense of duty, its impartiality and mastery of organizational problems in the face of official, clearly formulated tasks of a specialized nature. . . . But here we are concerned with political, not bureaucratic achievements, and the facts themselves provoke the recognition which nobody can truthfully deny: That bureaucracy failed completely whenever it was expected to deal with *political* problems. This is no accident; rather it would be astonishing if capabilities inherently so alien to one another would emerge within the same political structure." (1417) The control of the administrative apex of the bureaucracy by bureaucrats thus leads to politically irresponsible and ineffective direction of bureaucratic activity. In times of peace and domestic tranquillity this might not be terribly serious; but when crisis occurs, the results can be devastating.

B. Ineffectiveness and irresponsibility are not the only costs of uncontrolled bureaucratic domination. In addition, Weber argues, it tends to maximize the covert influence of big capitalist interests in the administration of the state. "The big capitalist interests of the present day, like those of the past, are apt, in political life—in parties and in all other connections that are important to them—to prefer monocracy [instead of collegial control such as parliament]. For monocracy is, from their point of view, more 'discreet'. The monocratic chief is more open to personal influence and is more easily swayed, thus making it more readily possible to influence the administration of justice and other governmental activity in favour of such powerful interests." (283–284) While the influence of large capitalist interests is by no means negligible even where there are strong parliaments (especially, Weber argues, when parties are organized as "political machines" as was common in the United States), those interests attain the most unrestricted scope when bureaucracy is the least controlled.[6] This combination of a predominance of capitalist influence behind the scenes with irresponsible and ineffective political leadership of the state bureaucracy, Weber felt, characterized Germany from the time of Bismarck. The only way out of this situation, Weber argued, was for professional politicians to replace bureaucrats in the top administrative positions. For this to be possible, a strong parliament was essential.

Proposition 4. *"Only a working, not merely speech-making parliament, can provide the ground for the growth and selective ascent of genuine leaders, not merely demagogic talents. A working parliament ... is one which supervises the administration by continuously sharing its work."* (1416)

While Weber feels that only professional politicians can bring effective and responsible leadership to the bureaucracy, he does not feel that politicians are necessarily any more moral or

6. In a typical liberal manner, Weber contrasts the influence of big capital on state policy to a more diffuse influence of a plurality of organized groups. In effect he is saying that to the extent the top of the state apparatus is dominated by the bureaucracy, the interests of big capital will dominate over the interests of "society". It is possible, without doing much violence to the logic of Weber's argument, to recast this analysis in terms of the contrast between the interests of particular capitalists and the interests of the capitalist class as a whole. That is, Weber's argument is equivalent to saying that bureaucratic domination of the apex of the state apparatus tends to generate a preponderance of particularistic capitalist interests over the interests of the class as a whole within the state.

honest than are professional bureaucrats: "The motives of party members are no more merely idealist than are the usual philistine interests of bureaucratic competitors in promotions and benefices. Here, as there, personal interests are usually at stake." (1416) What is of critical importance, Weber argues, is that "these universal human frailties do not prevent the selection of capable leaders." (1416) Politicians can become potentially effective leaders not because they have necessarily better personal qualities than bureaucrats, but because they operate in an institutional context which develops political talents, selects for leadership positions those individuals who most successfully demonstrate those talents, and holds those leaders accountable for the political quality of their actions. If such an institutional context is absent, professional politicians will behave much like bureaucrats who occupy positions of power at the top of the administration. In modern, complex industrial society, Weber insists, the only institution that can accomplish these tasks of political recruitment, training, and accountability is a powerful parliament.

A strong working parliament accomplishes three essential things: first, it provides the institutional means for effectively controlling the unrestrained power of the bureaucracy; second, it generates the talented political leadership necessary for responsibly directing bureaucratic activity; third, it provides the mechanisms for holding that leadership accountable.

A. *Administrative supervision.* A working parliament's effectiveness in controlling the bureaucracy stems from the active involvement of parliamentary committees in supervising and investigating the activities of various bureaucratic departments: "There is no substitute for the systematic cross-examination (under oath) of experts before a parliamentary commission in the presence of the respective departmental officials. This alone guarantees public supervision and a thorough inquiry. . . . The parliamentary right of inquiry should be an auxiliary means and, for the rest, a whip, the mere existence of which will force the administrative chiefs to account for their actions in such a way as to make its use unnecessary." (1418) Through such investigatory committees, the parliament shares in the work of administration by examining bureaucratic records, formulating legislative measures to improve bureaucratic performance, adjusting budgets for various departments, and so forth.

B. *Leadership creation*. Parliamentary investigation and committee work is also one of the basic means for developing the leadership qualities of politicians: "Only such intensive training, through which the politician must pass in the committees of a powerful *working* parliament, turns such an assembly into a recruiting ground not for mere demagogues but for positively participating politicians. . . . Only such co-operation between civil servants and politicians can guarantee the continuous supervision of the administration and, with it, the political education of leaders and led." (1420) At the same time, a powerful parliament generates talented political leadership in at least three other ways. First, the sheer fact of power attracts individuals with leadership qualities; a powerless parliament makes a political career uninviting.[7] Second, not only does power attract leadership talent, but also the process of parliamentary political battles cultivates that talent, particularly the ability to recruit allies and make the necessary compromises to establish a solid following. Third, the "natural selection" of the competitive struggle for power tends to push the more capable leadership into the top positions. In this process, political parties play an absolutely key role. As in all modern mass associations, there is a strong tendency for political parties to become bureaucratized and for the party functionary to replace talented politicians in positions of power. It is only when the stakes of parliamentary struggle are high, when victory brings real power to the party, that this tendency towards bureaucratic ossification is counteracted; a political party cannot afford to keep talented political leadership from rising if it hopes to be successful.

7. "In the face of the powerlessness of parliament [in Germany of 1917] and the resulting bureaucratic character of the ministerial positions, a man with a strong power drive and the qualities that go with it would have to be a fool to venture into this miserable web of mutual resentment and on this slippery floor of court intrigue, as long as his talents and energies can apply themselves in fields such as the giant enterprises, cartels, banks and wholesale firms. . . . Stripped of all phraseology, our so-called monarchic government amounts to nothing but this process of *negative selection* which diverts all major talents to the service of capitalist interests." (1413)

C. *Political accountability*. Finally, strong parliamentary institutions contain built-in mechanisms of accountability. When top administrative positions are filled by bureaucrats through behind-the-scenes deals, there is no way to hold them publicly accountable for their activity: "Unofficial patronage, then, is the worst form of parliamentary patronage—one that favours mediocrity since nobody can be held responsible. It is a consequence of our rule by conservative civil servants. . . . Patronage in this system is not in the hands of politicians and parties, which might be held responsible by the public, but works through private channels. . . ." (1429–1430) Where top positions are filled through open, parliamentary struggles, however, a certain minimum accountability is assured: "The politician, and above all, the party leader who is rising to public power, is exposed to public scrutiny through the criticism of opponents and competitors and can be certain that, in the struggle against him, the motives and means of his ascendancy will be ruthlessly publicized." (1450)

While the accountability that accompanies electoral campaigns does not by any means prevent demagogy, it does tend to make the demagogue more politically responsible. Beyond electoral accountability, a strong parliament itself has the power (through parliamentary inquiry, votes of no confidence, etc.) to hold the top administrative leadership accountable for its actions. This interplay of competing parties, accountable, elected leadership, and investigative parliamentary committees creates a political structure that, Weber felt, would guarantee a minimum political responsibility on the part of the political leadership.

Weber's expectations about the benefits of a strong parliament were relatively limited. He certainly did not feel that it would automatically create a happy and prosperous society or even solve all of the political ills of industrial society. But he did feel that all other alternative political structures would not even be able to guarantee the minimum political effectiveness of a working parliament. In particular, he argues that for a variety of different reasons, monarchy, (1406) "passive" democracy, (983, 1453) and "active mass" democracy will all inevitably strengthen the purely bureaucratic control of the bureaucracy. The most important of these for the comparison with

192

Lenin is active mass democratization—the process of expanding in various ways the scope of participation of citizens in political life. Two of the principles of active democratization are: "(1) prevention of the development of a closed status group of officials in the interest of a universal accessibility of office, and (2) minimization of the authority of officialdom in the interest of expanding the sphere of influence of 'public opinion' as far as practicable. Hence, wherever possible, political democracy [i.e., active democracy] strives to shorten the term of office through election and recall, and to be relieved from a limitation to candidates with expert qualifications." (985) The result is that while passive democratization tends to encourage bureaucratization, the principles of active democratization tend to work against bureaucratization.

This might lead one to believe that the most expansive, most "mass" active democratization would provide the best safeguard against bureaucratic domination. No, Weber says. Just as monarchic government cannot possibly supervise the bureaucracy, neither can a truly active *mass* democracy.

By "mass democracy" Weber means democratic states which lack significant and powerful "*free* representative institutions" (i.e., representative institutions in which the representatives are not narrowly mandated but rather are "free" to engage in political bargaining, struggle, etc.). Such democracies take one of two forms: either they are "direct democracies" or "plebiscitary democracies". The former Weber feels cannot exist in a large and complex society. They would simply be technically impossible. The closest thing in modern society to direct democracy is "the Soviet type of republican organization where it serves as a substitute for immediate democracy since the latter is impossible in a mass organization."[8] (293) Soviet assemblies (as an ideal type) are characterized by imperative mandates, recall at any time, short terms of office, and other characteristics derived from the principles of direct democracy.[9]

8. Whenever Weber discusses "soviets" in *Parliament and Government* and *Economy and Society*, he treats them as an "ideal-type" organization that adapts the principles of direct democracy to the conditions of modern society. Nowhere does he discuss them as a concrete historical phenomenon or present any empirical data on the actual functioning of soviets.

9. The basic characteristics of direct democracy as elaborated by Weber are: (a) short terms of office, if possible only running between two general meetings of

Weber feels that the prospects for such mandated representative institutions to control bureaucracy are quite limited. Mandated assemblies would work reasonably well, Weber argues, only as long as there were no significant antagonisms between (and within) the representatives' constituencies. As soon as serious conflicts occur, a mandated assembly would become completely impotent since the representatives would be prohibited from negotiating compromises. They would be forced to return to their constituency to alter their mandated position on every significant issue, thus making effective political bargaining impossible. The result would be a complete paralysis of the assembly and thus an incapacity to supervise effectively the bureaucracy. As soon as the principle of imperative mandates is relaxed, however, the representative ceases to be simply the delegated agent of the electors and begins to exercise real authority over them. The result is that the "soviet" form of direct democracy is transformed into the beginnings of a "parliamentary" system.

Plebiscitary democracy (i.e., formal government through mass votes on issues and leadership) is equally impractical: "The plebiscite as means of election as well as of legislation has inherent technical limitations, since it only answers 'Yes' or 'No'. Nowhere in mass states does it take over the most important function of parliament, that of determining the budget. In such cases the plebiscite would also obstruct more seriously the passing of all bills that result from a compromise between conflicting interests, for the most diverse reasons can lead to a 'No' if there is no means of accommodating opposed interests through negotiation. The referendum does not know the *com-*

---

the members; (b) liability to recall at any time; (c) the principle of rotation or of selection by lot in filling offices so that every member takes a turn at some time (making it possible to avoid the position of power of technically trained persons or of those with long experience and command of official secrets); (d) strictly defined mandate for the conduct of office laid down by the assembly of members (the sphere of competence is thus concretely defined and not of a general character); (e) a strict obligation to render an accounting to the general assembly; (f) the obligation to submit every unusual question which has not been foreseen to the assembly of members or to a committee representing them; (g) the distribution of power between large numbers of offices each with its own particular function; (h) the treatment of office as an avocation and not a full time occupation. (289)

promise upon which the majority of laws is based in every mass state with strong regional, social, religious and other cleavages." (1455) Since real government cannot in fact be conducted through constant referenda and plebiscites, there is a strong tendency for such systems to degenerate into "caesarist" forms of leadership selection: "Active mass democratization means that the political leader is no longer proclaimed a candidate because he has proved himself in a circle of *honoratoires*, then becoming a leader because of his parliamentary accomplishments, but that he gains the trust and faith of the masses in him and his power with the means of demagogy. In substance this means a shift toward the *caesarist* mode of selection." (1451)

The critical characteristic of such caesarist leadership (i.e., leadership directly selected by a show of *mass* confidence) is that it is not accountable to a working, powerful parliament. Because of his position of enormous power and prestige, such a leader usually has at his disposal all of the means necessary to guarantee mass support. But in the end, he is little different from a hereditary monarch in his capacity to control the bureaucratic apparatus, and like monarchic government, caesarist leadership tends to generate uncontrolled bureaucratic domination.

The only way out of these impasses, Weber maintains, is through active parliamentary democracy. While in any modern, mass state a certain tendency towards caesarism is inevitable, parliamentary institutions have the capacity to control such tendencies, and in so doing, to control the bureaucracy as well. Neither one-man rule, of either the caesarist or monarchical variety, nor mass rule, of either the soviet or plebiscitary variety, can accomplish this.

Lenin's Argument
The basic question that underlies Lenin's analysis in *The State and Revolution* is quite different from Weber's: How can the state be made to serve the interests of the working class? or alternatively, what is the relationship between the state apparatus and the goals of a socialist revolution? Such questions had particularly poignant implications in the summer of 1917, when the essay was written. The February Revolution had already occurred, establishing a bourgeois "constitutional"

government; the October Revolution was brewing. Such a conjuncture sharply raised a central theoretical issue that has preoccupied much writing and political struggle on the Left for a century: Should the state be considered an essentially *neutral apparatus* that merely needs to be "captured" by a working-class socialist political party for it to serve the interests of the working class, or is the apparatus of the state in capitalist society a distinctively *capitalist apparatus* that cannot possibly be "used" by the working class, and as a result, must be destroyed and replaced by a radically different form of the state?[10] Lenin very decisively takes the latter position, arguing that the "dictatorship of the proletariat" is incompatible with the bourgeois state apparatus, and therefore that the capitalist state must be smashed and replaced by new revolutionary "soviet" institutions.

Although much of the essay takes the form of a polemic against the more reformist perspective, Lenin's analysis does contain a fairly coherent theory of the state, bureaucracy, and the implications of socialism for state structure:

Proposition 1. *"The state is a product and a manifestation of the irreconcilability of class antagonisms. The state arises where, when and insofar as class antagonisms objectively cannot be reconciled. And, conversely, the existence of the state proves that class antagonisms are irreconcilable. . . . The state is an organ of class rule, an organ for the oppression of one class by another. . . . The state is a special organization of force: it is an organization of violence for the suppression of some class."* (267, 268, 280)[11]

10. These two conceptions of the state are frequently designated the "state in capitalist society" vs. the "capitalist state" theories. The writings of C. Wright Mills, G. William Domhoff, and to a much lesser extent Ralph Miliband fall mainly into the former, whereas Lenin and the French "structuralist" Marxists (Althusser, Poulantzas, and others) fall into the latter. The critical difference between the two centres on whether the state is analysed primarily in terms of who controls it (capitalists, elites, bureaucrats, etc.) or in terms of what kind of a state it is (feudal state, bourgeois state, socialist state, etc.). Of course, there is no necessary reason why the two perspectives cannot be combined.

11. All page references are to the one-volume edition of *Selected Works*, London 1969, unless otherwise specified.

Lenin adopts with very little modification the classic Marxian conception of the state. The state is defined not only in terms of the *means* at its disposal (the control of violence), but also in terms of the *ends* it serves (class domination and suppression of class struggle). This function is characteristic of all states, Lenin argues, including a socialist state; what differs is the class being oppressed and the class which rules. In a capitalist state, the bourgeoisie rules and the proletariat is suppressed; in a socialist state, the proletariat rules and the capitalist class is suppressed. All states imply repression.

Proposition 2. *"A democratic republic is the best possible political shell for capitalism, and therefore, once capital has gained possession of this very best shell . . . it establishes its power so securely, so firmly, that no change of persons, institutions or parties in the bourgeois-democratic republic can shake it."* (273)

This is the critical part of Lenin's argument. He argues not merely that capitalists happen to control the political institutions of a capitalist society, but also that those institutions are structured in ways which guarantee that control. In particular Lenin views parliament as a perfect instrument for ensuring capitalist domination. This is true for two reasons: First, parliament is an institution that mystifies the masses and legitimates the social order; second, the structure of capitalist society ensures that the bourgeoisie will necessarily control parliament.

A. *Mystification and legitimation.* The central way that parliament mystifies political life, according to Lenin, is that it appears to be the basic organ of power in the society, and thus gives the appearance that the people's elected representatives run the state, when in fact all important decisions are made behind the scenes: "Take any parliamentary country, from America to Switzerland, from France to Britain, Norway and so forth—in these countries the real business of 'state' is performed behind the scenes and is carried on by the departments, chancelleries and General Staffs. Parliament is given up to talk for the special purpose of fooling the 'common people'." (296) Lenin argued that parliaments in capitalist society must necessarily be "mere talking-shops" since important state functions are controlled by the executive apparatus (the bureaucracy), and thus they necessarily become sources of political mystification.

B. *Bourgeois control of parliament.* Even if parliaments did have some residual power, they would still be instruments of capitalist class domination because of the direct control of parliament by the bourgeoisie: "[Bourgeois parliamentary democracy] is always hemmed in by the narrow limits set by capitalist exploitation, and consequently always remain, in effect, a democracy for the minority, only for the propertied classes, only for the rich. . . . Owing to the conditions of capitalist exploitation, modern wage slaves are so crushed by want and poverty that 'they cannot be bothered with democracy', 'they cannot be bothered with politics'; in the ordinary peaceful course of events the majority of the population is debarred from participation in public and political life. . . . If we look more closely into the machinery of capitalist democracy we see everywhere, in the 'petty'—supposedly petty—details of the suffrage (residential qualification, exclusion of women, etc.), in the technique of the representative institutions, in the actual obstacles to the right of assembly (public buildings are not for paupers!), in the purely capitalist organization of the daily press, etc., etc.—we see restriction after restriction upon democracy. These restrictions, exceptions, exclusions, obstacles for the poor seem slight . . . but in their sum total these restrictions exclude and squeeze out the poor from politics, from active participation in democracy." (326)

The net result is, according to Lenin, that the masses only get "to decide once every few years which member of the ruling class is to repress and crush the people through parliament—this is the real essence of bourgeois parliamentarism." (295)

Proposition 3. Bureaucracy is the basic structure through which the capitalist class rules. Furthermore, bureaucratic organization is suited only for capitalist domination.

Lenin bases this proposition on three arguments: bureaucracy is functional for capitalism; bureaucrats, big and small, are dependent on the bourgeoisie; and bureaucratic organization makes popular control of administration impossible.

A. *Bureaucracy is functional for capitalism.* "The development, perfection and strengthening of the bureaucratic and military apparatus", Lenin writes, "proceeded during all of the numerous bourgeois revolutions which Europe has witnessed since the fall of feudalism." (284) As class struggle intensified with the development of capitalism, the progressive expansion and centralization of the bureaucratic apparatus became necessary:—"in its struggle against the [proletarian] revolution, the parliamentary republic found itself compelled to strengthen, along with repressive measures, the resources and centralization of governmental power. All revolutions perfected this machine instead of smashing it. The parties that contended in turn for domination regarded the possession of this huge state edifice as the principal spoils of the victor" (282: quoting Marx, from the *Eighteenth Brumaire*).

Finally, the latest stages of capitalist development, Lenin argues, have led to an even greater level of bureaucratization: "Imperialism—the era of bank capital, the era of gigantic capitalist monopolies, of the development of monopoly capitalism into state-monopoly capitalism—has clearly shown an extraordinary strengthening of the 'state machine' and an unprecedented growth in its bureaucratic and military apparatus against the proletariat both in monarchical and in the freest, most republican countries." (286)

Bureaucratization is thus seen by Lenin as a functional response by the capitalist state to the pressures of class struggle which accompany the development of capitalism.[12]

12. Not only does capitalism tend to result in the bureaucratization of bourgeois state institutions, it also tends to bureaucratize working class organizations: "We cannot do without officials under *capitalism*, under *the rule of the bourgeoisie*. The proletariat is oppressed, the working people are enslaved by capitalism. Under capitalism, democracy is restricted, cramped, curtailed, mutilated by all the conditions of wage slavery, and the poverty and misery of the people. This and this alone is the reason why the functionaries of our political organizations and the trade unions are corrupted—or rather tend to be corrupted—by the conditions of capitalism and betray a tendency to become bureaucrats, i.e., privileged persons divorced from the people and standing

B. *Dependence of bureaucrats on the bourgeoisie.* This is most obvious in the case of top bureaucratic positions, since these tend to be distributed as political spoils among the bourgeois and petty bourgeois parties. The "restricted nature" of bourgeois democracy guarantees that a revolutionary working-class party would never be able to partake in these spoils and thus could never control the top administrators. Furthermore, Lenin argues, this dependency on the bourgeoisie involves not merely the top echelons of the bureaucracy, but the apparatus as a whole: "In their works, Marx and Engels repeatedly show that the bourgeoisie are connected with these institutions [the bureaucracy and the standing army] by thousands of threads. Every worker's experience illustrates this connection in an extremely graphic and impressive manner.... In particular, it is the petty bourgeoisie who are attracted to the side of the big bourgeoisie and are largely subordinated to them through this apparatus, which provides the upper sections of the peasants, small artisans, tradesmen and the like with comparatively comfortable, quiet and respectable jobs raising their holders above the people." (283)[13]

C. *The separation of bureaucracy from the people.* For the working class to become a "ruling class" it is essential that institutions exist through which workers can "rule". Bureaucratic organization, Lenin insists, makes such mass participation impossible. This is a crucial part of Lenin's argument, for it ensures that the sheer existence of bureaucracy tends to further capitalist interests (or, at a minimum, to impede the realization

---

above the people. That is the *essence* of bureaucracy; and until the capitalists have been expropriated and the bourgeoisie overthrown, even proletarian functionaries will inevitably be 'bureaucratized' to a certain extent." (347) This bureaucratization of working class organizations, in Lenin's analysis, tends to undermine the political strength of the organization and the confidence of the people in their leadership. Such tendencies toward bureaucratization are thus also functional for capitalist interest.

13. In terms of the discussion in chapter 2 Lenin is in effect arguing that state bureaucrats are either directly bound to the bourgeoisie (top officials) or occupy contradictory class locations which link their interests at least partially to the bourgeoisie. Non-bureaucratic employees of the state—transportation workers, postal workers, janitors, etc.—would not be linked to the bourgeoisie in this way.

of working class interests). The key characteristics of bureaucratic organization which separate it from the masses are:

(1) appointment of officials rather than election, and particularly, the impossibility of recall;

(2) the high salaries and special privileges of officials, which concretely tie their interests to the bourgeoisie, create an aura of "official grandeur" about them, and place them "above the people"; and

(3) the restricted quality of bourgeois democracy, which separates legislation from administrative activity and prevents the active participation of the people in either. While the conditions of life strongly impede active participation in democratic politics in general, the separation of legislative activity from administrative activity absolutely prohibits any mass participation in administration.

If Lenin's analysis of the relationship of bureaucracy and parliament to capitalism is substantially correct, then it is clear that these state structures offer little or no possibility of being "captured" and used for the interests of the working class. Even *if* parliament could be captured by a revolutionary working-class majority and even *if* that parliament somehow had real power, still, Lenin argues, "it is clear that the old executive apparatus, the bureaucracy, which is connected with the bourgeoisie, would be unfit to carry out the orders of the proletarian state." (304) Thus, if the working class wishes to take power as a new ruling class and organize society in its own interests, it has no other choice than to destroy the old structures and create new ones.

Proposition 4. Socialism requires the complete destruction of bourgeois state institutions and their replacement by a new form of complete democracy or proletarian democracy (or, equivalently, proletarian dictatorship).

What will be the basic principles of these new institutions and how will they differ from the old structures? To begin, let us look at parliament: "The way out of parliamentarism is not, of course, the abolition of representative institutions and the elective principle, but the conversion of the representative institutions from talking shops into 'working' bodies. 'The Commune was to be a working, not a parliamentary, body, executive and legislative at the same time' " [quoting Marx]. (296) The model of this proletarian representative assembly was the short-lived Paris Commune of 1871: "The commune substitutes for the venal and rotten parliamentarism of bourgeois society institutions in which freedom of opinion and discussion does not degenerate into deception, for the parliamentarians themselves have to work, have to execute their own laws, have themselves to test the results achieved in reality and to account daily to the constituents. Representative institutions remain, but there is *no* parliamentarism here as a special system, as the division of labour between legislative and executive, as a privileged position for the deputies. We cannot imagine democracy, even proletarian democracy, without representative institutions, but we can and must imagine democracy without parliamentarism. . . ." (297)

"Democracy introduced as fully and consistently as conceivable", writes Lenin, "is transformed from bourgeois to proletarian democracy". (293) But as in all democracies, proletarian democracy still constitutes a "state", i.e., an organization of violence for the suppression of some class. Thus, proletarian democracy is at the same time a dictatorship of the proletariat: "Simultaneously with an immense expansion of democracy, which for the first time becomes democracy for the poor, democracy for the people, and not democracy for the money-bags, the dictatorship of the proletariat imposes a series of restrictions on the freedom of the oppressors, the exploiters, the capitalists." (327)

Administration, meanwhile, would cease to be organized bureaucratically and would gradually become democratized until, eventually, "the whole population, without exception, [would] proceed to discharge state functions." This, of course, would not happen overnight: "Abolishing the bureaucracy at once, everywhere and completely, is out of the question. It is a utopia. But to smash the old bureaucratic machine at once and to begin immediately to construct a new one that will make possible the gradual abolition of all bureaucracy—this is not a utopia . . ." (297) This new form of administration would differ from traditional bureaucracy in a number of critical respects, while in other respects it would be very similar to what Weber would call "bureaucratic" organization. To begin with the obvious differences: "The workers, after winning political power, will smash the old bureaucratic apparatus, shatter it to its foundations and raze it to the ground; they will replace it with a new one, consisting of the very same workers and other employees against whose transformation into bureaucrats the measures will at once be taken that were specified in detail by Marx and Engels: (1) not only election, but recall at any time; (2) pay not to exceed that of a workman; (3) immediate introduction of control and supervision by all, so that all may become 'bureaucrats' for a time and that, therefore, nobody may be able to become a 'bureaucrat'." (343)

The last of these three characteristics of socialist administration—mass participation in control and accounting—is clearly the most problematic. Lenin knew that such participation would necessarily be limited initially, but he was convinced that "the accounting and control necessary for this [the smooth running of production] have been simplified by capitalism to the utmost and reduced to extraordinarily simple operations—which any literate person can perform—of supervising and recording, knowledge of the four rules of arithmetic and issuing appropriate receipts." (337) The social conditions for mass participation in administration had also been created by capitalism and would be further developed by socialism: "The development of capitalism in turn creates the preconditions that enable all to take part in the administration of the state. Some of these preconditions are universal literacy, which has already been achieved in a number of the most advanced capitalist countries, then the 'training and disciplining' of millions of workers. . . . The possibility of this destruction [of bureaucracy] is guaranteed by the fact that socialism will shorten the working day, will raise the people to a new life, will create such conditions for the majority of the population as will enable everybody, without exception, to perform 'state functions', and this will lead to the complete withering away of every form of state in general." (336, 349)

Underlying this discussion of the possibilities of democratizing administrative control is a sharp distinction which Lenin draws between the roles of *bureaucrats* and *technical experts*: "The question of control and accounting should not be confused with the question of the scientifically trained staff of engineers, agronomists and so on. These gentlemen are working today in obedience to the wishes of the capitalists, and will work even better tomorrow in obedience to the wishes of the armed workers." (337) The bureaucratic dimension of bourgeois administration thus centres on the way "control and accounting" are organized rather than on the total organization of the administration. In fact, Lenin regards the non-bureaucratic, technical aspects of bourgeois administration extremely favourably: "At the present the postal service is a business organized on the lines of a state-capitalist monopoly. Imperialism is gradually transforming all trusts into organizations of a similar type, in which, standing over the common people, who are overburdened and starved, one has the same bourgeois bureaucracy. But the mechanism of social management is here already at hand. Once we have overthrown the capitalist . . . we shall have a splendidly equipped mechanism, freed from the 'parasite', a mechanism which can very well be set going by the united workers themselves, who will hire technicians, foremen and accountants, and pay them all, as indeed all state officials in general, workmen's wages." (298–299)

This "splendidly equipped mechanism" is the "scientifically trained staff" responsible for the technical work of administration which is quite distinct from the "parasitic" bureaucratic structures of control and accounting. While the latter must be smashed by the working class, the former can be "captured" and used by the workers. The "complete democracy" Lenin stresses so much is limited to a democratization of control, not a democratization of technical expertise as such. The result would be that: "We shall reduce the role of state officials to that of simply carrying out our instructions as responsible, revocable, modestly paid 'foremen and accountants' (of course with the aid of technicians of all sorts, types and degrees)." (298) The democratization is also explicitly not meant to negate all subordination and authority in organization. To begin with, as Lenin says many times: "We are not utopians, we do not dream of dispensing at once with all administration, with all subordination. . . . No, we want the socialist revolution with people as they are now, with people who cannot dispense with subordination, control and 'foremen and accountants'. The subordination, however, must be to the armed vanguard of all the exploited and working people, i.e., to the proletariat. . . . We, the workers, shall organize large-scale production on the basis of what capitalism has already created, relying on our own experience as workers, establishing strict, iron discipline backed up by the state power of the armed workers."(298)

Beyond the problems of authority inherited from the old order, moreover, Lenin argues, there will always be a certain amount of subordination and authority which is technically determined: "The technique of all these enterprises [large-scale industrial production] makes absolutely imperative the strictest discipline, the utmost precision on the part of everyone carrying out his allotted task, for otherwise the whole enterprise may come to a stop, or machinery or the finished product may be damaged." (342) Finally, the proletarian state would be quite centralized, but it would be a quite different kind of centralism from that of capitalist societies: It would "oppose conscious democratic, proletarian centralism to bourgeois, military, bureaucratic centralism." (301)

Lenin was unwilling in *The State and Revolution* to give more than a very general image of what the structures of a socialist society would be like. He strongly felt that to attempt to construct *a priori* blueprints for the "good" society was a form of utopianism. He argued that the concrete forms of the socialist state would emerge in a dialectical process from the attempt at building socialism: "To develop democracy to the utmost, to find the forms for this development, to test them by practice, and so forth—all this is one of the component tasks of the struggle for the social revolution. Taken separately, no kind of democracy will bring socialism. But in actual life democracy will never be 'taken separately'; it will be 'taken together' with other things, it will exert its influence on economic life as well, will stimulate *its* transformation; and in its turn it will be influenced by economic development, and so on. This is the dialectics of living history." (320)

Comparisons

There is a very curious combination of close convergences and polar divergences between Weber's and Lenin's analyses of politics and bureaucracy. The basic starting points of their discussions are quite different: Weber is generally concerned with the problem of the *formal rationality* of political structures and in particular with the factors that contribute to political effectiveness and responsibility; Lenin, in contrast, is much more concerned with questions of *substantive rationality*, with the relationship of state structures to the class *ends* that they serve. Both arguments, however, pivot around a very similar critique of bureaucratic domination and of parliamentary institutions that are purely "speech-making" assemblies (Weber) or "talking shops" (Lenin). Although in *The State and Revolution* Lenin never specifically addresses the problem of leadership effectiveness and responsibility which is so important to Weber, he does agree with Weber that when representative institutions are powerless, the real centre of power shifts to the bureaucracy. Both men agree that this tends to facilitate the political domination of purely capitalist interests. There is even one aspect of the solution to the problem that both Lenin and Weber share: the need to create representative institutions that are active, *working* bodies. But they differ substantially in the overall thrust of their conclusions: Lenin calls for the replacement of bureaucracy and parliamentary representation by "soviet" political institutions; Weber argues that soviets are unworkable and advocates instead the development of powerful, elitist working parliaments. The following comparison will try to illuminate the critical differences in the underlying assumptions about the social world which lead to these different conclusions.

Before examining those assumptions, it will be useful to juxtapose Lenin's and Weber's general arguments. (In order to make the steps in the arguments parallel, the order and form of the propositions have been somewhat changed from the presentation in the two previous sections.)

Weber	**Lenin**
1. When parliament is merely a speechmaking assembly, the result is uncontrolled bureaucratic domination, which serves the interests of	1. With parliament being merely a talking shop, the real centres of state power are located in the bureaucracy, which is controlled by and

capitalists and produces ineffective and irresponsible political leadership.

2. However, bureaucracies are inevitable and necessary given the conditions of modern technology and production, and the mass scale of the modern state.

3. Since bureaucracy cannot be eliminated, the problem is to create guarantees that will prevent bureaucrats from overstepping their proper place and controlling the political direction of the bureaucracy.

4. It is therefore necessary to develop institutions that will be able to create politically responsible and competent political leadership to direct that supervision.

5. This can only be done through a strong, working parliament which can control the bureaucracy.

serves the interests of the capitalist class.

2. Bureaucracy is not a technological imperative necessitated by modern technology and mass administration; it is a specifically *political* imperative for the stability of capitalism and the domination of the bourgeoisie.

3. In a capitalist society it is inevitable that representative institutions will be mere talking shops designed to fool the people; nothing can prevent the bureaucracy from being the real centre of power in advanced capitalist societies.

4. If socialism is to be established, institutions must be created that make it possible for the working class to be organized as the ruling class and that will make the masses politically sophisticated, class conscious participants in state administration.

5. This can only be accomplished by smashing parliament and bureaucracy and replacing them by a dictatorship of the proletariat organized in working assemblies and soviet administration.

The assumptions underlying these two trains of reasoning will be discussed under four general headings: (1) the determinants of organizational structure; (2) the nature of the state and politics; (3), organizational structure and accountability; (4) contradictions and the limits on the possible.

The Determinants of Organizational Structure

One of the serious difficulties in comparing Weber's and Lenin's conceptions of the determinants of organizational structure is that they use terms such as "bureaucracy", "technician", and "official" in quite different ways. In part, these different usages reflect merely semantic differences, but in important ways they also reflect theoretical differences.

Lenin differentiates between three basic organizational functions—policy-making, control-accounting, and "administration"—in his analysis of bureaucracy and the state, whereas Weber makes the distinction between only two—policy-making and administration.[14] We will leave the discussion of policy-making to the next section (on the nature of the state) and focus here on the implications of Lenin's distinction between technical-administrative functions and accounting-control functions.

Throughout his analysis of bureaucracy, Lenin stresses the distinction between "bureaucrats" and "technicians". The former role corresponds to the control and accounting functions in organizations; the latter, to the technical-administrative functions. Weber does not ignore the issue of control and accounting in his discussion of bureaucracy, but he does not regard them as a distinctive function in the same way that Lenin does. Nowhere, moreover, does Weber emphasize the distinction between technical and bureaucratic roles in bureaucratic organizations. Control and accounting are partially absorbed as an integral part of the administrative func-

14. I am using the word "administration" here in a way that does not entirely correspond to either Lenin's or to Weber's usage, although it is closer to Lenin's. Lenin uses the expression "administration" to describe that aspect of public bureaucracies that would be left when bureaucrats would be replaced by officials elected by the people. I will use the term as a general expression to describe the function of executing policies or carrying out orders formulated by the political directorate.

tion of carrying out policy and partially absorbed in the function of policy-making itself.

This problem of the control and accounting functions in bureaucratic organizations bears directly on the question of the determinants of organizational structure. Both Lenin and Weber agree that those structural characteristics most closely related to the technical-administrative function are substantially determined by the technological and material conditions of modern society. But unlike Weber, Lenin does not feel that the control and accounting functions are determined in this same way. While the technical features of production may have become increasingly complex with capitalist development, Lenin argues that the strictly control and accounting functions "have become so simplified and can be reduced to such exceedingly simple operations of registration, filing and checking that they can be easily performed by every literate person". (294) In capitalist society these intrinsically simple functions of control and accounting are in the hands of bureaucrats, "i.e., privileged persons divorced from the people and standing above the people" (347), not because it is *technically* necessary or efficient, but because it is *politically* necessary for the bureaucratic apparatus to be effective in controlling the proletariat. This separation of officials from the people is further mystified by the "official grandeur" of bureaucratic positions, which has led most workers to *believe* that they would be incapable of participating in administration. Finally, the factual absence of any participation by the people in politics has meant that these skills, even though fundamentally simple, have not been cultivated in most workers. The result is a pervasive mystification of the entire apparatus of the state. Weber, needless to say, disagrees strongly with Lenin. He feels that the administrative tasks of the bureaucracy—including the control and accounting activities—are extremely complex and that the masses are in fact incapable of effectively performing them.

The Nature of the State and Politics:
Elite-Organization vs. Class-Structure

The different assumptions that underlie Lenin's and Weber's conceptions of the state are reflected in their very definitions of the state. Weber first defines the notion of "organization" and then defines the state as a special kind of organization.

organization: "A social relationship which is either closed or limits the admission of outsiders will be called an organization when its regulations are enforced by specific individuals: a chief and, possibly, an administrative staff." (48)

political organization: "A 'ruling organization' will be called 'political' insofar as its existence and order is continuously safeguarded within a given territorial area by the threat and application of physical force on the part of the administrative staff." (54)

the state: "A compulsory political organization with continuous operations will be called a 'state' insofar as it successfully upholds the claim to the *monopoly* of the *legitimate* use of physical force in the enforcement of its order." (54)

Weber then makes the important following elaboration: "It is not possible to define a political organization, including the state, in terms of the end to which its action is devoted. All the way from the provision for subsistence to the patronage of art, there is no conceivable end which *some* political association has not at some time pursued. From the protection of personal security to the administration of justice, there is none which *all* have recognized. Thus it is possible to define the 'political' character of an organization only in terms of the *means* peculiar to it, the use of force." (55) At the core of this definition of the state, therefore, there is an individual—the chief—and his staff which have at their disposal a distinctive kind of means—the monopoly of the legitimate use of force. Under certain circumstances the "chief" might be a group of people—a collegial body—but it is *never* a "class". Together the chief and his staff constitute an elite which controls this special kind of organization and uses it for a wide variety of purposes.

Lenin's notion of the state also centres around the use of force but it differs from Weber's definition in two central respects:

First, *the state is assumed to serve a specific function*, the suppression of class struggle and the maintenance of the domination of the ruling class (whatever that class might be). An institution or structure which did not serve such a function could not be a state in Lenin's analysis.

Second, *the state is conceived more as a "structure"* than simply an organization controlled by an elite.[15] Of course, in many ways Lenin also conceives of the state as a special organization and frequently he discusses the concrete "connections" between the bourgeoisie and the state, the specific ways in which they influence it and control it. When Lenin discusses the state in these terms, he is not particularly inconsistent with Weber's usage. What is different is that Lenin also sees the state as an apparatus that by its very structure supports the domination of a particular ruling class. What is most important to Lenin about the "policy-making function" is not primarily the concrete individuals who make the policies, but rather the class whose rule is guaranteed by the structures within which those policies are formulated.

In short, Weber's concept of the state centres on the ways in which *elites* control a particular kind of *organization*; Lenin's conception of the state centres on the ways in which *classes* rule through a particular kind of *structure*.

Organizational Form and Accountability

The difference between an elite-organizational and a class-structural conception of the state bears directly on Weber's and Lenin's treatments of the problem of powerless parliaments and bureaucracy. Weber sees the powerlessness of parliament and the resulting uncontrolled domination of the bureaucracy as fundamentally an *organizational and leadership problem*, the only solution for which is the creation of a special organizational form—a strong working parliament. Whether or not such a strong working parliament will exist in a particular situation Weber largely attributes to contingent historical circumstances, to the actions of great men and the accidents of great events. In the case of Germany, the potential for the development of a viable working parliamentary organization

15. "Structure" is a much broader and more complex notion than "organization". Lenin, of course, does not formalize his concept of the state in these terms and thus would not have had the occasion to define "structure". The important point in the present context is that when the state is regarded as a "structure", it is no longer conceived of as a tightly bounded instrument (organization) which can be "controlled"; rather, it is conceived of as a complex network of institutions, organizations, and social relationships, or, to use Nicos Poulantzas's expression, "the organizing matrix behind institutions". (See *Political Power and Social Classes*, London 1973, p. 115n.)

had been severely damaged by the anti-parliamentary policies of one statesman, Bismarck.

Lenin sees the issue very differently. Parliaments are powerless and bureaucracies tend to be the site of the "real work of government" not because of some particular organizational failure, but because of the *structural requirements* of the stable domination of the capitalist class. Especially, in the "age of imperialism", when class struggle has become particularly intense and working class political parties potentially very strong, the bourgeoisie cannot rely on representative institutions to guarantee its rule, and thus it has tended to turn increasingly to the "executive" as the primary structure of class domination. The problem is not that parliamentary committees are not strong enough, that certain parliaments lack the formal constitutional right of inquiry, or that any particular statesman adopts strategies that undermine the stature of parliament. The problem is that parliament has ceased to be functional as an organ of class domination (but not as an instrument for legitimation—thus the maintenance of parliaments as "talking shops") for the bourgeoisie, and as a result, over a period of time, class conscious political leaders of the capitalist class have taken steps to see to it that parliamentary power has been reduced. From Lenin's perspective, therefore, the particular policies of a statesman like Bismarck, or the organizational failures of a particular kind of parliament should be understood as the *occasion* for the ascendancy of bureaucratic domination, but not as the crucial *cause* of that ascendancy.

Given Lenin's analysis of the causes of the powerlessness of parliaments and of bureaucratic domination, he sees the solution not in terms of organizational reform designed to cultivate effective leadership, but rather in terms of revolutionary change in the underlying class structure of the society (i.e., replacing the bourgeoisie by the proletariat as the ruling class). This does not mean that organizational structure is unimportant to Lenin. He spends a great deal of time, after all, saying how the specific structures of the capitalist state are incompatible with working class rule. But he treats those organizational characteristics as conceptually subordinate to the question of the class structure as such. Organizational structure becomes a kind of intervening variable that stabilizes and generalizes the rule of a particular class, that rule being rooted in the basic class relations of the society. As a result of this emphasis on the class determination of organizational structure, Lenin never systematically deals with the problem of organizational accountability. The problem of accountability is solved for Lenin not by creating special organizational devices for controlling leadership, but by transforming the class structure within which any organizational form will operate. The assumption is that without such a transformation, no organizational form whatsoever could create a political leadership responsible and accountable to the working class, and that once the question of class domination is practically dealt with, the solution to the specifically organizational problems will be relatively straightforward.[16]

In Weber's analysis, Lenin's formulation is quite inadequate. Classes as such cannot rule; only individuals and small groups can actually run the state. At best such elites can formally be the representatives in a general way of a "class" and govern "in its name".[17] What is decisive for the character of a society to Weber is much less which class the elite represents than the organizational structure of domination with which it governs. What matters most in modern society, whether capitalist or socialist, is the enormous power of the bureaucracy, and the most important political issue is whether or not organizational

16. This subordination of organizational issues to class structure creates an important asymmetry in Lenin's analysis. Because Lenin can observe the organizational consequences of bourgeois class domination, he can in considerable detail attack those organizational structures and show how they would be incompatible with proletarian rule. But since proletarian class domination does not yet exist, he cannot observe the organizational consequences of that class structure, and thus he is forced to remain quite vague about what those organizations would look like: "That is why we are entitled to speak only of the inevitable withering away of the state, emphasizing the protracted nature of this process and its dependence upon the rapidity of the development of the higher phase of communism, and leaving the question of the time required for, or the concrete forms of, the withering away quite open, because there is *no* material for answering these questions." (333)

17. Weber's position on the question of "class rule" is similar to that of Karl Kautsky, who insisted that a class "can only dominate but not govern." Lenin totally rejected such a position. In *The Proletarian Revolution and the Renegade Kautsky*, Lenin wrote: "It is altogether wrong, also, to say that a class cannot govern. Such an absurdity can only be uttered by a parliamentary *cretin* who sees nothing but bourgeois parliaments, who has noticed nothing but 'ruling parties'."

forms will be created to contain that bureaucratic domination. In short, unless the organizational problem of accountability is solved, it matters little which class formally dominates. Lenin argues the exact opposite: unless the problem of class rule is solved, it matters little whether or not leadership is formally accountable.

The Meaning of Contradictions and the Limits on the Possible

Weber and Lenin suffer from complementary forms of theoretical underdevelopment, which have critical consequences for their ultimate conclusions. To state the contrast in somewhat simplified terms: Weber has an elaborate theory of organizational contradictions, but an underdeveloped theory of social contradictions; Lenin has a relatively developed theory of social contradictions, but a limited theory of organizational contradictions.

This theoretical underdevelopment has two critical consequences in Lenin's analysis. First, in Lenin's analysis of capitalist society, there is a partial fusion of his critique of capitalism as such and a critique of complex organizations. Bureaucratic organization is condemned because it serves capitalist interests in a capitalist society. While this may be true—even Weber says as much—it does not follow that this constitutes a criticism of bureaucracy as such. Without a theory of organizations, a theory of the internal dynamics and processes of organizations, it is not possible to see which criticisms should be directed at the distinctively capitalist context of bureaucracy and which should be directed at the bureaucratic structures themselves. While Lenin is probably correct that such a theory of internal, organizational processes can be understood only in the context of an analysis of class relations, his critique of capitalist organizational structures suffers from not developing such a theory.

Second, in Lenin's analysis of socialism there is virtually no analysis of the internal contradictions of soviet structures of organization. Lenin certainly does see conflict *between* soviet institutions and the "remnants" of capitalist society, but he does not see any contradictions *within* the organizational structures of soviets themselves. Lenin felt that the main threat to the viability of soviet organization came from the tendencies towards bureaucratization surviving from bourgeois society. In his analysis, two processes were seen as potentially counteracting these bureaucratic pressures: (1) The vanguard party of the proletariat would actively assume the leadership role in building soviet institutions. The party would struggle against bureaucratic elements and would directly intervene in state activities to strengthen the participation of the masses in state administration. (2) As soviet organization became more and more pervasive, it would tend to inhibit the growth of bureaucracy. Since direct democracy and bureaucracy are antithetical principles of political organization, Lenin implicitly reasons that as the former becomes stronger and expands, the latter will necessarily become weaker and decline.

Weber would have sharply disagreed with Lenin's model of soviet organization in two main respects. First, he would have questioned the possibility of any political party being capable of operating in ways to strengthen soviet institutions. While the "vanguard party" might be formally committed to such intervention, Weber would argue that unless the leadership of the party were somehow systematically held accountable for their actions, there would be no guarantee that they would not themselves undermine soviet institutions. This would be especially likely since, like all mass organizations in modern society, the party itself would, in Weber's view, inevitably become bureaucratized. Second, Weber would strongly differ with Lenin's view of the relationship of direct democracy to bureaucratic growth: far from reducing bureaucratic tendencies, soviet institutions and all other forms of direct democracy (or plebiscitary democracy) in fact tend to increase bureaucratization. Thus, there is a fundamental contradiction in soviet organization, Weber would argue: on the one hand, soviets increase workers' *formal* participation in government and make the state seem much more democratic; on the other hand, soviet institutions would significantly increase bureaucracy, thus reducing substantive democracy and the real power of the working class.

Lenin never really provided a systematic answer to the first criticism, at least not in *The State and Revolution*. His fundamental belief was that the vanguard party, in which he had enormous faith, would in fact function as a positive force for building soviet institutions, but he provides little reasoning to support this belief. In a curious way, the vanguard party occupies a position in Lenin's analysis parallel to the working parliament in Weber's: The party is an elite organization led by professional revolutionaries trained in the art of politics and capable, after the revolution, of providing firm leadership of the state apparatus in the interests of the proletariat. The critical problem is the lack of an adequate theory of the mechanisms which produce and reproduce this "leadership" capacity. For Weber the problem was fairly simple: the competitive political struggle of competing parties within a working parliament provided the structural mechanism whereby such a parliament could generate the necessary leadership to control the bureaucracy. Lenin never develops as specific a notion of precisely how the party would fulfil that role and of what mechanisms would keep the party responsive to the working class.[18]

Against the second criticism Lenin does have an implicit defence which rests on two assumptions: first, a belief in the essential simplicity of the control and accounting functions of administration and the capacity for the average worker to manage such functions; second, a belief that it was only the control and accounting functions, not the "purely technical" functions, that posed a serious threat of bureaucratic anti-democratic power. If both of these assumptions were correct, then it would be reasonable that literate workers, organized in democratic soviets, could gradually take over the control and accounting functions of administration and thus check the tendencies towards bureaucratization. If either assumption is incorrect,

18. Calling the Party the "vanguard" and proclaiming its leadership role does not help to articulate the real mechanisms which substantively tie it to the working class as a class and make the Party a vehicle for meaningful working class rule. Ralph Miliband has formulated this serious problem in Lenin's writings well: "What is the relationship between the *proletariat* whose dictatorship the revolution is deemed to establish, and the *party* which educates, leads, directs, organizes etc.? It is only on the basis of an *assumption* of a symbiotic, organic relationship between the two, that the question vanishes altogether; but while such a relationship may well have existed between the Bolshevik Party and the Russian proletariat in the months before the October Revolution, i.e., when Lenin wrote *The State and Revolution*, the assumption that this kind of relationship can ever be taken as an automatic and permanent fact belongs to the rhetoric of power, not to its reality." See "The State and Revolution", *Monthly Review*, Vol 11, No 11, 1970.

however, then Weber's criticisms would have to be taken more seriously.

The first assumption has a certain face validity to it. Given a general spread of education among workers, a shortening of the work week as a result of production for use instead of exchange and a general ideological commitment for mass participation in such control and accounting functions, it is at least plausible that such activities could be organized eventually in a genuinely democratic manner. While the immediate conditions for such democratic control of control and accounting might have been extremely unfavourable in Russia in 1917—because of mass illiteracy, the small size of the working class, the difficulty in shortening the work week to provide time for politics, etc.—nevertheless the longer term prospects were potentially much brighter.

The second assumption—that experts do not pose a threat of bureaucratic usurpation—is more problematic. Weber's basic argument is that the purely technical expert, by virtue of his necessary control over information and knowledge, his familiarity with the files, etc., is in a strategic position to appropriate power. Certainly the Chinese experiences of the conflict between "reds" and "experts", in which there have occurred strong tendencies for technical experts to encourage the growth of bureaucracy, reflects the potential forces for bureaucratization that lie within what Lenin considered to be the purely technical aspects of administration. While it is still an unresolved question whether or not a revolutionary, mass democratic control of the proletarian state is possible, the organizational problems and contradictions of such control are considerably more complex than Lenin acknowledged.[19]

Let us now look more carefully at the theoretical one-sidedness of Weber's analysis. In some ways Weber is much more slippery than Lenin. Lenin was a political militant. He was interested in highlighting points polemically, not in cov-

19. Lenin might have been correct that pure experts do not pose much of a direct threat of usurping political power. However, because of their positions of control over information, they may potentially be able to undermine or neutralize the political initiative of the working class. In this sense, they have considerable negative power—power to obstruct. This could create a sufficient political vacuum to allow bureaucrats proper to assume a much more important political role.

ering all his tracks for potential scholarly critics. Weber was an academician, who skilfully qualified most of the theoretical claims which he made. While Lenin almost entirely ignored the theoretical problems of organizational contradictions, Weber was careful at least to touch on everything. His problem is generally less one of absolute omissions, than of the relative emphasis and elaboration he gives various theoretical issues. In particular, his analysis lacks a developed conception of social contradictions within which organizational processes occur. This affects Weber's analysis in three inter-related ways.

First, Weber tends to ignore or minimize the relationship of the growth of bureaucracy (and the development of the state apparatus in general) to class struggle in capitalist society. Weber's basic model of bureaucratic development centres on the need for rational, predictable administration for capitalist enterprises to be able to make efficient calculations in their production decisions. The central variable which underlies the explanation is the need for *rationality*. Lenin emphasizes the need in capitalist society for the bureaucratic *repression* of class struggle. Both of these models are developmental and dynamic rather than static, since both of them predict a progressively increasing level of bureaucratization in capitalist society. The difference is that Weber's model describes a harmonious rationalization process, while Lenin's depicts a contradictory social control process. Without denying the validity of Weber's insights, his model clearly represents a one-sided understanding of bureaucracy and the state.

Second, the absence of an elaborated theory of social contradictions raises serious questions about Weber's notion of "responsible" and "effective" political leadership. Weber sets out his argument as if political responsibility, effectiveness and competence are purely technical questions concerning the means rather than the ends of political life. Such political effectiveness, Weber argues, requires political leaders to have certain special skills that enable them to pursue competently whatever political goals they and their party are committed to. However, "responsibility" and "effectiveness" have very different meanings depending upon the total social structure in which that leadership operates. To be a "responsible" and "effective" political leader in the context of parliamentary politics in a capitalist society *necessarily* implies furthering the *substantive* goals of capitalism by accommodating oppositional forces to the requirements of capitalist social order. This is not because of the malevolence of such party leadership, and it is not because of the purely internal tendencies towards bureaucratization and oligarchy within political organizations. Rather, it is because of the essential content of the processes of political effectiveness and responsibility, given the constraints of operating within the structural framework of capitalist institutions.

As Weber stresses, to be an effective political leader in a parliamentary system means to know how to negotiate compromises and form political alliances. This means that a "responsible" leader must refrain from pursuing demands and goals that are non-negotiable. Once a particular bargain is reached, he must uphold it and try to prevent his constituency and party from undermining it. Leadership effectiveness thus requires the acceptance of political goals that are compatible with the functioning of the existing social order. This does not mean, of course, that change is prohibited, but it does constrain change within limits determined by the structures of capitalist society.

Effectiveness and responsibility are thus not "neutral" dimensions of technical, formal rationality; they intrinsically embody certain broad political orientations. In fact, it can be said that the more responsible and effective the leadership of political parties (of the right and the left) is, the more they will orient their political activity towards consensus, negotiation, compromise, and accommodation, i.e., the more solidly will their goals fall within the limits of system-compatibility. Effectiveness and responsibility thus become transformed into manipulation and mystification.

The easy answer to these objections would be to deny the existence of real social contradictions in a capitalist social order. For if unresolvable class antagonisms do not exist, if there really does exist a potential for genuine social consensus, then the compromises and bargains negotiated through parliamentary politics could be conceived in terms of a purely technical political effectiveness. Although there are parts of Weber's writings that seem to approach this pluralist image of a fundamentally harmonious social order, he more generally acknowledges the existence of social classes with antagonistic and even irreconcilable class interests. Given this acknowledgement of real class divisions, Weber's plea for responsible, effective political leadership becomes a programme for stabilizing and strengthening capitalist hegemony.

Third, even aside from the question of the meaning of leadership effectiveness and responsibility, Weber's solution to the problem of bureaucratic domination in capitalist society—the creation of strong parliamentary institutions—tends to minimize the relationship of parliamentary institutions to class domination. While Weber does say that a weak parliament is functional for capitalist interests, he definitely does not say that parliaments are weak because of capitalist class domination. They are weak because of weak parliamentary traditions, constitutional obstacles, the policies of particular statesmen, rather than because of the basic requirements of capitalist domination. At best in Weber's discussion of parliaments, such social contradictions are treated as background variables; they are never systematically integrated into his analysis.

Just as Lenin's "solution" in effect abstracts the problems of constructing socialism from the real organizational contradictions of soviet institutions, Weber's "solution" abstracts parliamentary institutions from the social contradictions of capitalist society. While it might be true that a strong working parliament would be an effective check on bureaucracy if such a parliament could exist, it seems highly questionable that such an institution is possible given the contradictions of advanced capitalist society. Weber, of course, was very pessimistic about the long-term durability of parliaments. His pessimism, however, was always based on the organizational problems faced by parliaments when confronting the ever-expanding bureaucracy; he almost never discussed the relationship of parliamentary power to the general social contradictions in capitalist society.

Elements of a Synthesis:
Class Struggle and Organizational Structure

Lenin never believed that a socialist revolution would instantly demolish bureaucratic structures. To imagine such an immediate transformation was, he always insisted, utterly utopian. However, Lenin did not anticipate the durability of bureaucratic structures after the revolution, and he certainly did not expect to see a widening rather than a narrowing of the scope of bureaucracy. In the Eighth Party Congress in 1919, Lenin acknowledged the problem of persistent bureaucracy. "We have been hearing complaints about bureaucracy for a long time," he wrote; "the complaints are undoubtedly well-founded". After briefly discussing the relative success in the debureaucratization of the judicial system, Lenin then went on to explain: "The employees in the other spheres of government are more hardened bureaucrats. The task here is more difficult. We cannot live without this apparatus; every branch of government creates a demand for such an apparatus. Here we are suffering from the fact that Russia was not sufficiently developed as a capitalist country. Germany, apparently, will suffer less from this because her bureaucratic apparatus passed through an extensive school, which sucks people dry but compels them to work and not just wear out armchairs, as happens in our offices."[20] Several years later, in a letter concerning the reorganization of the council of people's commissars written in 1922, Lenin seemed much more despondent about the problem: "We are being sucked down by the rotten bureaucratic swamp into writing papers, jawing about decrees, drawing up decrees—and in this sea of paper, live work is being drowned."[21]

How did Lenin explain this persistence of bureaucratic forms and the difficulty of their eradication? Two themes underscore most of his accounts of the problem: (1) the low level of *culture*

20. *Collected Works*. Vol 29, Moscow 1965, p. 182.

21. In this letter Lenin went on to suggest what should be done about the bureaucratic morass: "work out written regulations for the bringing forward and consideration of questions, and check not less than once a month, you personally, whether the regulations are being observed and whether they are achieving their object, i.e., reduction of paper work, red tape, more sense of responsibility on the part of the People's Commissars, replacement of half-baked decrees by careful, prolonged, business-like checking-up on fulfilment and by checking of experience, establishment of personal responsibility (in effect, *we have complete irresponsibility at the top* . . .)" *On the Soviet State Apparatus*, Moscow 1969, pp. 331–332.

Ironically, in Weber's terms Lenin's suggestions amount to an intensification of bureaucratic structures, especially in the injunction to establish written regulations and regular check-ups on their application. It should also be noticed

and education of the Russian masses;[22] and (2) the low level of *economic* and industrial development of the Soviet Union.[23] Nowhere, to my knowledge, does Lenin emphasize the specifically *political* dynamic at work in the reproduction and extension of bureaucratic structures in the post-revolutionary state apparatus.

We thus have a curious irony: Lenin correctly understands that bureaucratic organizations are not technically necessary, but rather are socially generated by the political imperatives of class domination; yet, his explanations of continuing bureaucracy after the revolution are primarily in terms of economic and ideological (cultural) factors, not political ones. Weber, on the other hand, saw bureaucracy as strictly technically-economically necessary, but saw the solutions to the "problem" of bureaucracy in exclusively political terms. While one might

---

that in this letter Lenin bemoans the *irresponsibility* of the top of bureaucratic offices, much as Weber criticized the irresponsibility of the top levels of the Prussian bureaucracy.

22. For example, in his discussion of bureaucracy at the Eighth Party Congress, Lenin contrasts the *legal* obstacles to direct democracy in the bourgeois republics with the *cultural* obstacles in the Soviet Republic: "We can fight bureaucracy to the bitter end, to a complete victory, only when the whole population participates in the work of government. In the bourgeois republics not only is this impossible but *the law itself prevents it....* What we have done, was to remove these hindrances, but so far we have not reached the stage at which the working people could participate in government. Apart from the law, there is still the level of culture, which you cannot subject to any law. The result of this cultural level is that the Soviets, which by virtue of their programme are organs of government *by the working people*, are in fact organs of government *for the working people* by the advanced sections of the proletariat, but not by the working people as a whole. Here we are confronted by a problem which cannot be solved except by prolonged education." *Collected Works*, Vol 29, p. 183.

23. Aside from frequent general references to the "low level of development", Lenin makes the following specific reference to economic conditions and bureaucracy in his pamphlet "The Tax in Kind": "The evils of bureaucracy are not in the army, but in the institutions serving it. In our country bureaucratic practices have different economic roots [from those in bourgeois republics], namely, the atomised and scattered state of the small producers with their poverty, illiteracy, lack of culture, the absence of roads and *exchange* between agriculture and industry, the absence of connection and interaction between them." At the end of the essay he suggests that trade and exchange relations would help to alleviate bureaucratic evils: "Exchange is freedom of trade; it is capitalism. It is useful to us inasmuch as it will help us overcome the dispersal of the small prod er, and to a certain degree combat the evils of bureaucracy; to what extent t! can be done will be determined by practical experience." *Collected Works*, Vol 32, p. 351.

be able to explain this absence of a political discussion of bureaucracy in Lenin after the revolution in terms of the political conditions and struggles which he faced, nevertheless, the absence of such an analysis leaves his theory of bureaucracy seriously incomplete.

What we need to do, therefore, is to link more systematically the social-economic determinants of bureaucratic structure to the political determinants. The model of determination in Figure 4.1 attempts to lay out the basic shape of these relationships. Of particular importance in the present context are the diverse ways in which the forms of political class struggle are linked to the social-economic structure, the political organizational capacities of classes and the bureaucratic structure of the state. First, the forms of political class struggle are structurally limited by the underlying social-economic structure, and structurally selected by the organizational capacities of classes and the structure of the state apparatus. Secondly, political class struggle transforms the social-economic structure, political capacities and the structure of the state itself. Finally, the forms of political struggle mediate the relations of determination between the social-economic structure, political capacities and the structure of the state. Most importantly in the present discussion, this means that depending upon the nature of these struggles, the effects on state structures of the same underlying social-economic conditions will be different.

In terms of this heuristic model, Weber's analysis can be seen as primarily examining the linkages on the outside of the diagram. Weber paid particular attention to the ways in which social-economic conditions (or more precisely, technical-economic conditions) set limits on the structure of the state (rationalization and bureaucratization in response to the technical needs of industrial society); and the ways in which the political organizational capacities (the strength and vitality of parliamentary institutions) selects specific kinds of bureaucratic structures from within those limits (greater or lesser control of the bureaucracy by responsible, political leadership). Lenin was also concerned with the relationship of the social-economic structure to the structure of the state apparatuses (capitalist class domination produces bureaucratic administration), but he was much more interested than Weber with the

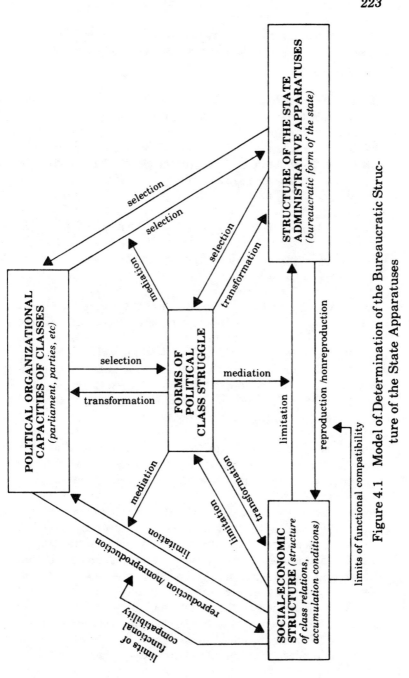

Figure 4.1 Model of Determination of the Bureaucratic Structure of the State Apparatuses

inside of the diagram: the ways in which class struggle is shaped by social and political structures and the ways in which class struggle transforms those structures.

Neither theorist, however, explicitly grappled with the relationship of mediation in a systematic way. It is this relationship which is particularly important in understanding the resilience of bureaucratic organization in the post-revolutionary period in the Soviet Union. Lenin was absolutely correct that the low cultural and economic level of Russia meant that it would be impossible immediately to destroy bureaucratic structures in the state, and that as a result it was of tremendous importance to create the economic and ideological preconditions for a full transition to socialism. What Lenin underestimated, however, was the importance of creating the political preconditions for the control of bureaucratic structures. In the terms of the present discussion, this would have meant specifying how political struggles could mediate the relationship of economic and cultural conditions to state structures and thus affect the shape and strength of those inevitable bureaucratic structures. To the extent that Lenin saw the problem in political terms, it was mainly as a "selection" problem: i.e., how the party might intervene in various bureaucratic organizations to improve the quality of their administration, to eliminate excesses, etc. (see footnote 20 above). He did not see this problem primarily in terms of a genuine political mediation process.

If this is the correct way to pose the problem of the relationship of political struggle to bureaucratization, then the question is: what kind of mediation was necessary? What forms of political struggle could have had the result of reducing the pressures towards bureaucratic expansion generated by economic and social conditions? What developments in the post-1917 period were most decisive in shaping the political mediations which actually did occur? Without pretending to have an adequate answer to these questions, it can be said that the progressive erosion of intra-party democracy as well as inter-party competition (i.e., the prohibition on the formation of intra-party factions and the abolition of all parties other than the Bolsheviks) were among the key developments in this process of political mediation. A deeper form of proletarian democracy would not have eliminated bureaucracy; and it would not necessarily have guaranteed that the bureaucracy which continued to function would have been more efficient. But it would have changed the political terrain on which that bureaucracy was reproduced, by creating a broader mass of politically trained and sophisticated workers. This is not to say that such choices *could* have been made by the young Soviet Republic given the enormous pressures which it confronted. It might well have been utopian to attempt a thorough-going proletarian democracy in the 1920s. But whatever the causes of the choices which were made, the longer term consequence of the specific political mediatjons which historically emerged ·after the Revolution was to reproduce and strengthen bureaucracy and to undermine the political capacity of the working class.

This is the fundamental truth to Weber's analysis: bureaucratic power feeds on the political incapacity of non-bureaucrats and reinforces that incapacity. In his analysis, the pivotal category of non-bureaucrats was the parliamentary elite, and thus he was preoccupied with the problem of how to develop their political capacity. Within Marxist theory, the critical category of non-bureaucrats is the working class. The decisive question is, therefore, how to develop and strengthen the political capacity of this class, i.e., how to forge strong and meaningful social relations among workers at the political level. This can only be accomplished through the direct participation of workers in political struggles and political organizations —which means that after a socialist revolution, it is essential that the institutions of proletarian democracy be constantly defended and deepened.

In the following chapter we will examine what such political mediation means in contemporary capitalist societies.

5

Conclusion: Socialist Strategies and the State in Advanced Capitalist Societies

In *The State and Revolution*, Lenin dismissed bourgeois representative democracies as "mere talking shops". Since the real centres of political power lay in the state bureaucracy, even parliamentary victories by working class parties would not give the working class control of the state. As for the bureaucracies themselves, they were structured in such a way as to make it impossible for the working class to participate directly in the exercise of bureaucratic power. Since parliaments were impotent and bureaucracies impregnable, the only way in which the working class could attain state power was to smash the state apparatus as a whole.

These judgements were based on the historical experiences of bourgeois democracies in the first part of the 20th century. Sixty years have passed since then. Capitalism has progressed from the period of the consolidation of monopoly capitalism to the emergence of diverse forms of state-directed monopoly capitalism. The pivotal contradictions of the accumulation process have shifted from the rising organic composition of capital to an incipient politicization of the accumulation process through state intervention at the level of production. The class structures of capitalist societies have changed drastically: the traditional petty bourgeoisie has shrunk to a small proportion of the population, contradictory locations within class relations have increased, and simultaneously, many of those contradictory locations are becoming increasingly proletarianized. The question is thus posed: to what extent are Lenin's evaluations still valid under contempory historical conditions? In what ways can parliamentary victories of working class parties contribute to a socialist revolution? Or, more broadly, how can the capitalist state be used in the struggle for socialism in advanced capitalist societies? Such questions are being posed with a renewed urgency as European communist parties move away from traditional Leninist answers and seem prepared to participate fully in the institutional framework of the capitalist state.

In the rest of this chapter, we will explore these issues by linking the analysis of the capitalist state and bureaucracy in the previous chapter with our earlier discussion of capitalist crisis and class formation. Specifically, we will examine the thesis that *in advanced monopoly capitalism it is possible to use the democratic capitalist state apparatus as a basis for (ultimately) destroying the capitalist state itself.*[1] There are some indications that this thesis, in one form or another, is at least tentatively being advanced by certain tendencies within European Communist Parties.[2] In much clearer terms, this general thesis has been supported by a variety of political tendencies to the left of the Communist Parties.[3] As a general stance towards

1. It is important to note that this thesis does not pertain to the capitalist state in general, nor even to the democratic form of the capitalist state in general, but specifically to the democratic form of the capitalist state under the conditions of advanced monopoly capitalism. The historical specificity of this claim is one of the things (among others indicated below) which differentiates it from social democratic strategies.

2. For example, Santiago Carrillo, the Secretary-general of the Spanish Communist Party, expresses this basic thesis in his book *Eurocomunismo y Estado* (Barcelona: Critica, 1977): "The state apparatus as a whole continues to be an instrument of the dominant class. This continues to be a Marxist truth. The State is not above classes, it is not an arbiter between them. . . . Without transforming the state apparatus all socialist transformation is precarious and reversible. . . . The problem is not only to arrive to the Government. The problem still is *how to transform the state apparatus.*" (pp. 18, 66, emphasis in the original.) The tactfulness of the language (transformation instead of destruction of the state) should not obscure the central theoretical point being made: the state apparatus itself has a class character and that unless that class character is fundamentally changed, any transition to socialism will be thwarted. The claim that it is possible to use this bourgeois apparatus in the process of its own transformation should not be confused with the liberal claim that it is not a bourgeois apparatus in the first place.

3. See, for example Lucio Magri, in a recent interview: "Italy, Social Democracy and Revolution in the West: an Interview with Lucio Magri", *Socialist Revolution* No. 36, 1977. Magri argues that a socialist strategy in advanced capitalism involves participation in parliamentary activity but it is not limited

228

the capitalist state, this thesis must be differentiated from both the traditional social-democratic position and the traditional Leninist position.

The traditional social democratic position, at least since World War I, is that it is possible to use the capitalist state as a basis for a transition to socialism without at the same time destroying the capitalist state itself. The state apparatus is thus viewed as an essentially neutral instrument, capable of being used by different class forces for radically opposed ends. Socialism is viewed as a series of policies, or reforms, which can be effectively implemented through the democratic state apparatus of capitalist society. While this does not imply that such a reform process will necessarily be smooth or uncontested, it does imply that there are no inherent structural limits to such reforms embedded in the very character of the state itself.

The traditional Leninist position has generally rejected the possibility of using the capitalist state in the transition to socialism.[4] The structural limits imposed by the capitalist state

to electoral activity. "The problem is to add to the traditional forms of representative and parliamentary democracy the new forms of direct democracy expressed through the councils, the women's movement, the movement of young people, and the unemployed workers' movement, and to achieve an ever greater level of activation and organization of the masses. It is necessary to use the opportunities offered by bourgeois democracy against bourgeois democracy itself. . . . When we speak of a government of the left, we are not thinking of a sort of Kerensky government—the reformist left parties going into the government and helping us open the road to revolution. Rather, we propose that the left parties, although not yet having full control over state power, use the government itself to help the mass movement grow and to create the space and the instruments for coordination of the mass movement." (pp. 130–131) A similar stance is adopted by Ralph Miliband in the concluding chapter of his book *Marxism and Politics* (Oxford 1977): "[The transition to a socialist society] both *includes* and *requires* radical changes in the structures, modes of operation and personnel of the existing state, *as well as* the creation of a network of organs of popular participation amounting to 'dual power'. The 'reformist' strategy, at least in this 'strong' version of it, may produce a combination of direction and democracy sufficiently effective to keep the conservative forces in check *and* to provide the conditions under which the process of transition may proceed" (p. 189).

4. It is always dangerous to talk about "the" Leninist position, since a wide variety of political orientations have at different times and places adopted the label "Leninist". The position outlined here under this designation is not necessarily restricted to Leninists, and certainly not all groups which have called themselves Leninist have invariably held this position. But I do think that it represents the central thrust of the traditional Leninist views of the capitalist state and the correct strategies of socialist movements with respect to that state.

are thought to be so narrow that any attempt at using that state apparatus will necessarily have the effect of reinforcing bourgeois domination. The capitalist state cannot be captured and used by the working class; it must be destroyed. Such a stance does not prevent purely tactical and conjunctural demands *on* the capitalist state for certain kinds of policies or reforms, but it does argue against a strategy of trying to control the capitalist state apparatus itself.[5] Not only would such a strategy fail on its own terms; its net effect would only be to strengthen the capitalist state and make the task of smashing the state that much more difficult.

The thesis that the capitalist state can be used for its own destruction differs from both of these more traditional stances towards the capitalist state. Like the social democratic position, this thesis accepts the possibility of the Left systematically using the democratic capitalist state for socialist objectives (or at least for helping to create the preconditions for socialism). But unlike the social democratic position, the capitalist state is understood as imposing definite structural limitations on any socialist transformation. Thus, like the Leninist position, the

5. Lenin in particular argued that the capitalist state should be used tactically in the struggle for socialism. His emphasis was generally on the importance of engaging in parliamentary struggles as a way of educating the masses. For example, in 1920 he wrote: "Participation in parliamentary elections and in the struggle on the parliamentary rostrum is *obligatory* on the part of the revolutionary proletariat *specifically* for the purpose of educating the backward strata of *its own class*, and for the purpose of awakening and enlightening the undeveloped, downtrodden and ignorant rural masses. Whilst you lack the strength to do away with bourgeois parliaments and every other type of reactionary institution, you must work within them because it is there that you will still find workers who are duped by the priests and stultified by the conditions of rural life. . . . In Western Europe, the backward masses of the workers and—to an even greater degree—of the small peasants are much more imbued with bourgeois-democratic and parliamentary prejudices than they were in Russia; because of that, it is *only* from within such institutions as bourgeois parliaments that Communists can (and must) wage a long and persistent struggle, undaunted by any difficulties, to expose, dispel and overcome these prejudices." See *Left-Wing Communism: An Infantile Disorder*, in *Selected Works*, London 1969, pp. 546, 551. However, while Lenin vehemently attacked the "ultra-left" for denying tactical participation in bourgeois parliamentary democracy, to my knowledge he never argues that a workers' government in a bourgeois democracy could transform the very capitalist character of the capitalist state through a series of structural reforms. The capitalist state may well be a vital *arena* for class struggle, but it cannot be *used* strategically by a workers' party in order to destroy the capitalist state.

thesis acknowledges the necessity of ultimately destroying the very structure of that state in order to make possible a sustained transition to socialism. The strategy embodied in the thesis breaks with traditional Leninism, however, in arguing that under the conditions of advanced capitalism, it is possible for the Left to control the capitalist state apparatus (or at least parts of it) and to use that apparatus systematically in the attack on capitalist state power itself.

The modes of determination discussed throughout this book may help us to understand more rigorously the logic of this thesis. Two relations of determination are particularly important.[6] First, state interventions are *structurally limited* by the underlying class structure of the society and *selected* by the structure of the state apparatuses. This means that certain forms of state intervention are made impossible by the basic social structures of the society, and that within the range of possible interventions, a narrower set of possibilities are selected by the state apparatuses (i.e., the apparatuses establish limits within limits). Second, the class structure of the society generates *limits of functional compatibility* on the effects of state interventions. That is, within the range of all structurally possible state interventions, only certain interventions can be considered optimal for the reproduction of capitalist society as a whole; other interventions are compatible with that reproduction but not optimal (i.e., they have contradictory effects), and still other possible interventions are actually non-reproductive of capitalist social relations. An intervention by the state which falls outside of the limits of functional compatibility sets in motion a chain of consequences which will either lead to a negation of that state activity, or eventually to a break with the structure of capitalism itself.[7]

6. Figure 1.7 in Chapter One presents a model of determination which corresponds fairly closely to the present discussion. The only difference is that a relation of limitation should be added between economic structure and state policies.

7. In these terms, a "perfect" capitalist state, from the point of view of the bourgeoisie, would be one in which the state apparatuses were organized in such a way that only those state interventions which were optimally reproductive for capitalism would be selected within the range of structurally possible interventions. Such a coincidence of the limits of structural possibility and the limits of functional compatibility would doom any attempt by the working class to "use" the capitalist state to failure. Such a perfect capitalist state cannot exist

Now, the thesis that the capitalist state can be used to destroy the capitalist state can be reinterpreted as a thesis about the possibility of the noncoincidence between these two kinds of limits in a capitalist society: *the limits of what is structurally possible need not correspond to the limits of what is functionally compatible with the requirements of reproducing capitalism.*[8]

The premise of the strategy of using the state to destroy the state is that in advanced capitalism the instrumental control of the summits of the state apparatus by the Left can serve to widen this gap between the structural limits on the state and the functional effects of the state.[9] The implicit reasoning goes

---

because the capitalist state is not simply the product of bourgeois domination, but of class struggle. The ruling class may rule, but not just as it pleases. This means that the extent to which the interventions of the state will be optimal for the capitalist class is always problematic. Many Marxist theoretical works on the state nevertheless adopt the view that the capitalist state is such a perfect apparatus for the bourgeoisie. The assumption is made that the capitalist state is universally functional for reproducing the dominance of the capitalist class, and thus the two modes of determination discussed above are fused into a single relation of determination. The "functionalist" cast to some of Poulantzas's early work (see especially *Political Power and Social Classes*, NLB London 1973) comes in part from this fusion of the limits of structural possibility and the limits of functional compatibility.

8. If the theoretical claim is to be made that there is inevitably a coincidence of the limits of functional compatibility with the limits of structural possibility, then it is necessary to demonstrate the social mechanisms which guarantee such a coincidence. In the absence of a discussion of these mechanisms, the claim for coincidence becomes ideological rather than scientific. The one tradition within Marxism which has attempted to outline such concrete mechanisms is so-called "instrumentalist" research on the ruling class. In this tradition of research, it is the concrete ties of the capitalist class to the state apparatus which guarantee the coincidence of the activities of the state (limits of the possible) with the interests of the bourgeoisie (limits of functional compatibility). However, it is only if the bourgeoisie is thought to be both omniscient and omnipotent that the empirical demonstration of such ties to the state can be translated into a theory of the *necessary* coincidence of the limits of the possible and the functional. Such an assumption implies that history can be understood simply in terms of class domination rather than class struggle.

9. The degree of non-coincidence between the limits of the possible and the limits of the functional is not fixed for all time. Rather, it is a variable non-coincidence. In certain historical conjunctures such a non-coincidence is very restricted, in others it is very broad. The degree to which such a non-coincidence occurs is a measure of the extent to which the basic class contradictions of the society have been internalized into the state. The fundamental reason why the strategy of using the capitalist state to destroy the state may be a plausible strategy in advanced capitalism, but not in earlier forms of capitalism, is that

something like this: because of the gap between the class selectivity of the state and the class functionality of the state, a Left government can potentially enact certain reforms (i.e., structurally possible interventions) which have the effect of changing the structure of the state itself in ways which erode the class selectivity of the state apparatuses. As the class selectivity of the state structures is eroded, the possibility of nonreproductive state interventions increases. Such interventions can potentially change the class structure itself in ways which broaden the structural limits on the state, thus increasing the gap between structural limits and functional compatibility still further. At some point such a process leads to a qualitative transformation (destruction) of the class character of the state itself. Once this occurs, a new type of state structure is established which can function to build socialist relations of production rather than simply undermine capitalist relations. Such a transformation represents a revolutionary break with capitalism.[10]

It is one thing to make an abstract claim about the theoretical possibility of such a contradiction between the limits of structural possibility and the limits of functional compatibility of capitalist state interventions, and another thing to demonstrate the historical reality of this possibility. Certainly in the case of the United States, the above scenario of progressively eroding the class character of the state has little immediate plausibility.

---

the structural changes embodied in the capitalist state (greater role in accumulation, the welfare state, etc.) have considerably increased this internalization of class contradictions within the state. This internalization of contradictions, of course, only generates the potential for an increased gap between the class selectivity of the state and the class functionality of the state. The extent to which this potentiality becomes an actuality is determined by class struggle (through a relation of mediation).

10. At first glance, this series of propositions may seem extremely voluntaristic: by an act of will, a socialist government can somehow transcend the constraints of capitalist structures. The argument, however, is not that a Left government can voluntaristically ignore the constraints imposed by the capitalist character of the capitalist state. Those constraints are real and limit the options of any government. Rather, the argument is that the structural contradictions of late capitalism create conditions within which political struggles can have the effect of gradually shifting the constraints themselves. It is not a question of political will-power, but of the objective contradictions within the state—the gap between the limits of the possible and the limits of the functional—which make possible such transformations of the state itself.

Both because of the weakness of the Left in general and because of the (still) relatively untarnished hegemony of the capitalist class, the gap between structural possibilities and functional effects of the state offers little opening for such strategies in the United States.[11]

The situation in parts of Western Europe appears quite different, and it is there that the strategy of using the capitalist state to destroy the state has received the most attention. The organizational capacities of the working class are greater than in the United States and the internal contradictions of the capitalist state more intense. If the strategy is to be plausible in the current period, it will be in Europe rather than the United States that it will be tested.

I do not have a sufficiently broad understanding of current developments in Western Europe to provide a rigorous analysis of alternative socialist strategies. What I can try to do is indicate the general developments in advanced capitalism which impinge on the strategy of using the state to destroy the state. My general conclusion will be that the conditions of advanced capitalist societies *simultaneously* generate new possibilities for such a strategy and recreate obstacles to any attempt by socialist forces to use the capitalist state. The decisive task of any socialist strategy is to grapple with this intensely contradictory situation, rather than to ignore the contradictions in the polemical defence of a specific choice.

This discussion of the strategic implications of developments in advanced capitalism will focus on four issues: 1. the relationship of immediate to fundamental interests of the working class in advanced capitalism; 2. the relationship of state bureaucracy to the class formation; 3. the dialectical rela-

11. This is not to say that the scenarios of socialist revolution presented by various vanguard Marxist-Leninist parties in the United States are more plausible than the strategy of using the state to destroy the state. The problem is that in the United States in the late 1970s no strategy for socialism is particularly plausible. This is not because of a failure of revolutionary imagination on the Left, but because the historical conditions within the United States make it difficult to assess the chain of consequences which flow from a given strategy. In a sense, therefore, the crucial immediate question for the American Left is less "how to make a revolution", but rather "how to create the social conditions within which we can *know* how to make a revolution". In the common parlance of the Left in the United States, this is referred to as "putting socialism on the political agenda", i.e., creating the ideological and political conditions in which socialism is viewed as a serious alternative within the working class.

tionship of class capacities of the working class to the capitalist state; 4. the problem of repression.

1. Fundamental and Immediate Interests

Parliamentary competition has generally been one of the basic mechanisms by which struggles for the fundamental interests of the working class become displaced onto struggles for immediate interests.[12] Electoral campaigns tend to encourage promises of immediate benefits of constituencies, and the structural prerequisite for a party to "deliver the goods" is a healthy capitalist economy. Furthermore, the attempt by socialist parties to create an electoral majority has always necessitated electoral appeals to voters outside of the working class, and this too has tended to undercut electoral campaigns around the fundamental interests of the proletariat.[13] The end result is that "responsible" parliamentary parties of the Left generally restrict their programmes to reforms which are compatible with the reproduction of capitalism, and this means that immediate interests of the working class tend to replace fundamental interests in party programmes.

While there are some exceptions to this pattern—as when left parliamentary parties act to strengthen the legal rights of working class organizations, thus facilitating the development of the class capacities of the working class—nevertheless, the typical effect of parliamentary competition on left parties has been to shift their real programmes from fundamental to immediate interests. This is the traditional pattern. The question, then, is whether the new contradictions of advanced capitalism allow the Left to link fundamental interests to reforms over immediate interests within the framework of democratic bourgeois politics? It would be a serious mistake to argue that somehow in advanced capitalism, socialist and communist parties have been liberated from the pressures and constraints faced by earlier parties. Indeed, it can be argued that since these

12. See chapter 2 above for an extended discussion of immediate and fundamental interests.

13. For an extremely interesting and important discussion of this process of erosion of fundamental interests within socialist electoral parties, see Adam Przeworski, and John Sprague, "A History of Western European Socialism", paper presented at the Annual Meeting of the American Political Science Association, September, 1977.

parties are likely to come to power under relatively unfavourable economic conditions, their first order of business will be to stabilize and revitalize the accumulation process. In the short run this could imply a fairly serious constraint on even the pursuit of immediate interests of the working class (higher wages, more jobs, better housing, etc.), but it certainly would constrain the pursuit of more fundamental interests.

Nevertheless, the specific contradictions of advanced capitalism do open up a new terrain for joining immediate and fundamental class interests of the working class. Two specific developments are especially important. First, since the Second World War there has occurred a partial erosion of the purely commodified character of labour power. The most striking form of this decommodification of labour power centres on welfare state policies which reproduce labour power even when it cannot be sold as a commodity on the labour market. The mildest form of this decommodification is unemployment insurance, which guarantees the reproduction of wage-labourers during periods when they cannot find employment. Other forms include state subsidies to families for child support, state welfare for the handicapped, for the aged, etc. To a greater or lesser extent, all of these forms of state transfers break the linkage between subsistence and the market, i.e., they undermine the commodity status of labour power.[14] Labour power is also partially decommodified through the reduction of the portion of the life cycle during which an individual labourer sells his/her labour as a commodity (i.e., through the lengthening of schooling, through earlier retirement and through longer life).[15] Again, this implies a partial weakening of the link between selling labour power as an exchange value, and the reproduction of people through the consumption of use-values.

Of course, the counter-tendency also exists within capitalism. Most notably, the rapid incorporation of vast numbers of women

14. One of the crucial consequences of this partial decommodification of labour power is a weakening of the effectiveness of the reserve army of labour as a way of disciplining the working class. Unemployment no longer holds the terror for workers that it once did, even though it is still unquestionably a hardship on most workers. (See chapter 3 above.)

15. This point was suggested by Adam Przeworski. See his "The Process of Class Formation: from Karl Kautsky's *The Class Struggle* to recent debates", *Politics and Society*, 1977.

into the labour force since the 1940s implies that an increasing proportion of women's labour is commodified. Thus, while the growth of the welfare state partially decommodifies all labour power, an increasing proportion of the population spends at least part of their lives selling their labour power as a commodity.

The critical point in the present context is that this partial decommodification of labour power potentially undermines the assumption that the "natural" organization of production requires labour power to function as a commodity. To the extent that such decommodification of labour power deepens, then struggles for improvements of the standard of living of workers will tend to be progressively displaced from direct wage struggles (struggles over the exchange value of labour power) to struggles over the provision of use-values by the state. This in turn may make it easier to challenge at the ideological level the commodity status of labour power itself.

The second way in which the specific contradictions of advanced capitalism potentially allow for a closer linkage of immediate and fundamental interests concerns the progressive politicization of the accumulation process itself. As was argued at some length in the discussion of contemporary crisis dynamics in chapter 3, the solutions to the present world economic crisis will involve much more profound interventions of the state into the production process itself. Such interventions will take many forms: more pervasive levels of state planning, state controls over investments and flows of capital, the direct organization of broader spheres of production by the state, etc. All of these contribute to an erosion of the unrestricted sway of commodity relations in the economy, i.e., increasingly exchange-value criteria are replaced by use-value criteria (ultimately political criteria) in the process of resource allocation within capitalist economies. To be sure, an attempt will be made politically to subordinate such use-value criteria to the needs of commodity production itself. However, the very fact that such allocations pass through the state opens the door for their political contestation in ways which are impossible so long as accumulation is directed entirely within "private" corporate boardrooms.

Such a shift away from pure commodity relations may be essential for the reproduction of capitalism itself, but it simultaneously contradicts one of the basic requirements for the reproduction of capitalist relations: the displacement of conflicts from fundamental to immediate interests. The increasing intervention of the state within accumulation means that purely economic conflicts between capital and labour immediately become political conflicts; while the erosion of market rationality means that those political conflicts will more directly pose the question of the class content of the state interventions within production itself. Again, this means, at least potentially, that conflicts between labour and capital over immediate interests can more easily be linked to questions of fundamental interests.

Both of these developments—the partial decommodification of labour power and the politicization of accumulation—only *potentially* provide a basis for linking immediate and fundamental interests of the working class. They can also serve to reinforce a split between the two. The partial decommodification of labour power, for example, poses new divisions within the working class between those workers whose labour is completely commodified (full time wage labourers) and workers whose labour is less commodified (students, pensioners, unemployed, underemployed). Instead of challenging the assumption of labour power as a commodity, therefore, the partial decommodification of labour power could potentially become a material basis for deepening the hostilities between workers with strong and weak positions in the market. Similarly, the politicization of accumulation need not link immediate to fundamental class interests. Instead of raising the issue of the class content of the process of resource allocation in a capitalist society, such a politicization can simply reproduce at the political level the belief that the strengthening of capitalist institutions and capital accumulation is in the interests of everyone.

The extent to which these developments will lead to a stronger linkage of immediate and fundamental class interests or to a continued displacement of fundamental onto immediate interests depends, therefore, on the ways in which class struggles in general, and socialist politics in particular, intersect these contradictions. In terms of our discussion of modes of determination, the effects of these contradictions are mediated by class struggle.

The policies of a socialist government around the question of full employment are especially important in shaping the effects of the partial decommodification of labour power. If a full employment policy takes the form primarily of stimulating economic growth in order to provide greater employment through the market (i.e., classical Keynesian programmes), then the commodity status of labour power might even be reinforced. If, however, a full employment policy was centred around a reduction of the average hours worked per worker, with state subsidies to workers to provide compensating income supplements, then full employment would be consistent with a continued decommodification of labour power.

Perhaps even more importantly, the stance a socialist government takes toward the contradictions embedded in the politicization of accumulation will have a significant impact on the possibilities of linking struggles over immediate and fundamental interests. The temptation of any government in a capitalist state, including a Left government, is to try to obscure the class character of its own activity. If austerity measures are necessary to prevent the flight of capital, such policies are likely to be portrayed as necessary for "national prosperity and economic recovery". Instead of arguing that such measures reflect the constraints of the capitalist mode of production, they will be defended in terms of neutral technical criteria which essentially obscure the contradictions between state interventions which stabilize capitalism and the fundamental interests of the working class. A Left government can adopt another stance: it can try to make the class content of its own interventions explicit, showing how in spite of Left control within the state apparatus, the bourgeoisie remains the ruling class and is thus capable of constraining the state itself. Of course, proclamations that the capitalist class constrains the state can be an excuse for inaction and immobility rather than a basis for demystifying the class character of the state itself. It is not enough to proclaim the constraints of capital; it is necessary for the policies of the state constantly to push up against those constraints, materially demonstrating the limits of possibility within the existing social structure. If this is done, the politicization of accumulation in advanced capitalism can become the basis for asserting the necessity of progressively joining the struggles for immediate and fundamental interests, i.e., for attacking the constraints themselves.

2. Bureaucracy and Class Formation

Lenin insisted that in the parliamentary republic the real work of government took place in the bureaucracies, not in parliaments. If a left government is to have any chance of instituting policies which serve the fundamental interests of the working class (anti-capitalist policies) it is essential that it not only be capable of legislating such policies, but of actually implementing them. This requires a capacity to control the actual workings of the bureaucracy. If the bureaucracy is sufficiently autonomous from control by elected bodies—as Weber indicated was the case in Prussia in the early 20th century—then anti-capitalist state policies are likely to be neutralized in the actual process of state intervention.

As in the case of the relationship of immediate to fundamental interests, the Left confronts very contradictory prospects on the question of controlling the state bureaucracy. On the one hand, the power of state bureaucracies has if anything increased over the past half century, further eroding the capacity of parliamentary majorities to define decisively state policy. The saga of increasing centralization of the state apparatus and decreasing influence of legislative bodies has been told many times.

On the other hand, pervasive contradictions have emerged within the state bureaucracies themselves which pose new possibilities for the Left. Whereas Lenin could refer to the bureaucratic personnel of the state apparatus as tied to the bourgeoisie "through a thousand threads", which guaranteed their loyalty to the capitalist class, the class character of state bureaucratic positions can no longer be characterized in such a simple manner. As was argued in the discussion of class in Chapter 2, many positions within the bureaucracy should be considered contradictory class locations between the working class and the bourgeoisie, and many others should be viewed as essentially proletarian in character (excluded from both the creation and execution of state policy). Furthermore, there are certainly some reasons to believe that many of the contradictory locations within the state apparatuses are being increasingly proletarianized in late capitalism. The growth of trade unionism among state employees in the United States, for example, would tend to support the view that contradictory locations within the state are being drawn closer to the working class. As the state attempts to rationalize its own labour processes in order to counter the fiscal crisis of the state, this tendential proletarianization of civil servants will if anything increase.

Such a proletarianization of positions within the state apparatus significantly changes the relationship of bureaucratic structures to the class struggle. While it remains the case that bureaucratic structures still act as a barrier against any direct influence of the working class on the administration of state policies, the emerging class relations within the bureaucracy mean that substantial portions of the bureaucratic personnel are potential allies of the working class in class struggles. This means that with socialist governments in power, parts of the bureaucracy, at least, are likely to throw their weight behind the Left, rather than sabotage the Left. The problem of resistance from top levels of the bureaucratic structure would remain, but it will be potentially easier to counter such resistance if lower levels of the state bureaucracy can be drawn into working class organizations.

The proletarianization of state employees, including lower level bureaucratic personnel, does not imply that people in such positions will automatically join forces with the working class in socialist struggles. At the level of immediate interests, a fairly deep division between state workers and non-state workers continues to exist because of the link of state sector wages to taxation. The organization of state workers into unions and the intensification of their struggles with the state over immediate interests can have the effect of increasing the conflict between state workers and other workers. To the extent that state workers are mobilized only around purely economistic demands, their proletarianization is unlikely to tie them more closely to the working class as a whole.

In order for the proletarianization of state workers to contribute to an erosion of the barriers between the working class and the bureaucracy, therefore, it is essential that state workers also be organized around political demands—demands for better social services, for smaller classes in the schools, for client and consumer participation in the management of state services, and so forth. The strategy of socialist penetration of the capitalist state, of using the state to destroy the state, will depend heavily upon the success of the Left in organizing state workers around such political demands. To the extent that state bureaucratic personnel remain unorganized by the Left, the Weberian dilemma of parliamentary control of the bureaucracy would undermine the effectiveness of any Left government. To the extent that substantial segments of the bureaucracy are mobilized into working class formations, Lenin's insistence that the bureaucratic structure of the capitalist state negated any possibility of the working class using parliament for anti-capitalist ends would need to be qualified.

3. Working Class Capacities and the Capitalist State

The eventual possibility of a revolutionary break with capitalism in advanced capitalist societies depends upon the organization and strength of the working class. The most decisive issue in the strategy of using the capitalist state to destroy the state is thus: *in what ways can the control of the government by the Left contribute to expanding and deepening the class capacities of the working class?*[16] If a Left parliamentary victory were to lead to a demobilization and disorganization of the working class, then even if such a government were to enact a series of progressive reforms, it is inconceivable that it could create the conditions for a socialist transformation.

As Poulantzas has effectively argued, one of the central functions of the capitalist state is precisely to disorganize the working class while simultaneously organizing the bourgeoisie. This disorganization of the working class is accomplished above all by the essential institutional structures of the capitalist state. The privatized character of voting, the canons of equality before the law, the denial of "class" as a juridical category, and so on, all serve to transform people from members of a class into individual, atomized citizens.[17] To the extent that the working

16. Lucio Magri strongly emphasizes this issue. He argues that it is less the intrinsic character of the reforms enacted by a Left government that matters than the relationship of such reforms to the mass struggle. (See footnote 3 above.)

17. For an extended discussion of such processes of disorganization of the working class, see Poulantzas, *Political Power and Social Classes*.

class is formed into a class in spite of such processes of atomization, the repressive apparatus of the state functions to limit
the growth of the organizational capacities of the working class
and to channel such organizations toward objectives which
divide rather than unite the working class as a class.

It would be extremely utopian and idealist to suppose that an
electoral victory of a Left coalition would somehow allow a Left
government to be unconstrained by this basic function of the
capitalist state. The disorganization of the working class is an
effect of the very structure of the capitalist state; it is not
primarily a question of a "policy" of the government of the
capitalist state. *As long as a capitalist state remains a capitalist
state, therefore, it will continue to have such disorganizing effects
on the working class.*

This being said, the question becomes: To what extent can a
Left government act to *minimize* the disorganizing effects of the
capitalist state? To what extent can it actively erode the structural basis of those effects?[18] Answers to these questions are
pivotal to the strategy of using the capitalist state to destroy the
state. Fundamentally, "destroying the *capitalist* state" means
destroying the structures of that state which systematically
undermine the class capacities of the working class and thus
make it impossible for the working class to become a ruling class.

Answering these questions involves two major tasks: first,
analysing what actions a Left government would have to pursue
once in power in order to erode the structural basis of the

18. These questions presuppose that the atomization of the working class is a
variable rather than constant effect of the structure of the capitalist state. There
are two sources of this variation: first, different variations of the structure of the
capitalist state will generate differing degrees of disorganization of the working
class; and second, the same structure will produce differing degrees of disorganization depending upon the conditions of class struggle (for class struggle
always mediates the effects of state structures). The strategy of using the state
to destroy the state presupposes both sources of variation: the control of the
government by the Left can push the capitalist state towards the minimal pole of
disorganization of the working class through structural change of the state
itself, and class struggles can mitigate the disorganizing effects of the state. All
Marxists, of course, would acknowledge the mediating role of class struggle (if
not, it would be impossible to organize the working class), but they differ
strongly on their views of the first source of variation of disorganization of the
working class. The traditional social democratic view would be that the state
does not necessarily disorganize the working class at all (i.e. it is a neutral
apparatus), while the traditional Leninist view would be that possible variations in disorganizing effects were extremely limited or non-existent.

atomizing effects of the state; and second, analysing the pre-conditions necessary for the Left to be able to engage in such actions if it gained control of the government.

State actions which potentially minimize the disorganization of the working class. The disorganization of the working class, as was observed above, is accomplished through two sorts of mechanisms: the direct repression of the expansion of working class capacities, and the atomization of political life through the structures of the capitalist state. The first of these is more easily influenced by a Left victory than the second, but the second is more important if the capitalist character of the capitalist state is to be eventually destroyed.

Any electoral victory by the Left is likely to be accompanied by considerable initiatives from the working class, ranging from the formation of neighbourhood councils to factory occu-pations. The reaction of the new government to such initiatives will have long-term consequences for the ultimate success or failure of the regime in building the capacities of the working class. Upon coming to power, a Left government would be under considerable pressure to prove that it was "responsible", cap-able of maintaining order and controlling its own ranks. The temptation under such circumstances would be for the gov-ernment to crush such popular movements, or at least to create conditions which would be highly unfavourable to their expan-sion. Threats of various sorts from the capitalist class—ranging from withdrawal of investments to political disruption to mili-tary intervention—would add considerably to the pressure to repress such initiatives from the working class. To a large extent, the capacity of the government to withstand such pres-sures and to provide some sort of protective umbrella for the growth of popular social movements will determine the longer-term prospects for more fundamental structural change.

A Left government would not simply be under pressure from the bourgeoisie to repress popular mobilization. It would also be under pressure from conservative socialist forces within the government itself to control social movements, especially those involving significant participation of the extra-parliamentary revolutionary left. Again, the temptation of the government under such pressures would be, at a minimum, to withdraw any institutional support for those movements, and perhaps even to actively repress the extra-parliamentary revolutionary left.

Such a systematic repression of a Left opposition would seriously undermine the possibilities of using the state to expand the class capacities of the working class. It might seem somewhat of a contradiction, but a socialist government within a capitalist state needs a healthy, politically active left opposition outside of parliament. In the absence of an organized opposition on its left, it would be extremely difficult for a socialist coalition in power to avoid gradually moving toward the right under the pressures of the constraints of the capitalist state. In a complementary way, of course, such a left opposition must be a "loyal" opposition in the sense of refraining from purely destructive tactics aimed at wrecking the coalition in power. It is only under conditions where an extra-parliamentary revolutionary Left offers critical support to a socialist parliamentary government and yet continues to engage in political work outside of the constraints of the capitalist state, that the parliamentary parties themselves will be able to contribute to building the political capacities of the working class.[19]

The policy of adopting a generally non-repressive stance toward popular social movements as a way of expanding the class capacities of the working class is fairly straightforward, even if it will confront serious opposition. The problem of effecting structural reforms of the capitalist state itself in order to undermine the atomizing effects of the state is much more

19. A policy of sheltering social movements by a Left government poses potential risks to the regime, in addition to the obvious possibility of direct threats from the capitalist class. On the one hand, not all popular social movements are animated by the Left, and a generally non-repressive stance towards popular mobilization may give the Right greater room for manoeuvre. Repressive responses selectively directed towards right-wing organizing might be effective, but such repression would potentially undermine the legitimacy of the government as a "constitutional" regime among various middle strata which otherwise might support the government. On the other hand, not all extra-parliamentary left forces may be a "loyal" opposition. Some will undoubtedly direct much of their energy against the regime itself, arguing that it is deceiving and coopting the working class. If such opposition took the form of sabotage or other highly disruptive tactics, the government might be impelled to try to control such groups. Yet once the government begins to repress one segment of the revolutionary Left, it becomes more difficult to protect tendencies within a "loyal" revolutionary Left opposition as well.

problematic.[20] But if the class capacities of the working class are to develop, such reforms are of critical importance.

Perhaps the most important way by which the structure of the democratic capitalist state atomizes the working class is by limiting popular political life to voting, to periodically casting a ballot as private individuals for political representatives. The key issue involved in minimizing such atomization is to expand the ways in which people can directly participate in politics as members of organized collectivities. In order to accomplish this it is necessary to establish primitive organs of direct democracy on the fringes of the state administration. Such structural changes would include such things as community planning boards linked to neighbourhood councils, client-worker committees in state services, delegates from factory councils on state planning bodies, self-management (*auto-gestion*) structures in state industries, and so on. In each of these new quasi-democratic forms of state administration, the critical issue is not simply the greater participation of individuals in political processes, but rather the participation of individuals *as members of class-based collectivities* within politics. If this occurs, then such forms of limited "debureaucratization" of the state can serve partially to replace the individualized and privatized forms of political participation embodied in voting, with more collective and public forms of political life. The collective-public character of this participation could potentially widen and deepen the social relations within the working class and this in turn would serve to strengthen the class capacities of the working class.

Within the framework of the capitalist state, such a dissolution of the state apparatus would of course be limited in scope, constantly thwarted by the constitutional and economic impediments to working class democracy. Rules of due process would continually impinge on the initiatives of grass roots organizations attempting to participate in the new "democratic" forms of state administration. Bureaucratic prerogatives would undermine the effectiveness of attempts at administrative decentralization. The necessity of working

20. For a relatively early discussion of the problem of reforming the capitalist state in ways which enlarge the power of the working class, see André Gorz's discussion of "non-reformist reforms" in *Strategy for Labor*, Boston 1967.

40-hour weeks would undermine the vitality of popular participation within political organs. It is precisely because of factors such as these that it is impossible for a Left government within the capitalist state to eliminate atomized politics. The most that can be hoped for is that a limited erosion of bureaucratic structures will contribute to expanding working class capacities and that such policies will serve as a concrete demonstration in embryo of the alternative to bourgeois representative institutions. To the extent that this occurs, then the experience of the constraints on such a programme of debureaucratization could itself contribute to demonstrating the necessity of more fundamental transformations beyond the limits of capitalist structures.[21]

Preconditions for a Left government to be able to minimize the disorganizing effects of the capitalist state. In order for a Left government to adopt a generally non-repressive stance toward social movements and even to begin a minimal erosion of the bureaucratic structure of the capitalist state, two pre-conditions are necessary: First, it is essential that the Left gain control of the government on the basis of a mobilized working class with strong, autonomous organizational capacities. Second, it is important that the ideological hegemony of the bourgeoisie be seriously weakened prior to a Left electoral victory. These two conditions are dialectically linked, but it will be helpful to discuss them in turn.

If the Left were to come to power through the typical dis-

21. A word should be said about the relationship between this analysis of the possibilities for a limited dissolution of the state (partial debureaucratization) and the classic revolutionary theory of "dual power". Dual power refers to the relatively brief period during a revolutionary situation in which a new, revolutionary state apparatus is first established and exists alongside the apparatus of the old regime. In effect, there are two states, competing with each other for popular support. The revolutionary state, in these terms, is external to the old apparatus. The perspective of a Left government within a capitalist state adopting structural reforms which reduce the atomizing effects of the state is a scenario of changes internal to the old state apparatus. In a sense it can be interpreted as an argument about the possibility of creating primitive forms of socialist political institutions within the fabric of the capitalist state. This does *not* imply that it will be unnecessary at some point to break qualitatively with the structures of the capitalist state and that such a break might involve the creation of a dual power structure. The claim is simply that it is possible to prepare the political terrain for such a break through structural changes within the capitalist state itself.

organized political relations of electoral politics—if, for example, the Left won an election in a period of economic crisis more because of the collapse of bourgeois parties than because of its own organizational base—then it would be very difficult to imagine how it could even tentatively adopt policies which would significantly expand the capacities of the working class. The crucial way, by which a Left government can potentially contribute to the consolidation and expansion of the capacities of the working class is to link various working class organizations directly to the processes of state intervention. The irony is that unless those organizations already have considerable vitality and cohesion prior to an electoral victory, then such participation in state activity is likely to generate manipulative, co-optive forms of corporatism rather than a strengthened capacity of the working class. Even under the best of conditions with the best of intentions, the pressures for efficiency and control will diminish any genuine contribution by working class organizations to a planning process. From a bureaucratic point of view it is much more convenient for such participation to be purely formal rather than substantive. Only strong and autonomous working class organizations genuinely rooted in the working class (i.e., constituting working class capacities) would be able to counter such tendencies. Given the heavy political and economic pressures faced by a Left government once in power, it will be impossible to wait for such organizational capacities to develop if they are not already present.

A relatively weak organizational capacity of the working class would also make it difficult for a Left Government to control effectively the bureaucratic apparatus of the state, let alone to initiate programmes to erode the bureaucratic structure of that apparatus. Any programme of restructuring bureaucratic agencies in ways which would allow for genuine participation by grass roots organizations would be impossible without the co-operation of at least the rank and file workers in the bureaucracy. Again, in the absence of strong working class organizations with already well-established linkages to state workers prior to an electoral victory of the Left, it is difficult to see how such changes could be successfully made.

The reverse side of the necessity for strong working class organizational capacities as a precondition for efforts by a Left government to counter the atomizing effects of the capitalist state, is the necessity for the hegemony of the bourgeoisie to be relatively weakened. The crucial aspect of "hegemony" in this context is the capacity to define *ideologically* what kinds of social alternatives are possible at a given moment. (Hegemony must be contrasted with "domination", which refers to the capacity to *enforce* a certain range of social alternatives regardless of whether people believe other alternatives are possible or not.) If the hegemony of the bourgeoisie is more or less intact, then it would be difficult for any socialist government to adopt programmes which seriously attempted to expand the scope of political participation of the masses. In order for such mass participation to have its desired effects—the expansion of the class capacities of the working class—it is essential that people participate in a committed and energetic way. Unless there was already a fairly pervasive socialist consciousness within the working class, it is unlikely that such commitment would be sustained over an extended period.

For these reasons, it is essential that the Left not simply attempt to achieve a parliamentary majority (a difficult enough task, needless to say), but that it do so in ways which build the organizational capacities of the working class (i.e., strengthen social relations among workers) and challenge the ideological hegemony of the capitalist class. This means both drawing more and more people into the organizations of the working class and linking those organizations to longer-term socialist objectives. In order to accomplish this, electoral struggles must be systematically linked to grass roots social movements, electoral strategies must be oriented as much around local and regional levels of government as around national levels of government,[22]

22. The strategic emphasis of the Italian and French Communist Parties on building a base at the local and regional levels of government, before attempting to form a government at the national level, could potentially contribute to the strengthening of the organizational capacities of the working class prior to assuming a dominant role in the central government. The critical question, then, is the extent to which the control of the local state apparatuses by the Left has fostered or undermined the organizational capacities of the working class in societies like Italy and France. Have Communist city governments in Italy, for example, underwritten neighbourhood councils, giving them greater resources and scope of action, or have such governments tended to restrict neighbourhood councils, undermining their initiatives, coopting their leadership? Systematic,

party programmes must be sensitive to popular initiatives and not be formulated exclusively through top-down, bureaucratic directives, socialist cultural activity must reach broader masses of the people, and so forth.

These arguments about the necessity of undermining capitalist hegemony and creating durable organizational capacities of the working class prior to a Left electoral victory do not imply that capitalist hegemony must be completely shattered or that the working class must already have an organizational capacity sufficient to enable it to become the ruling class. On the contrary: the strategy of using the state to destroy the state assumes that it is only through structural changes within the capitalist state that capitalist hegemony can be definitively undermined and that the capacities of the working class can develop to the point where a decisive break with capitalism becomes possible. The point here is that a certain level of working class organizational capacity and of the disintegration of bourgeois hegemony is necessary for the control of the government by the Left to provide a basis for ultimately destroying the capitalist state. If these pre-conditions are not met, then a socialist electoral victory is likely to produce, at most, a series of relatively progressive reforms, but reforms which do not shift the basic balance of class forces in the society. If, on the other hand, they are met, then the government can potentially adopt reforms which contribute to an expansion of the capacities of the working class. Such expanded capacities would in turn potentially accelerate the erosion of bourgeois ideological hegemony, and this in turn would create conditions allowing for a further consolidation of working class capacities.

4. The Problem of Repression

Ruling classes do not rule by hegemony alone; they also rule through domination. An attack on the ideological hegemony of the bourgeoisie will not create a socialist society unless it becomes translated into an attack on the domination of the bourgeoisie. The strategy of using the capitalist state to destroy the capitalist state is implicitly an argument about such a

---

comparative case studies of Italian cities would be extremely useful for answering such questions.

possibility. To argue that structural changes within the capitalist state can facilitate a strengthening of the organizational capacities of the working class is to argue that it can make such a challenge to bourgeois domination possible.

The problem, of course, is that the bourgeoisie may not wait for the class capacities of the working class to reach such a level. The bourgeoisie would certainly respond vigorously to state interventions which appeared to be shifting the balance of class forces in favour of the working class. Initially the response would probably be various forms of economic sabotage (capital flight, cutting off credits by international financial institutions, embargoes, etc.). Under normal conditions, such actions would so seriously constrain the possibilities of state activity and so severely undermine the economic security of the population, that they would effectively reverse the pattern of state interventions.[23] This is what it means to say, after all, that the bourgeoisie is the dominant class even when working class parties hold the reins of government.

In advanced capitalism, however, the effectiveness of such economic sabotage by the bourgeoisie may be less pervasive than in earlier periods. The greatly increased role of the state in accumulation means that a much larger proportion of social resources are managed by the state rather than directly by private capital. This would, in principle, somewhat mitigate the impact of economic sanctions by the capitalist class. Furthermore, the weakening of bourgeois ideological hegemony and the strengthening of working class organizational capacities implies that in some countries, at least, large sections of the working class may be prepared to weather the hard times which capitalist sabotage would provoke. While it would be a serious mistake to underestimate the economic leverage that the capitalist class still possesses in every capitalist society, such leverage might not be sufficient by itself to topple a Left government or force it into submission.

This, then, raises the fundamental question of armed counter-revolution, of the possibility that the capitalist class

23. This is precisely what it means to say that there are "limits of functional compatibility" imposed on state interventions. Interventions which fall outside those limits set in motion a chain of consequences—in this case, escalating forms of economic class warfare—which eventually lead to a reversal of the policy or to a break with the system of capitalist domination.

would attempt a military coup or perhaps even an invasion by imperialist forces to destroy a democratically elected socialist government. Perry Anderson has expressed this issue well: "The logic of Marxist theory indicates that it is in the nature of the bourgeois state that, in any final contest, the armed apparatus of repression inexorably displaces the ideological apparatuses of parliamentary representation, to re-occupy the dominant position in the structure of capitalist class power. This coercive State machine is the ultimate barrier to a workers' revolution, and can only be broken by pre-emptive counter-coercion. . . . An insurrection will only succeed if the repressive apparatus of the State itself divides or disintegrates—as it did in Russia, China or Cuba. The consensual 'convention' that holds the forces of coercion together must, in other words, be breached."[24] The historic lesson of Chile underscores the theoretical rationale of this argument. It is ultimately the capacity of the bourgeoisie to destroy violently any peaceful attempt at constructing socialism that makes such attempts so precarious.

At some point, a Left parliamentary regime either has to abandon its socialist objectives or directly confront and challenge the repressive apparatus of the state. In such a confrontation the decisive issues become the extent to which the ideological unity of the military itself has been eroded by socialist struggles, the extent to which that military apparatus can call on external imperialist forces for assistance, and the extent to which the class capacities of the working class have been fortified or weakened during the period of socialist parliamentary rule. While a confrontation with the military may be inevitable, it is not necessarily inevitable that the military win such a confrontation.[25]

24. Perry Anderson, "The Antinomies of Antonio Gramsci", *New Left Review* No. 100, 1977, pp. 76–77.

25. It is because of this threat of military intervention that Western European Communist parties ascribe such importance to the current international equilibrium of forces. Their hope is that the general balance of power between the US and the USSR will make it unlikely that direct military intervention would occur if a Left government came to office. This does not mean, however, that the threat of internal military counter-revolution can be treated lightly. Even in Chile, where American involvement was quite important in the fall of the Allende Government, it was unnecessary for the United States to invade the country directly. Any socialist strategy in advanced capitalism must therefore

The purpose of this chapter has not been to provide an historical judgement of the actual practices of specific political parties, nor to attempt a forecast of the likely strategies which will be pursued in the future. Rather, the intention was to explore the logic of a particular strategic alternative facing the left and to examine the social conditions which will shape the possibilities of success for such a strategy. It remains to be seen whether the strategy of using the capitalist state to destroy the class character of that state will ever be generally accepted by the organized left in Western Europe or elsewhere. Perhaps even more importantly, even if the strategy were sincerely held as a theoretical position, it remains to be seen whether in practice any socialist government in a capitalist state could resist the enormous pressures to abandon such a strategy.

In the end, it is the character of class struggles during a period of socialist parliamentary rule which will determine the plausibility of the strategy of using the capitalist state as a basis for destroying the capitalist state. While there are important new possibilities for socialist transformation generated by the contradictions of late capitalism, those contradictions do not uniquely determine the success or failure of specific strategies for socialism. The extent to which the strategy can succeed, therefore, depends in large measure on the extent to which communist and socialist parties systematically and continually attempt to strengthen the class capacities of the working class—which in turn depends upon the complex ways in which class struggle itself mediates the diverse processes of class formation, state activity and social change.

---

involve serious organization within the military itself, efforts at changing life within the military in order to break down the social and ideological isolation of the army from the working class and so on.

Bibliography

Aaronowitz, Stanley, Russel Jacoby, Paul Piccone and Trent Schroyer. "Notes and Commentary: Symposium on Class", *Telos*, No. 28, 1976.

Althusser, Louis. *For Marx*, London: New Left Books 1977.

Althusser, Louis and Etienne Balibar. *Reading Capital*, London: New Left Books, 1970.

Amin, Samir. "Toward a Structural Crisis of World Capitalism", *Socialist Revolution*, No. 23, 1975.

Anderson, Perry. *Lineages of the Absolutist State*, London: New Left Books, 1974.

————. "The Antinomies of Antonio Gramsci", *New Left Review* No. 100, 1977.

Baran, Paul and Paul Sweezy. *Monopoly Capital*, New York: Monthly Review Press, 1966.

Bertaux, Daniel. *Destins Personnels et Structure de Classe*, Paris: Presses Universitaires de France, 1977.

Boddy, Raford and James Crotty. "Class Conflict and Macro-Policy: The Political Business Cycle", *Review of Radical Political Economics*, Vol. 7, No. 1.

————. "Wage Push and Working Class Power: A Reply to Howard Sherman", *Monthly Review*, Vol. 27, No. 10, 1976.

Bowles, Sam and Herb Gintis. *Schooling in Capitalist America*, New York: Basic Books, 1976.

Braverman, Harry. *Labor and Monopoly Capitalism*, New York: Monthly Review Press, 1974.

Bullock, Paul and David Yaffe. "Inflation, the Crisis and the Post-War Boom", *Revolutionary Communist*, No. 3/4, 1975.

Burawoy, Michael. *The Organization of Consent: Changing Patterns of Conflict on the Shop Floor, 1945–1975*, Ph.D. Dissertation, University of Chicago, Department of Sociology, 1976.

Carchedi, G. "On the Economic Identification of the New Middle Class", *Economy and Society*, Vol. IV, No. 1, 1975.

―――. "The Reproduction of Social Classes at the Level of Production Relations", *Economy and Society*, Vol. IV, No. 4, 1975.

―――. *On the Economic Identification of Social Classes*, Routledge & Kegan Paul, 1977.

Cogoy, Mario. "Les Théories Néo-Marxistes, Marx et l'Accumulation du Capital", *Les Temps Modernes*, September–October, pp. 396–427, 1972.

―――. "The Fall in the Rate of Profit and the Theory of Accumulation", BCSE, Winter, pp. 52–67, 1973.

Del Rio, Alfredo. *Class Struggle and Electoral Politics in Chile, 1958–1973*, Ph.D. Dissertation, Department of Sociology, University of Wisconsin, 1978.

Desai, Meghnad. *Marxian Economic Theory*, London: Gray-Mills Publishing, 1974.

DeVroey, Michael. "The Separation of Ownership and Control in Large Corporations", The Review of Radical Political Economics, Vol. 7, No. 2, 1975.

Edwards, Richard. "Alienation and Inequality: Capitalist Relations of Production in Business Enterprises", Ph.D. Dissertation, Department of Economics, Harvard University.

Ehrenreich, Barbara and John Ehrenreich. "The Professional-Managerial Class", *Radical America*, Vol. 11, No. 2, 1971.

Esping-Anderson, Gösta, Roger Friedland and Erik Wright. "Modes of Class Struggle and the Capitalist State", *Kapitalistate* No. 4–5, 1976.

Freedman, Francesca. "The Internal Structure of the Proletariat", *Socialist Revolution*, No. 26, 1975.

Friedland, Roger. *Class Power and the Central City: The Contradictions of Urban Growth*, Ph.D. Dissertation, Department of Sociology, University of Wisconsin, 1977.

―――. "Class Power and Social Control: The War on Poverty", *Politics and Society*, Vol. 6, No. 4, 1976.

Friedland, Roger, Alexander Hicks and Ed Johnson. "Class Power and Redistribution", *American Sociological Review*, Vol. 43, No. 1, 1978.

Gedicks, Al. "Ethnicity, Class Solidarity and Labor Radicalism among Finnish Immigrants in Michigan Copper Country", *Politics and Society* (forthcoming), 1977.

———. *The Radical Finns of Northern Minnesota: A Study in the Development of Working Class Politics*, PhD. Dissertation, Department of Sociology, University of Wisconsin, 1978.

Giddens, Anthony. *The Class Structure of the Advanced Societies*, New York: Harper and Row, 1973.

Gillman, Joseph. *Prosperity in Crisis*, New York: Marzani and Munsel, 1965.

Glyn, Andrew and Bob Sutcliffe. "The Critical Condition of British Capital", *New Left Review*, No. 66, 1971.

———. *British Capitalism, Workers and the Profit Squeeze*, London: Penguin Books, 1972.

Gold, David, Clarence Lo, and Erik Olin Wright. "Some Recent Developments in Marxist Theories of the State", *Monthly Review* (in press), 1975.

Hill, Judah. "Class Analysis: United States in the 1970's" (pamphlet), Emeryville, California, 1976.

Hodgson, Geoffrey. "The Falling Rate of Profit", *New Left Review*, No. 84, 1974.

Keat, Russel and John Urry. *Social Theory as Science*, London: Routledge & Kegan Paul, 1976.

Koshimura, Shinzaburo. *Theory of Capital Reproduction and Accumulation*, edited by Jesse Schwartz, Kitchner, Ontario: DPG Publishing Co., 1975.

Laibman, David. "The Organic Composition of Capital: A Fresh Look at Marxian Accumulation Theory". Unpublished Ms., 1974.

Lenin, V. I. *The State and Revolution*, in *Selected Works* (one volume edition), London: Lawrence and Wishart, 1969.

———. *Collected Works*, vol. 29, vol. 32, Moscow: Progress Publishers, 1965, Vol. 33, 1969.

———. *On the Soviet State Apparatus*, Moscow: Progress Publishers, 1969.

Levine, David. *Accumulation and Technical Change in Marxian Economics*. Unpublished Ph.D. Dissertation, Economics, Yale University, 1973.

Lo, Clarence. "The Functions of U.S. Military Spending", *Kapitalistate*, No. 3, 1975.

258

Luria, Daniel. *Suburbanization, Homeownership and Working Class Consciousness*, Ph.D Dissertation, Department of Economics, University of Massachusetts, 1976.

Mage, S. H. *The Law of the Falling Tendency of the Rate of Profit*, Unpublished Ph.D. Dissertation, Columbia University, 1963.

Mandel, Ernest. *Late Capitalism*, London: New Left Books, 1975.

Marglin, Stephen. "What Do Bosses Do?" *Review of Radical Political Economics*, Vol. 6, No. 2, 1974.

Martinelli, Alberto. "Nation States and Multinationals", *Kapitalistate*, No. 1, 1973.

Marx, Karl. *Capital*, Vol. 1, Penguin/NLR, London, 1976.

———. *Capital*, Vol. III, New York: International Publishers, 1967.

Mattick, Paul. *Marx and Keynes*, Boston: Porter Sargent, 1969.

Miliband, Ralph. "The State and Revolution", *Monthly Review*, Vol. 11, No. 11, 1970.

Nicolaus, Martin. "Proletariat and Middle Class in Marx", *Studies on the Left*, No. 7, 1967.

O'Connor, James. "Productive and Unproductive Labor", *Politics and Society*, Vol. 5, No. 3, 1975.

———. *The Fiscal Crisis of the State*. New York: St. Martin's, 1973.

Offe, Claus. "Structural Problems of the Capitalist State", in Von Beyme (ed.), *German Political Studies*, Vol. 1, Beverly Hills, California: Sage Publishing Co., 1974.

———. "The Theory of the Capitalist State and the Problem of Policy Formation" in Leon Lindberg, et al., (eds.), *Stress and Contradiction in Modern Capitalism*, Lexington, Massachusetts: D.C. Heath.

Perrone, Luca and Erik Olin Wright. "Lo Stato Nella Teoria Funzionalista e Marxista-Strutturalista", *Studi di Sociologia*, Vol. XI, 1973.

Poulantzas, Nicos. *Political Power and Social Classes*, London: New Left Books, 1973.

———. "On Social Classes", *New Left Review*, No. 78, 1973.

———. *Classes in Contemporary Capitalism*, London: New Left Books, 1975.

Przeworski, Adam. "The Process of Class Formation from Karl

Kautsky's *The Class Struggle* to Recent Debates", *Politics and Society* (Vol. 7:4), 1977.

Reich, Michael. *Racial Discrimination and the White Income Distribution*, Ph.D. Dissertation, Department of Economics, Harvard University, 1973.

——. "Who Benefits from Racism?" *Journal of Human Resources* (forthcoming), 1978.

——. *Racial Discrimination and Class in the United States*, Princeton University Press (forthcoming), 1979.

Roach, John M. "Worker Participation: New Voices in Management", *Conference Board Report No. 564*, New York: The Conference Board, 1973.

Rowthorn, Bob. "Skilled Labour in the Marxist System", *Bulletin of the Conference of Socialist Economists*, pp. 25–45, September 1974.

——. "Late Capitalism", *New Left Review*, No. 98, 1976.

Rush, Harold M. F. "Job Design for Motivation: Experiments in Job Enlargement and Job Enrichment", *Conference Board Report No. 515*, New York: The Conference Board, 1971.

Schwartz, Jesse. *The Subtle Analysis of Capitalism*, Santa Monica: Goodyear Publications, 1977.

Stinchcombe, Arthur. *Constructing Social Theories*, New York: Harcourt, Brace & World, 1968.

Stone, Katherine. "The Origins of Job Structures in the Steel Industry", *Review of Radical Political Economics*, Vol. 6, No. 2, Summer, 1974.

Sweezy Paul. *The Theory of Capitalist Development*, New York: Monthly Review Press, 1942.

——. "Some Problems in the Theory of Capital Accumulation", *Monthly Review*, Vol. 26, No. 1, 1974.

Szymanski, Al. "Trends in the American Working Class", *Socialist Revolution*, No. 10, 1972.

Therborn, Göran. *What does the Ruling Class do when it Rules?* London: New Left Books, 1978.

Urry, John. "Towards a Structural Theory of the Middle Class", *Acta Sociologica*, Vol. 16, No. 3, 1973.

Weber, Max. *Economy and Society*, ed. by Guenther Roth, New York: Bedminster Press, 1968.

——. "Politics and Government in a Reconstructed Germany", Appendix II in the Roth edition of *Economy and Society*.

Wright, Erik Olin. *Class Structure and Income Inequality*, unpublished Ph.D. Dissertation, Department of Sociology, University of California, Berkeley (available from University Microfilms, Ann Arbor, Michigan), forthcoming by Academic Press, 1979, as *Class Structure and Income Determination*.

————. "Class Boundaries in Advanced Capitalist Societies", *New Left Review*, No. 98, 1976.

————. "Alternative Perspectives in the Marxist Theory of Accumulation and Crisis", *The Insurgent Sociologist*, Fall 1975.

————. "To Control or To Smash Bureaucracy: Weber and Lenin on Politics, the State and Bureaucracy", *Berkeley Journal of Sociology*, Vol. XIX, 1974.

Wright, Erik Olin and Luca Perrone. "Classi Sociale, Scuola, Occupazione e Reddito in U.S.A.". *Quaderni di Sociologia*, Vol. XXIV, No. 1–2, 1975.

————. "Marxist Class Categories and Income Inequality", *American Sociological Review*, Vol. 42, No. 1, 1977.

Yaffe, David. "The Marxian Theory of Crisis, Capital and the State", *Economy and Society*, Vol. 2, 1973.

————. "The Crisis of Profitability, A Critique of the Glyn-Sutcliffe Thesis", *New Left Review*, No. 80, 1973.

Zeitlin, Maurice. "Corporate Ownership and Control: The Large Corporation and the Capitalist Class", *American Journal of Sociology*, Vol. 79, 1974.

Name Index

Subject Index

10 Questions Commonly Asked by the Patient with a Newly Formed Stoma

Theresa Porrett

INTRODUCTION

Following stoma forming surgery patients will have many questions about the stoma and how it might affect their lifestyle, work and social activities. Some of the questions commonly asked by patients are discussed in this chapter. The advice outlined in the answers is general in nature and if you have any doubts or concerns about an individual patient's queries it is essential that you involve the stoma care nurse (SCN). Equally, if patients have specific concerns regarding their stoma management or surgery you should advise the patient to discuss these with their SCN or the consultant who performed their surgery as they will be able to advise the patient more specifically, bearing in mind the underlying condition and the surgical procedure performed.

LEARNING OBJECTIVES

By the end of this chapter the reader will be able to:

❏ discuss the main issues and concerns experienced by patients following stoma formation;
❏ explain the national and local support mechanisms available to stoma patients;
❏ identify the clinical staff who can support patients and address any specific concerns they may raise.

COMMONLY ASKED QUESTIONS

Patients have many information needs and will be given a large amount of information at all stages of their treatment

REFERENCES

Allison, M. (1996) Discharge planning for the person with a stoma. In: C. Myers, ed. *Stoma Care Nursing*. Arnold, London.

Black, P. (2000) *Holistic Stoma Care*. Baillière Tindall, London.

Brady, V.A. (1980) Community care of the stoma patients. *Nursing* **1**, 741.

Curry, A. (1991) Returning home with confidence. Discharge planning in stoma care: a conceptual framework. *Professional Nurse* **6**, 536–9.

Davenport, R. (2003) Post operative stoma care. In: D.C. Elcoat, ed. *Stoma Care Nursing*. Hollister Ltd, Berkshire.

Ewing, G. (1989) The nursing preparation of stoma patients for self care. *Journal of Advanced Nursing* **14**, 411–20.

Kelly, M. & Henry, T. (1992) A thirst for practical knowledge: stoma patients' opinions of the service they receive. *Professional Nurse* **7**, 350–6.

Taylor, P. (2003) Community aspects of stoma care. In: D.C. Elcoat, ed. *Stoma Care Nursing*. Hollister Ltd, Berkshire.